Lindsey Davis

FALCO

The Official Companion

CENTURY

Published by Century 2010

2 4 6 8 10 9 7 5 3 1

First published in Great Britain in 2010 by
Century
Random House, 20 Vauxhall Bridge Road,
London SW1V 2SA

www.randomhouse.co.uk
www.lindseydavis.co.uk

Addresses for companies within The Random House Group Limited
can be found at: www.randomhouse.co.uk

The Random House Group Limited Reg. No. 954009

A CIP catalogue record for this book
is available from the British Library

ISBN 9781846056734

The Random House Group Limited supports The Forest Stewardship
Council (FSC), the leading international forest certification organisation.
All our titles that are printed on Greenpeace approved FSC certified paper carry
the FSC logo. Our paper procurement policy can be found at
www.rbooks.co.uk/environment

Mixed Sources
Product group from well-managed
forests and other controlled sources
www.fsc.org Cert no. TT-COC-2139
FSC © 1996 Forest Stewardship Council

Design and layout by Roger Walker

Printed and bound in Great Britain by
Clays, St Ives Plc

This was in the Olden Days, when the Romans were top nation, on account of their classical education, etc.

SELLAR AND YEATMAN

The story is this man's adventure in search of a hidden truth, and it would be no adventure if it did not happen to a man fit for adventure ...

CHANDLER

Key to Abbreviations

The Course of Honour   [CH]

The Falco Novels in chronological order:

The Silver Pigs	[SP]
Shadows in Bronze	[SB]
Venus in Copper	[VC]
The Iron Hand of Mars	[IHM]
Poseidon's Gold	[PG]
Last Act in Palmyra	[LAP]
Time to Depart	[TTD]
A Dying Light in Corduba	[DLC]
Three Hands in the Fountain	[THF]
Two for the Lions	[TFL]
One Virgin Too Many	[OVTM]
Ode to a Banker	[OB]
A Body in the Bath House	[BBH]
The Jupiter Myth	[JM]
The Accusers	[AC]
Scandal Takes a Holiday	[STH]
See Delphi and Die	[SDD]
Saturnalia	[SA]
Alexandria	[AL]
Nemesis	[NM]

Contents

Introduction

*As the girl came running up the steps, I decided
she was wearing far too many clothes ...* [SP]

With these words I launched the career of Marcus
Didius Falco, the Roman informer, in 1989. Twenty
years and twenty books later, he has discerning and
devoted followers worldwide and I have had a wonderful career. It seems time to offer the *Companion* volume
so many readers have asked for.

It won't be a textbook, definitely not a full handbook of Roman life.[1][2] There are hundreds of excellent
books on the Roman world, written and illustrated by
experts, something I have never claimed to be. The
Internet is crowded with information, some of it even
reliable. I will mention some of my sources, but remember, that's what they are – the particular books, sites and
museums that I used for the series. For serious study
you should seek out your own. I shall merely touch on
aspects of Roman life that have caused puzzlement. My
opinions may be grumpy and maverick. On the other
hand, I hold those opinions because, after twenty years
of loving and living with this subject, I think I am right.

I won't create a comprehensive encyclopaedia of
every character, place, murder weapon, stuffed vineleaf
and cockroach in the books. How ghastly that would
be! My intention is to shed light on how the books are
written, why I tackle particular subjects and what I
believe to be important in portraying my characters. I
will talk a little about my own background, because that
is what made me think, imagine, believe, love and hate
the way I do. My early life partly explains where the
books came from. This is probably as much as I will ever
write autobiographically, containing family anecdotes
even my family have forgotten, because families and the
mad myths that colour their generations are central to
the Falco series.

I wanted to give you glossy illustrations, pull-out
maps and give-away models. Sadly, we are constrained

to simple and black-and-white illustrations; this is 'due to the Recession' (*That old story!* Falco would scoff). Rodney Paul, who has always created our maps, has produced some brilliant technical drawings of Roman inventions; Bernard Frischer has very kindly allowed us to use stills from 'Rome Reborn'. Many photographs are from my own collection, so while they may not be of the best professional standard, they are the specific photos Richard and I took on our trips, my personal reminders of useful things we saw. They go back over twenty years and often I can't tell now who took which, when it was – or even where. We never catalogued anything; we just piled them into drawers. You may disapprove, but this is one authentic source of the books' relaxed style. For us, life was too short to keep minute records and until very recently I had no thought that we might one day need to impress the stern public.

Linda Hodgson and Roger Walker at Random House who designed this book have done wonders with the often unpromising material I offered them. And poor Katie Duce in Century editorial, who found herself unexpectedly landed with organising me on two books at once, has been kind, calm, and unfailingly efficient throughout. Beth Humphries has done a wonderful job of copy editing, as she always does. Vicki Robinson produced a professional, helpful index; she is not responsible for the joke entries someone slipped in afterwards.

People have been extremely generous with permissions; they are listed and thanked in the Acknowledgements. Mary Fox at Penguin went to particular trouble to unravel aged copyrights.

I want to give a special mention to the close team who encouraged and helped me slowly produce this book: my agent, Heather Jeeves, who lightly whipped me to finish, and my editor, Oliver Johnson, who championed the idea and scrutinised the manuscript as meticulously as ever. Janet Jenvey supervised my homework chart. And my great thanks to Ginny Lindzey and Michelle Breuer Vitt, for their contributions and unfailing interest.

This has been a hard, sad year for me personally. I lost Richard, and then Oliver resigned. To carry on with Falco, while surveying my past career, was a surreal experience. But it helped me remember why you, my loyal readers all around the world, enjoy and love the books so much. Even in times of trouble, that gives a validation to my life. I am very proud to have provided so much pleasure, intrigue and consolation. I cherish the friendships I have made, often with people I have never met or may never hear from. But I know you are there. This book, this little extra bit of fun, is all for you.

Lindsey Davis
London, 2010

Background, Writing and Research

The Author's Birth and Background

Anyone planning to be a writer needs to start *before they are born*.

People ask for advice. It's simple: be the child of a famous published author; use their surname. You will be published immediately. Join writers' cliques; your books will always be reviewed.

You must: be blond, stay young, be photogenic. Or, write in your eighties, a different ploy, which carries risks and leads to a short career. Even then, you must be a well-spoken charmer with snowy white hair and elegant attire.

Never reveal that you write in a paint-stained velour leisure suit, with orthopaedic inserts in your thermal slippers.

Once born: organise your book jacket biography. Work on a tramp streamer in the South Seas. Serve a prison term; treasure that transsexual's bigamy claims against you (boast or deny this, according to taste); catalogue your experiences with your pet lion cub (make it die in poignant circumstances). You must have an abusive father, a cheating husband, delinquent children and whimsical cats to write about. What else is there?

I knew none of this. I had no authors in my pedigree, though my father had done academic editing for Robert Maxwell's press. Connections in publishing have helped many new authors. But Mum made Dad give up his Maxwell work because she did not trust the man. In this, as in so many things, Joanie's perceptiveness glowed bright.

I was born in Birmingham. Many authors have come from there, though most keep quiet about it.

Brum has no Roman heritage. We pretend there is a 'fort' beside the Queen Elizabeth Hospital, but it's just a signal station. I grew up in an inventive manufacturing city with a strong Nonconformist background, still famous then for cars, guns, jewellery, chocolate, HP sauce. All gone, sadly. The dictionary definition of Brummagem is *counterfeit, sham, cheap and showy*, so like all Brummies, I droop under a permanent sense of shame.

My background was working-class. One grandfather was a foreman electrician – at the Gas Works – and the other a toolmaker. My cousin Jennie researches my mother's family; the Barkers were butchers and hairdressers. Auntie Eleanor had a wool shop, Flo and Glad a general store. Lovely Uncle Wally Stephens founded the Thor Hammer Company. Great-Grandfather Barker, who lived in the Black Country, had kept a pub; he drank a bottle of whisky a day and would brandish a shotgun at closing time. He was thought eccentric. For instance, he believed handkerchiefs were dangerous; people should blow their noses on a piece of old rag, then throw it in the fire.

... your relatives, given you by nature with no effort on your part ...
HORACE
(telling us something?)

And he was an atheist, a follower of Charles Bradlaugh, the Northampton MP who secured the right of affirmation (instead of taking a religious oath) for Members of Parliament and witnesses in court. Bradlaugh's Secular Society argued that freedom *from* religion was as much a human right as freedom *of* religion. One aim was to allow children to be withdrawn from religious assembly at school, though there were penalties for it: *Stand up, the little boy whose father does not believe in God!* Grandad Barker was so traumatised that our family never did this again – until me. My own secondary school had a strong religious foundation, but I was allowed to withdraw from the service at assembly so long as I promised not to do homework instead; I said, *I'll knit, then!* (Not meant as offensive, but a practical solution.) My Aran and Fair Isle became exemplary.

On Dad's side, his father was a toolmaker and his mother's father a lamp-lighter. My great-great-grandad was a clockmaker, Martin Benzing, from Germany. A Socialist who had wanted to assassinate Bismarck, allegedly he lay in wait in a park where the Iron Chancellor went riding. Bismarck trotted past, slapping his riding crop, which broke; he hurled it into the bush where Martin was lurking. He grabbed it and fled. True: I have the yellowed ivory handle.

Supposedly, a Benzing became the Benson of '&
Hedges' but of course I am not a tobacco heiress or I
could be a Celebrity Author and wear diamanté jump-
suits. Wealth stuck to my people only fitfully. Grandfather Davis went to Canada; a trustful man, he made a
fortune in apple orchards, but his partner stole the
money (twice). My father in turn left everything –
nearly half a million pounds – to a woman he met
through the small ads who, like a villainess in Falco,
claimed *she wasn't good with money*. The worst part of
this was my estrangement from Dad. Incidentally, it was
long after I invented Geminus.

As you see, my people lacked privilege. They all had
trades or shops, though, rather than labouring or being
servants. My family were not the intellectual class,
effete, snooty and unable to wire an electric plug. We
had no goofy twerps in plus-fours at big country-house
parties, no female pioneers in Edwardian skirts sipping
cocoa at early women's colleges. Ours was an urban
Victorian heritage: the Barkers doing moonlit flits
when they could not pay the rent; Mum (young and
appealing) being dispatched to beg pub landlords to
send Grandad home so he didn't spend all his wages;
Grandma Davis hiring a barrel organ to raise money for
the Jarrow miners. On both sides of my family was at
least one man whose wife died in childbirth, after
which – whatever gender historians maintain – the
widower brought up the children.

> *My old man said 'Follow the van!' and don't dilly-dally on the way ...*
> MUSIC HALL SONG

The Barkers were one such family. It was said that
Grandad could get his wife pregnant just by hanging up
his trousers on the end of the bed. Seven children survived, though we know there were others. A terrible
tale is told that when my grandmother was in labour
the last time, the doctor came downstairs and said, *I
can't save your wife, but I can possibly save the baby* – to
which Grandad said no. Thereafter he brought up the
rest with an iron hand, famously cooking with a dangling cigarette; the ash provided flavour. Stories of this
hungry, noisy, teeming tribe, and the songs Grandad
sang, permeated my childhood. Cousin Dorrell
remembers life at their house, with her as a child scam-
pering from room to room, not knowing where to
settle because there was always something exciting

The Barkers at leisure

going on somewhere else. Their catchphrase to visitors was *Come in, sit down, what'll you have to eat and drink?*

Another myth about the working classes is that: *the Victorian working man received his wages and his wife might never see a penny.* Grandad Davis knew his wife was the money-manager; he used to hand Lil his wage packet unopened. He died before I was born, but Grandma was a huge influence. She had friends everywhere; hers was another house where people constantly dropped in. A motto she gave me was: *Never stand when you can sit; never sit when you can lie down.* She was a tireless raconteur, a fund of stories. Dancing the tango with 'Mr Paul' Cadbury so everybody stopped to watch ... Helping a nun run away from her convent ... Grandad being chased by a policeman, for speeding (on his *bike)* all down the Pershore Road ... I'm sure there was one about Grandad having once seen a crowd set upon a police constable and kill him. And let's dispel another cosy myth: even after the Second World War the name of Winston Churchill was never mentioned, because of Gallipoli, where Gran had had three brothers killed, including Charlie, her favourite.

Grandad and Grandma at the allotment

My parents were a curious pair, made for one another and yet doomed by association. Neither went to Grammar School, though both could have; Mum's family could not afford it and Dad wanted to be out enjoying the world. So, they both worked at Boxfoldia and their first tryst was on a works outing, behind the summerhouse at Newnham College, Cambridge. They married during the war, in August 1942: 24–8–42 – not only a palindrome, but the probable anniversary of Vesuvius erupting in AD79.

I wish I had been at that wedding. Grandad Barker was so opposed, it was kept secret from him, but he found out and jumped on a bus to chase after the couple. When the registrar began, instead of 'Do you, Joan Margaret ...?' he used the wrong name. Even when he got it right, Mum paused for an endlessly long time before answering ...

Nonetheless it happened, as mistakes inexorably do. They lived in Bury at first, as Dad was posted up north; a mouse used to come out and warm itself in front of the fire and Lancashire hotpot became a staple of my childhood. Mum's brothers had told Dad not to expect any dinner because Mum would always have her nose in a book; she just bought herself a cookbook. Dad was sent to India, running wireless communications on the Khyber Pass. Travel abroad was life-changing, which may resonate in Falco. Mum worked at an industrial company where her work was so secret she *never* disclosed it. She had a traumatic ectopic pregnancy; no doctor believed her complaints of pain until she collapsed in the street. She nearly died. It happened on her birthday, which from then on she refused to celebrate.

They were then obliged to wait, but four years after the war ended, my parents produced me. It was a difficult birth; I was three days in an incubator, when Mum never saw me and was afraid I had died.

My earliest memory is when I was just a toddler. We lived briefly in a flat in Snow Hill, the very centre of Birmingham, where every time Mum ran out my nappies on the pulley washing line, they came in black with smuts.

Joan and Bill wonder what they have done ...

She used to take me for air and escape to St Philip's Cathedral churchyard, where I was equally frightened by tramps and pigeons. Dad, to his credit, gained a degree by correspondence course, some feat with me, a very mardy baby; he became a lecturer at what was then the College of Commerce, teaching public administration and politics. I next remember sitting on the path at our first little house in Ward End, surrounded by wallflowers and butterflies.

When I was three and a half, my brother Maxwell was born. He and I were always good friends though very different; I think he started taking clocks apart to see how they worked before he could talk. (For a long time he didn't bother to talk, because I did it for him.) Max had his first toolkit when most children were still on soft toys. He struggled at school; Mum had to help with his reading and I taught him his tables. I had a little blackboard because I wanted to be a teacher; in fact, I didn't have an 'imaginary friend', I had a complete imaginary class, with names, IQs and characteristics, whose careers I followed in real time for years.

To be a child in the 1950s was a mixture of opportunity and austerity. Birmingham had lost much of its housing stock, but now we lived in a new three-bed semi-detached, with metal windows, small gardens front and back, kitchen, bathroom, inside lavatory – even *French windows*. There was no central heating; in winter we had chilblains, we got dressed under the bedclothes, Jack Frost whitened the window glass, washing came in from the line solid with ice. Behind our row of houses lay 'the little field' – remains of a bomb site, a haven to play in. We were tough and sensible. Fathers just went and checked any new fly-tipping. Besides, it was nowhere near as dangerous as the flooded clay pit in the brickyard or the railway lines … Our play was grounded in imagination; toys were scarce, only given at Christmas and birthdays, though aunts and grandmas, or even close family friends, would slip a child some coppers, maybe even half a crown (you hid that, or it was 'saved' for you). I don't remember sweet-rationing, though I do remember it ending. Birmingham children had the benefit of Cadbury misshapes, which came in plain brown bags and were always the wrong ones – Turkish delight and toffee, never strawberry creams.

My class at primary school had forty-four children. Everywhere was painted green. Sometimes they still tested the air-raid sirens. We cut pencils in half to save money. For art we had a print of *The Laughing Cavalier* in the hall. Music was covered more ambitiously; members of the Birmingham Symphony Orchestra would visit, and enormous radios would be brought into class for *Time and Tune* and *Music and Movement* (we'd be in anguish that the radio wouldn't warm up in time for our favourite song). Although we preferred belting out 'A Song of the Western Men', we also learned to read a score, and studied ambitious pieces – Smetana's *Vltava*, Stravinsky's *Petrushka*. We learned things by heart; we did mental arithmetic and spelling tests. For general knowledge we had booklets stuffed with tables of weights and measures, or Kings and Queens of England. We'd collect the *I Spy* or *Observer* series; even as a townee, I knew my ragged robin from my cow parsley. Rosebay willowherb was easy, because of the bomb sites.

As her leg was made of wood And she did not want it known At the point on which she stood, She had fixed a rubber cone ...

I was encouraged to read. Mum still liked her nose in a book, mainly from the library, though we did own books (more Left Book Club than classics). I was a rapid reader. I hated the Birmingham library policy that children were allowed only one fiction ticket to two non-fiction; you could cheat if your parents lent theirs, which must have been how I once read three Biggles books in a day. Mostly I liked books with strong young heroines, orphans who fought off adversity, like the *Anne of Green Gables* Mum passed on, Hodgson Burnett's *Little Princess* and *The Secret Garden*. Other orphans were Edith Nesbit's well-meaning Bastables, which I preferred to *The Railway Children* even though, like *Little Women*, it had a female writer, with the insidious suggestion that you could earn money that way ...

Is Falco Biggles? – Discuss.

We had books ...

I came to some books through the radio: Noel Streatfeild, *Tom's Midnight Garden*, *Lorna Doone* (*Lorna Doone* still means Butterworth's *Banks of Green Willow*), *The Hobbit* ('Kaschei's Dance') – and eventually Rosemary Sutcliff's *The Eagle of the Ninth: Some time about the year* AD117 *the Ninth*

*Legion, which was stationed at Eboracum where York now
stands, marched north to deal with a rising among the
Caledonian tribes, and was never heard of again … Marcus
set the bundle carefully on the table. 'We have brought back
the Hispania's lost Eagle,' he said, rather muzzily, and very
quietly crumpled forward on top of it.* Ever since *The Flight
of the Heron,* I have known I do not belong to my
parents but am Bonnie Prince Charlie
(except when being Hornblower).

I cannot over-stress the importance of
radio. My family rarely went to the cinema,
and due to a mix of meanness and liberal
principles, we did not acquire a TV until I
was fourteen. I grew up with classical music
in the evenings, the Light Programme at
Grandma's, music-hall numbers, Kathleen
Ferrier – and radio drama, which is intri-
cately bound up with written fiction for me.
Saturday Night Theatre would introduce me
to classic detective stories. Perhaps that's
why the Falco novels are told in the first
person, as if he is talking to us in a radio play.

… we had radio.

Another great feature of radio, then later
TV, was comedy. My tastes are unfashionable; I preferred Michael Bentine of the Goons and never took to
Monty Python, loathing the deep misogyny of male
comics dressing up as hideous caricature women. I did
my weekend homework with *The Navy Lark* and
Round the Horne, before *Pick of the Pops;* and I loved the
Pythons' radio predecessor, *I'm Sorry I'll Read That
Again.* The point about these is that they had zany,
quick-fire sketches, irreverence, non sequiturs, songs,
in-jokes and catchphrases. Radio can do it, with a light-
ness of touch TV lacks; books do it. The facility to draw
on all aspects of cultural life, firing a glancing shot then
passing on rapidly, is special to the radio generation.
Think of Terry Pratchett or Douglas Adams. Certainly
think of Falco.

*A vast behind! … I think I am
a slice of rhubarb tart …*

My folks were upwardly mobile. The College of
Commerce became Birmingham Polytechnic. We
moved to a middle-class suburb, a 1930s house with dry
rot and treacly brown paint that had to be burned off;
we acquired central heating, a coke boiler that often

Author aged ten

jammed and blew off steam, bringing ceilings down and making the dog shit in terror all over the breakfast room (my brother had a dog; our new house had a 'breakfast room'). What we didn't have were friends. My father always had his colleagues at work but Mother was losing her contacts; my brother was put in a prissy primary school where the headmaster was over-keen on little girls and Max overheard a teacher sneer, *He's not as clever as his sister.* The rot had set in.

I had passed the exams to King Edward's, the Girls' High School. There I was given a superb education, made friends I still have today, was taught by wonderful women – and was provided with a base of my own outside the family. It was understood that to be female was irrelevant. If you were given the tools, you could master any discipline; if you had the talent, you could become anything you chose. I would be, indeed I still am, shocked to discover that the world does not always accept those principles. Clearly they underpin everything I have done as a writer.

My school was the making of me intellectually, and when things fell apart at home, it was the saving of me too.

Things had begun to change when we moved. My mother discovered that my father – gregarious, popular, spoiled and self-centred – had a long history of philandering (he always pooh-poohed this, but I heard his confessions to Mum). My mother – once gregarious and popular herself – became isolated and secretive. Divorce was rare, and carried a stigma. Instead, once Max and I were in bed, my parents quarrelled – shouting, slamming doors. I lay awake in dread, night after night, through most of my teen years. Eventually my mother had a nervous breakdown. Psychiatric treatment entailed barbiturates and a stay in hospital where she had electro-convulsive treatment. Now I know what that entails, I can hardly bear to think of it being imposed on a human being. If 'electric shock treatment' was given to prisoners of war, it would be denounced as torture. Psychiatrists say it works. I suggest it 'works' because patients who can do so, simply close down and look obedient to make the experience stop.

Mum came home. Her true personality was lost. We carried on. That was what you did. Families kept secrets. Even my brother and I never spoke about it; I never knew if he heard or understood what happened.

I passed my exams – though with very mixed results, a rarity at King Edward's which, then as now, excelled at training girls to pass. My results could be due to undiagnosed hay fever in the exam season, laziness about subjects where I needed to work, or my unhappy home life and lack of sleep. I mention it because these days when only rows of A*s count, people like me must suffer. Instead, I stayed for an extra term to do the Oxbridge entrance exams and Lady Margaret Hall at Oxford accepted me. So I went to the best university and now carry out a profession where I use scholarship and serious creativity. Think on, foolish grade snobs!

I had elected to read English because I was better at it, rather than History, which would have been my first choice. This proved right. My course was 'English Language and Literature'; I revelled in both parts equally. However much attention is paid to the history, Eng Lang and Lit are the true underpinnings of my work. I write novels first, historical novels second. Despite experimental moments, they are in the tradition of English fiction. Their important constituents are plot, character, dialogue and narrative approach. My tools are grammar and vocabulary. Selection of detail is a vital element, and that may be historical, but without the rest, everything would be banal. Plenty of banal novels are published, but you read mine because you have better taste.

In my second year at Oxford, a terrible event occurred. My brother Maxwell had always struggled at school; his genius was technical, not academic. We were both painfully shy in company, gauche with the opposite sex, crushed by failures. I at least always had a very sharp sensitivity whereas he was other-worldly. When he hit puberty he became depressed, ran away 'to think', complained of suicidal feelings.

Strings were pulled to get him into the psychiatric unit where my mother had been treated. He had the same regime of drugs and ECT. Staff thought he was

recovering and allowed him to go by himself to a day room, to play his guitar. The unit was on the fifth floor. It had safety locks on the windows, but Max simply unscrewed one. He went out and died of his injuries. He was seventeen.

My mother was prostrate. I accompanied my father to the inquest. The coroner concluded, *He just had a hard time growing up.* The verdict was simply that he killed himself. My parents were told that the unit would be moved. It wasn't. Some years later when other patients committed suicide there, I wrote to the psychiatrist, who used the tired justification *When people really want to kill themselves, they will.* It seems to me that with young people at least, whose problems are put down to adolescence, strenuous efforts to keep them safe might help them outgrow their difficulties and survive.

When I returned to college, I sat alone on my bed and thought, *Nothing will ever be as bad as this again.*

Sometimes I write about those whose lives are changed for ever by the actions of other people, and I do so with feeling. I probably had no inkling immediately that as a result I would never marry or have children, both of which I wanted. Men fled. I don't blame them; my family looked mad and I became a strange person for many years. Any who were strong enough to cope were too strong and would have swamped me. I won't ever write a misery memoir; I pity the people who do and those who are connected with them. But in a discussion of my work, this is a defining issue.

I don't say a writer must live alone; that is clearly untrue. But it helps. I always enjoyed writing and would probably one day have tried it, but I doubt if I would have left the civil service if I had had responsibilities. The poverty and uncertainty I then lived in for nearly five years could not have been imposed on others. Getting first published is so hard, I needed to work at it full time. It took four years to my first book – and as I was always refusing to follow trends, that was actually quite good going.

Most definitely, I have written the Falco series at one book a year, which is a very tough schedule. They are dense books, longer than some novels; such production was possible only because I had long quiet periods for writing. Richard and I had the closest companionship for over thirty years but I remained single; I did most of my creative work at times when I was alone in a quiet house.

I reject 'writing as therapy'; you need to filter and mould. What I know of life shines through my work, but no book of mine is intended to be autobiographical. It's partly ironic that the Falco series is so much about families. That said, my work has consoled me for grief and disappointment. My books will be what justify my existence. They gave me, too, financial independence to match the personal independence I had been forced to acquire.

When I was a small child, before my mother lost her happiness, she used to send me to sleep with lullabies; one was a Paul Robeson song that included the words *Do you want the moon to play with? The stars to run away with? They'll come if you don't cry ...*

She did know what I became, and it was a solace for her. For me, from the moment I held the first copy of the first book, I was playing with the moon and stars.

Being a Writer

Although I had always wanted to write, and knew that I wanted to write historicals, it was only in my last year as a civil servant that I began. That was in the dark days of Thatcher's Britain, when the career I had chosen, which once had been well-paid and respected, turned into something different. Those of us who should have been overseeing how taxpayers' money was spent and advising the government on policy issues were viewed only as numbers – unwanted numbers. Outside 'consultants' were brought in, with a remit to destroy systems and dispense with staff. We were distrusted, with our careers under threat and our rewards slashed.

I wrote a romantic novel to cheer myself up. I did so in secret. You should never say you are trying to write and never discuss work in progress until it is in print.

I saw an advert for the Georgette Heyer Historical Novel Prize, for unpublished manuscripts. I submitted mine, was shortlisted, and realised I might be able to do this. Not so simple – over five years, I submitted four scripts. Three reached the shortlist: one became a serial in *Woman's Realm*; one appeared ten years later as *The Course of Honour;* another was *The Silver Pigs.* I never won, not even with those two last books, now in print for decades and loved by readers around the world.

The prize deadline was always the end of August, so I wrote a book every year, ending then. Excellent training! I am, though, always as close to a deadline as I can be – ever since school where I would run down the corridor to shunt my essay into a pigeonhole, just as the teacher came to collect. I used to take my bundles up to London myself, to gain an extra day over posting them. I still hand-deliver to my agent.

After I had posted *The Course of Honour* by hand, I made my way slowly home. It was very hot. During the chillier midnight printing of my work (technology was slow back then), rather than turn the central heating back on, I had added extra clothes. I stood in Tottenham Court Road tube station, stifling in a thermal vest and a jumper. *As the girl came running up the steps, I realised she was wearing far too many clothes ...*

I went home and wrote the first page of *The Silver Pigs.* I had no idea who was speaking, in what period and background, or from which steps.

This answers one question rather unhappily, because when people ask, *Where do you get your ideas?,* obviously they do not want me to say, *From a thermal vest*!

And that's where Falco came from?

Could be. According to Richard, we were watching *Mike Hammer,* a TV series we liked, and *he* said, *You should write about a Roman detective ...*

I had let slip that I myself wrote for relaxation. Always a mistake. People want to know if your work has been copied up by scroll-sellers, or if you have given readings socially. Saying no shrinks your standing; saying yes makes their eyes glaze defensively. Though I mentioned that I sometimes toyed with the idea of hiring a hall to give an evening of my love poems and satires, it was said ruefully. Everyone, including me, was convinced it was a dream. [TFL]

For me, writing is a job. Ethereal forces don't provide inspiration. I had read detective stories and, significantly, heard detective dramas on radio. When I finished *The Course of Honour,* I had just finalised a large project, emptied my imagination and was ready for something new. My brain is a hot compost of ideas; many *could* be forked up, have the woodlice shaken off them and be worked into novels. Some were. Some still will be, perhaps.

For years, I kept folders with titles, disconnected paragraphs, even a page or two of dialogue between feisty heroines and covetable chaps. People who are trying to be authors are scared of letting a Big Idea escape. I had been a civil servant. My filing system is good. But none of my old folders contained anything like *The Silver Pigs.* The idea for a spoof gumshoe in the ancient world was new (and therefore exciting). I still have the old folders, though of course, now I've mentioned them, they will have to be shredded.

I came home and wrote that opening page. So I opened a new folder.

I still have that too: a beige Slimpick Wallet, slightly worn on the edges, with a few ink smears and one blob of what may be spilt tea. This folder, called 'Mickey Spartacus Notes', contains: timelines (five or six duplicates) of the First Century imperial period; lists; newspaper cuttings; a Port Guide to Civitavecchia (revised 6/84), a postcard of the Via Appia Antica; vocabularies; a Calendar of Holidays and Festivals (dated 1998); a hand-traced map of ancient Rome with coloured crayoning; and the original photo of 'Nux', a doggie who caught Richard's eye on a Greek island. There is a page of mathematical calculations, involving both linear and liquid measures, in  three colours of biro, which I believe to be an olive oil sum for *A Dying Light in Corduba.* Will I ever get to use the news-clipping: *Ferret Foils Police Stake-out?* ...

Did Falco come from there?

No; I opened the folder once he turned up. I hardly ever look at it now. My filing system's purpose, as Falco might scoff, is to lie in a cupboard looking neat.

Author and agent typically relaxing, in a Rome *hosteria*

So the answer is, I don't know. Tough luck, wannabe writers who plan to steal the pattern for Knit Your Own Falco.

I wrote the first book. I found an agent. She found us a publisher. Just like that? No. Several agents turned me down. Many editors said no to Heather.

It took four years, though it seemed much longer, to see *The Silver Pigs* in print. There was a delay at the end because apparently the book was printed in China and failed to arrive on time; a slow sampan, clearly.

The Writing Day: Do you have a routine?
If I wanted to work 9 to 5, I could have stayed in a 'real' job.

My deadline is fixed. My contract is non-negotiable, says Falco to Avienus, who supposedly has 'writer's block'. *And I shall deliver on time, like a true professional. The masterpiece will be rolled up neatly and fastened with a twist of string. There will be supporting proofs, cogently explained in exquisitely constructed sentences. Informers don't hide behind 'blocks'. The guilty go before the judge.* [OB] My system is to get the work done – 100,000 words every year. This is how:

My radio alarm turns on Radio 3, the classical music programme, at 7.30; during the next hour I wake up. In the following hour I get up. Nowadays, instead of buying my newspaper while the kettle boils I go for a healthy walk in the park and then buy it. (Not having a paper delivered derives from when I first began working at home; it makes me leave the house at least once every day and not become peculiar …)

I read the paper. I read the post. I look around the garden, I consider housework, mend stuff, do ironing. I walk upstairs to the study, turn on my computer, do financial tasks, read email. I make phone calls, write letters, order from catalogues. Then it is probably lunchtime. I turn off the computer and have lunch.

I go back. Now I write. I look at yesterday's work, polish it, move the work forward. It is concentrated. I do not mess about. When I am tired I stop.

I have a bath and my dinner. In fact I am still working. My relaxing brain will come up with really good ideas.

I do not write them down. I am off duty now. If I forget them, since I am a professional writer, I will just devise more tomorrow.

That's it.

Do you have a synopsis?

If I have a contract I send a few pages of notes to my UK editor, copied to my US editor if he has also bought the book. This is polite; it says what they have bought, and helps them prepare catalogues, etc. I often don't look at the outline again for a long time. My synopses are brief, though all authors differ. I hate prior detail; once I begin writing, I want the same thrill of discovery that the reader will have.

I begin at page 1 then power through. A typical Falco novel takes about four months of writing. Research continues simultaneously and may cause changes.

Do you use a computer?

I am a toolmaker's granddaughter. I use the best tools I can get.

The first thing I do when I buy a PC is to strip out all games and media samples. I do not allow email alerts. I don't listen to music; I blot out noises of fireplaces being installed or bitter cold when the boiler breaks down. I am focused.

I wake when I like … The shutters stay closed, for in the stillness and darkness I feel myself surprisingly detached from any distractions and left to myself in freedom; my eyes do not determine the direction of my thinking but, being unable to see anything, they are guided to visualise my thoughts. If I have anything on hand I work it out in my head, choosing and correcting the wording, and the amount I achieve depends on the ease or difficulty with which my thoughts can be marshalled and kept in my head. Then I call my secretary …
PLINY THE YOUNGER

However, if I hear screams or smell smoke nearby, I go to investigate.

Where do you work?

Once, it was on the dining-room table – in a room only about eight foot by eight. Every evening the work had to be tidied off, so dinner could be civilised.

First study, being prepared for dinner

My first Random House contract enabled me to buy a new house with its own study. By Millennium Year I had a house with a study and a library.

Study One had the airing cupboard in one corner, which I highly recommend. Hypothermia can set in when writers sit too still for too long. Other risks to health are RSI, arthritis, sight problems, headaches, weight gain and piles! The sedentary life is, literally, a killer. Working from home avoids many germs, but at public events you will gather viruses. Since by definition you have started off solitary, weird, despondent by nature and probably with the gene for hay fever and asthma, I advise writers to live close to their local surgery. Going there does give useful insights into human nature.

There are special UK tax rules for the self-employed who work at home, though these are beyond the scope of this volume. Sadly, they are beyond the scope of most writers, but I am at heart a bureaucrat. So for decent fiscal reasons, I always edit in the dining room, read in the lounge, think in the bath, do interviews on the bedroom phone (I was once on *Today* live, while secretly in bed), keep my sewing machine in my study and spare lightbulbs in the library. Pre-meetings with my agent and editor take place in the conservatory (the meetings tend to be outside the home).

Are you forced to make a lot of changes by your editor?

Not me. He tries. I say I'll think about it.

If a word or phrase makes Oliver pull up, I generally omit or alter that passage because if he bothered to find his pencil, something there is wrong.

In twenty years he has taught me a lot and I can write now to what I know he will like (or naughtily write things he will want to correct).

For *Venus in Copper* I had two editors, which was intriguing. Oliver had moved to Arrow, a paperback imprint; I was supposed to have a hardback editor. It was decided that Oliver and Paul Sidey at Hutchinson would *both* edit the manuscript. Oliver would then discuss their joint list of suggested changes with me. (Note 'suggested'. I am sure that is how editors see it.) They had different interests so produced two completely different sets of queries; I was heartbroken by the sheer amount and ended up in tears. It made me wonder; given that usually, only one of those lists would be considered yet a perfectly acceptable book would result, could one do without *both* editors and still – after the author's final draft tweaks – have a decent book?

Of course this is heresy.

Author and editor at a Fishbourne Palace event with curator David Rudkin (togate)

Indeed! [Editor]

Do you have any influence over book jackets?

In Britain I have the 'right of consultation' – an ambiguous concept.

Publishers like to 'refresh' a long series; I've been through it many times. When one re-jacketing was planned, I asked readers, via my website, what they thought. There were unexpected results, for instance that you *hate* the phrase 'Her new bestseller' and don't trust glowing quotes because you think money has changed hands. Scenes from the story were requested, which we did have for a while (it was really hard work for me because I had to brief the designers). Now, in anniversary year, the UK series is in four different liveries and two sizes; for those of you who want a complete collection, I can only apologise.

My US editor shows me jackets in advance, and we tweak them. On translations, sometimes I've never even seen the finished books; I'm almost never asked about their covers.

Generally, I just stick by my sad hope that people will pay for what is inside, not what gets stuck on the front. We have scanned some of the jackets [overleaf] I've had over the years just for *The Silver Pigs*. Each of these was thought by the publisher to be the best way to sell the book to readers … In fact there are common themes – plus an anachronistic Colosseum, and my name spelled wrong!

My favourite story concerned a major book chain considering the proposed jacket for *Three Hands in the Fountain*. We were on scenes from the books at the time, and that one showed Falco and Anacrites in the sewer. The retailers asked, could it be livened up; could there, for instance, be things floating in the water? I wasn't at the meeting (of course), but I heard there was a sudden silence as people worked out *what* might be floating in a sewer …

Jackets do lie: for instance, authors plead with their publishers to use a specially youthful photo.

Events

Once I was published, I had to meet the public. Juvenal had prepared me for this:

> Some peeling dump of a hall in the suburbs, its doors
>   all barred
> And bolted like the gates of a city under siege …
> hangers-on to sit at the end of each row, distribute the
>   applause …
> the cushioned front row chairs that have to be returned
>   double-quick, when the performance is over

Germany, Eichborn, 1991

UK, Sidgwick & Jackson, 1989

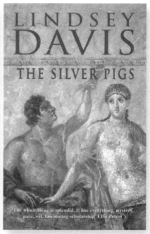

UK, Century, 2000

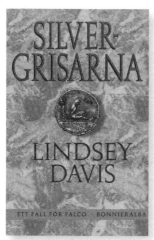

Sweden, Bonnier Alba, 1996

US, Crown, 1990

Japan, Kobunsha, 1998

Denmark, Klim, 1997

US, Ballantine, 1991

Germany, Knaur, 1993

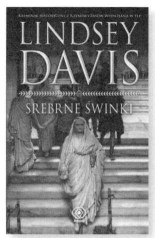

Poland, Rebis, 2010

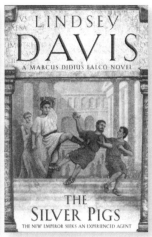

UK, Arrow, 2000

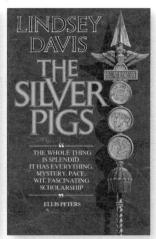

UK, Pan, 1990

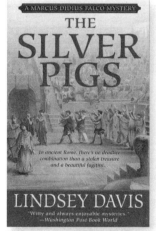

US, Minatour, 2006

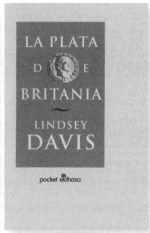

Spain, Edhasa, 1995

Spain, Edhasa, 1991

Italy, Tropea, 2002

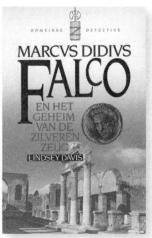

Netherlands, Unieboek, 1990

Spain (Catalan), Columna, 1997

I enjoy meeting readers but it gets more tiring every year. You can never relax, because there will always be some question you are not expecting. It can be lonely, you sometimes don't get to eat properly – but the good nights, with gales of laughter and lots of sales, make it worthwhile.

Favourite memory: overhearing a lady say excitedly to her friend: *She's lovely – she's so <u>ordinary!</u>*

Website

I didn't think I wanted a website; I didn't even have email or Internet access. I write about olden times, but new ideas don't frighten me; indeed if I had been timid I would not have entrusted this vital author tool to a person I had then never met. Ginny Lindzey from Texas took on that role and this is how she describes it:

Years ago, I realized that Lindsey should have a website and told her so. Once she was finally ready to embrace technology, the fun began.

See *Last Act in Palmyra*

We discussed what we (she) wanted and didn't want. We discussed organization. We discussed voice. And then Lindsey had to leave it to me, an amateur, to do the rest on blind faith because there was no way she could supervise my design work transatlantically. She had no idea what the site looked like until the day it was posted. That was an extraordinary amount of trust placed in a person she only knew from correspondence at that time.

The trust was well placed and our site was successfully launched in 1998. We took note of what worked and didn't work on the site. There have been several revisions, including the addition of the infamous 'Rants' page, which began when an American reader complained about the Arval Brothers apparently wearing wreaths of sweetcorn; this eventually raised some fundamental issues of whether British novels should be 'Americanized'.

Rant – 'an extravagant flight of words ... to rave in high-sounding language'
DR JOHNSON

We were famously praised in the UK publishing magazine The Bookseller*: 'It's the best author site I've ever visited. You get the feeling of an alert, steely intelligence and a good strong left hook to go with it.' And the article*

> concludes, 'Artistically, typographically and textually, this is an outstanding site.' This is wonderful praise for a couple of creative women who just put their heads together. Two things, I think, have made this an effective site. First, it is personally done. Lindsey doesn't just have a site created by some professional firm who have no idea what she is about. She writes the text, updates the diary, decides what goes in The Postbag, chooses the photos. Second, I've kept the site simple and focused on content, not bells and whistles. This site is personal; it is designed for Lindsey to communicate with her fans, and her fans with her.

One thing readers communicated was their desire for a Falco Companion!

Correspondence

From the start I had a lot of letters from readers. Many say, *I've never written to an author before,* so either I seem approachable – or that's just what readers politely say to authors. Email has increased the flow. Much of the correspondence brings me joy. Surprising numbers of people, both youngsters and those going back to education, have been inspired to study classical subjects – quite a responsibility! The Falco novels have helped women in labour, patients and their carers. One moving letter was from a young woman whose husband had died in Iraq, his last term of duty at least cheered by Falco. I like thinking that soldiers have Falco to provide escapism and keep them humane.

At my request readers sometimes provide little pen portraits. A website survey also helped determine who they are – men and women, aged from teens to nineties, rather a lot of teachers and academics, lawyers (one confessed to being no good), media people (surprising they owned up at all), retired folk, and every kind of occupation from beekeeper to knitting instructor, through cathedral curator to friars and jailors.

Just a few favourites:

Don't seek mass adulation. Be content with a small circle of readers – or are you mad enough To want your poems dictated in shabby schools? Not me.
HORACE

> On going into my local bookshop and asking was there any news? I was told after the guy looked you up on the screen, 'Both her next two novels have been cancelled. She's either retired or died.'
> (Dave Lee Tripp)

Suffice it to say, Falco is up there with chocolate!
(Vanessa Terry)

Two years ago I travelled on a cargo ship for five weeks.
Dear Lindsey, you saved my sanity. I lay on my bunk
and was transported through the First Century AD.
When one is surrounded by water and Russian sailors,
a book is of inestimable value.
(Mrs Barbara Young)

I hope that you will be amused rather than offended to
learn of a somewhat unusual use for one of your books.
My mother had the misfortune to be attacked by a
neighbour's large, aggressive dog in the garden of her
holiday home. On finding her ankle clenched between
sizeable canine teeth, my mother, rousing herself from
her lounger, swung her holiday read (a rather hefty
large-print version of See Delphi and Die*) above her*
head and felled the dog in one fair blow. I exaggerate; it
took two to knock the dog unconscious, the first merely
demonstrated that she meant business.

You will be pleased to know that my mother and the
dog were both unhurt by their respective ordeals. The
book fared worse, but retains some dignity, more than a
little battered and slightly grass-stained, in pride
of place on the bookshelf.
(Iola Robinson)

Radio

The Falco novels are being produced as BBC
radio drama productions. They are adapted for
radio by Mary Cutler, one of my oldest friends,
who was in my class at school, the senior
scriptwriter of *The Archers*. They are produced
in Birmingham by Peter Leslie Wild.

Anton Lesser is Falco and Anna Madeley
now plays Helena. I usually try to attend on at
least one day when the recordings are being
made, preferably the full 'read through'. I am
always amazed how much extra real actors can

Lindsey and Mary, giggling

add to words I wrote and thought I fully understood.
It's quite an emotional experience. There is an increas-
ing bond between the team too.

I feel that Mary does the best possible job. A great
deal has to be lost from the books and, sadly, it will

usually be Falco's musings – which, to me, are the main attraction. Some people complain the voices are not what they hear in their heads when they read. That's why I think nothing can beat books!

Film rights

A film called *The Age of Treason* was made, ostensibly of *The Silver Pigs*, though who would know it? It abandoned everything that makes the books special. Readers were very disappointed and I shall try to prevent that happening again. The BBC optioned the entire Falco series on what seemed decent terms (though I had doubts about their scripts). They bought *Rome* instead.

Film rights for all my books reside with me and I will consider options.

I never speculate on who would play Falco or Helena.

The Writing Process

What about writers of history? Do all their labours
Bring them bigger returns or merely consume
More midnight oil? With unrestricted licence
They pile up their thousand pages – and an
    enormous
Stationery bill.
JUVENAL

Creating a subject

There is a Creative Writing mantra: *write what you know.* Let's think about that for a satirical moment. I have never been a man or an ancient Roman; when I started to write I had not visited Italy; I was brought up a pacifist, have no connection with the police, to this day have never seen a dead body …

The Falco series shows what you can do with curiosity, hard work and imagination. Such qualities can earn enough for you to avoid ever having to get a job as a creative writing teacher.

Even so, some writing is more enjoyable for me. I hit upon my liking for passionate but dry historical writing with *The Course of Honour,* then with Falco I found the best idea in the world for me.

*You keep to the dress of everyday speech, but you're
    clever at the pointed
Juxtaposition; you've a fairly well-rounded diction;
    you're adept
At scraping unhealthy habits and nailing vice with a
    stroke of wit. Draw your material from there.*

That may be Persius saying *write what you know,* however.

Creating a hero

It is important for writer and readers to have sympathy with the lead character, or *some* character who is appealing, with whom you can identify. Where is the pleasure otherwise? Reading a novel is not a duty; nor is writing one. Both should be a joy.

Is Falco based on a real person? No. That's intrusive and a cop-out. Falco was specially created to do a special job. Yet he has qualities that I have known in a man, and liked, and loved. I hoped I would write about him for some time, though never dared imagine it would be twenty years. I built him to last.

I made him plebeian because it seemed more suitable, and was more to my own taste. He had to be hard. I made him an ex-soldier for that. I put him in Britain for a joke, during the Boudiccan Rebellion because he needed to be bitter about the past. He served in the Second Augustan legion, first because it was Vespasian's legion but mostly because this legion failed to turn up for the battle against Boudicca; this makes Falco and Petronius angry with the establishment, determined to leave the army, and sometimes inconvenienced by the past that was not their fault.

I gave him his best friend Petronius because it is traditional. A private investigator needs a police crony to leak official information, provide superior back-up, and occasionally arrest him just to give us a twinge.

He has a large family to overturn a stereotype. Philip Marlow has nobody. Falco is Italian. Being hampered by relatives' presence and family duties would help provide humour. Inventing a ridiculous family tree was a good game.

I was particular about choosing Falco's age. He has his thirtieth birthday in *The Silver Pigs.* Many people in

Down these mean streets a man must go, who is not himself mean, who is neither tarnished nor afraid. The detective in this kind of story must be this sort of man. He is the hero, he is everything. He must be a complete man and a common man and yet an unusual man. He must be, to use a rather weathered phrase, a man of honor – by instinct, by inevitability, without thought of it, and certainly without saying it. He must be the best man in the world and a good enough man for any world.
CHANDLER

the real Roman world would never reach this age, due to poor conditions and diet; large numbers of children died at birth or in their first few years, though the wealthy would live to seventy or older. I wanted Falco old enough to have knocked about the world; experienced, mature, able to impress people. He had to remain athletic and nimble, always capable in a fight. I did want him to have scope to change, so even by *A Dying Light in Corduba* he is: *older, mature, responsible, a seasoned state official: still stupid enough to take on any task, still put upon, still losing more than I ever gained.* He will move on still further in later books; for one thing, he will not always lose. However, I never expected to make him a rich man.

Leaving something unplanned keeps a series fresh.

Are you in love with him?

Oh get away! I was, and always will be, in love with someone else.

Creating a heroine

Curiously, Helena Justina was devised as a villain. Finally unmasked, she would have left Falco traumatised, carrying forward his bitterness about the woman who had so duped him ... But I wrote their love affair too well and couldn't part them.

I thought it a cliché to give my plebeian hero an aristocratic girlfriend. However, this allowed me to sustain a troubled love affair through several books. People *still* worry that I might break them up ... a good marketing plan.

Villainous characteristics worked: I made Helena clever, witty and scathing. Bad experiences with men let her match Falco's own slightly sour knowledge of women. A heroine needs a past to draw on just as much as a hero, though not too often, or readers feel left out. Helena is brave – essential for adventures. Mystery heroines must be feisty enough to ask questions, particularly awkward questions. Like Falco, she must be shrewd enough to evaluate answers and spot lies. She will be prepared – she will be *eager* – to take the lead in investigations. If Helena simply sat at home waiting to bandage Falco's wounds and listen devotedly to the story of his day, she would not be a *heroine*, merely a female character. But she is not a harridan; she has compassion and warmth.

This is important. I have written about Helena for twenty years. If I did not like her just as much as Falco, it would have been dire.

She is not perfect. She is above her ideal weight, cannot keep her hair up and would rather have her nose in a book than look after small children.

Practical point: I gave her children. I wanted to show that the Romans had contraception, but that it could fail for normal human reasons – in the heat of passion, people just don't use the stuff. But whenever Helena is pregnant, it gets in the way. Now every scene requires me to think, *Who is looking after the cute kids?* Falco is a *novus vir*, but half the time Helena has to do it. And I am not keen on cute kids; I prefer the dog.

Concerning sex: Helena likes it just as much as Falco. Every reader knows that – yet by modern clinical standards I have never described it. But a woman needs her mystery. I want people to like and admire her – but leave them curious for more.

Is she you?
No more than he is.

Creating a style

> *There are no fixed rules of style. They are governed by the usage of society and usage never stands still for any length of time. Many speakers hark back to earlier centuries for their vocabulary ... Others in seeking to confine themselves to familiar, everyday expressions, slip into an undistinguished manner. Both these practices, in their different ways, are a debased style (quite as much as the rejection of any expression that is not high-sounding, florid and poetical, avoiding the indispensable expressions in everyday use).*
> SENECA

I began with the 'gumshoe' authors' tone of voice. Chandler said, *I doubt that Hammett had any deliberate artistic aims whatever; he was trying to make a living by writing something he had firsthand information about. He made some of it up; all writers do; but it had a basis in fact; it was made up out of real things.* That said, Hammett and Chandler created a recognisable style, using short, terse sentences, a wry wit, startling imagery. Chandler learned the art of metaphor at Dulwich College rather than from the streets. So a classical education is responsible – the English literary style that goes back to Greek and Latin, appropriately for me.

My series is written in the first person because that seemed natural for a detective story. It makes for an informal conversational tone. This is visceral and vivid, which certainly helps when a shy, home-loving Englishwoman with hay fever writes as a macho, athletic man of the Mediterranean streets.

Then I think it's important to write of everything, especially things strange to us such as slaves or gladiators, as if to Falco they are perfectly ordinary aspects of life. Occasionally he can explain 'for any barbarians', but there must not be too much of that. Ginny Lindzey discussed imagery with me recently, mentioning the scene where Falco first arrives in Britain and describes it from the Roman point of view. *How the heck did you think that one up?* asked Ginny. It's a memory of a ghastly old Vaseline pot that lived in my bathroom cupboard for about thirty years … How the memory raised itself I have no idea. It works well because it's both visual and tactile; while Falco is portraying a backward Britain where people live in smoky round huts, he alludes to his own more sophisticated world, and also links to something we may recognise from ours.

Civilisation simply topped the province like a film of wax on an apothecary's ointment pot – easy enough to press your finger through. [SP]

Other techniques that matter are to have more knowledge – not just in the historical sense but about characters, for instance – than one uses; it's a cliché to say you must not insert great gobs of research, though the cliché is true. I try never to forget I am telling a story; I'm not there to show off or teach.

I developed a taste for upsetting stock situations – take the kiss between antagonists, where they traditionally melt into lust. My couple are just overwhelmed and embarrassed. *I had kissed her. Yet I still did not know what it was really like. I have known men who will tell you rough handling is what such women really want. They are fools. She was distraught. To be perfectly honest, I was distraught myself …* [SP] Later, it's better, truer, much more moving, when they do it honestly.

I also like to overturn clichés of the crime genre. There is a whole chapter in *Two for the Lions* where Falco's case has run into the ground; he explains that sometimes an investigator has to give up. *Life is not a fable, where stock characters seethe with implausible emotions, stock scenes are described in bland language, and every puzzling death is succeeded in regular progression by four clues (one false), three men with crackable alibis, two women with ulterior motives, and a confession which neatly explains every kink in events and which indicts the supposedly least obvious person – a miscreant any alert enquirer could unmask.* He rants on about coincidences, lies, implausible happenings and the fact that many murderers do get away with it – but of course, however many times he says this is a dead end, in a novel that cannot be allowed to happen. That's a bit of irony; I specialise in irony.

Timescale – *The Silver Pigs* takes place over eight or nine months. If I was allowed to write a long series, this would not work; Falco would die of old age. Besides, we want speed. Now most stories take place over a few weeks or months; in *One Virgin Too Many*, it is only ten days – because the missing child, trapped down a well, must be rescued alive.

I don't have space to dissect my style any further – nor is it in my interests commercially!

Influences

Manlius and Varga came swinging back home in the dead of night, arguing at the top of their voices with a gang of other artistic delinquents ... [PG]

People always want to know 'What are your influences?' Falco's tiny hand is frozen as he waits for the free-spirited fresco painters; I wonder how many readers have spotted the seepage from the opera *La Bohème*? I never noticed. I don't enjoy opera. I won't go to opera. I like music for its own sake. I want words you can hear and understand. I find most musicals watery. I only care about Gilbert and Sullivan and the repertoire of English satirical song. And Tom Lehrer. So do Manlius and Varga reveal an authentic influence? Of course not.

I am always very cautious about *influences*.

I suspect people want to believe I have based my writing on someone else's (perhaps because that is what they would do – or because some twerp of a tutor says to ask the question). For me, writing must be original. I deliberately chose the Roman period to be different. If the Falco novels are *influenced* by Sutcliff, or Chandler, or *Tristram Shandy,* or Giles cartoons, or *Round the Horne,* or Shakespeare, or *The Mikado,* or Liquidated Damages (building contracts), or Byron's *Don Juan,* or my mum … it is only a starting point. People who know me say, in astonishment, 'It sounds just like you!' Exactly.

You could just as well say my influences are 'Dido's Lament', Vaughan Williams' *Fantasia,* Tchaikovsky's *Pathétique* and all the other music Richard and I loved, especially with Julian Bream or Alicia De Larrocha … Or they are sausages, boeuf bourguignon, lemon meringue pie, bacon sandwiches (with HP sauce), macadamia nuts, pesto pasta, Stilton and Cheddar …

Or loathing pretension. Or needing to pay the mortgage.

Everything I have ever seen, heard, read; everyone I ever met; every place I remember lurks in the subconscious ready to give me ideas. Ideas are just an unopened packet of plasticine. It takes particular thumbs to mould them.

Enough of *influences.*

A Sharp Discourse on 'Errors'

And another thing!

I wonder at the vehemence of some people who have written to me about perceived mistakes. Often they are wrong. Sometimes they attack my publisher, as if I was their enemy, not a shared party in a contract. Complainents' fury is alarming. What is it supposed to achieve, to tick off a grown author like a naughty child? Are these ravers in the pay of jealous rivals, who hope I'll groan, *Why do I bother?* and retire? Grr.

I have thumped out novels steadily for twenty years. It would be a marvel if there were no mistakes. The books would be bland and safe, sterile pedantry, not full of creativity and cheery ideas.

My books are pored over in the production stages. They are edited, copy-edited, proof-read. After publishing, I collect mistakes diligently and they are corrected in new editions. When I am close to a text, I don't see spelling mistakes, homophones, omissions or repetitions. Some people in my family have dyslexia. My Oxford tutor said, generously, my problem is twofold: my brain works too fast for my hand and I am too interested in the ideas to see the words properly.

People who write to complain won't help by blind rage. I worry about their anger, and one day I myself will snap.

> *The boys with their feet on the desk know that the easiest murder case in the world to break is the one somebody tried to get very cute with; the one that really bothers them is the murder somebody thought of only two minutes before he pulled it off ...*
> CHANDLER

Research

How do you do your research? is the question I am asked most often.

Research sources and tools

> *The object of this history is to console the reader. History is not what you thought. It is what you can remember.*
> SELLAR AND YEATMAN

Tired researcher in shop doorway

I had a good classical education (Latin and some Greek), when this was mainly linguistic, with history and philosophy, but little social history. I was introduced to archaeology, a fascination I kept. But this is crucial: I read English at university. So: I use primary sources. I read academic works but if I think their authors are barmy, or just copying previous textbooks, I reject them. I will access the Internet for a 'quick fix', but I treat it as fundamentally flawed. Whenever possible, I go and have a look. For my Roman novels I generally visit Rome once a year, plus any country where that story is set.

I have been researching the Romans for twenty years. I really enjoy it. To me, that enjoyment is essential. I study in the way I was taught by rigorous women at Oxford: I soak myself in background material, then evaluate my findings using experience and common sense. I have a large library; I visit museums and sites. Finally, I let ideas bubble up and mould them into a plot. Ideas may be mulled for years – or never used at all.

This is my method. It works for my readers. Namby-pamby would-be writers who hope I'll give them a magic formula that requires neither work nor narrative skill will be disappointed. 'How do you use the history?' I use it to tell a good story. There is no other point.

As a novelist, my need for information covers a wider field than classics and archaeology. I don't just need ancient jewellery, wine, pots and hypocausts but geography, weather, plants, psychology and physical

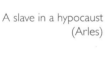

When I am fifty three or so, I would like to write a novel as good as Persuasion, *but with a modern setting of course. For the next thirty years or so, I shall be collecting material for it. If anyone asks me what I work at, I shall say, 'Collecting material'. No one can object to that. Besides, so I shall be.*
GIBBONS

A slave in a hypocaust
(Arles)

illness ... While writing a book I will be constantly burrowing for 'stuff'. This isn't just crackpot meticulousness. Every time a reader knows, or feels, that I have told them something right, whether it's a 'fact' or an insight into human nature, that increases their trust. This is the 'willing suspension of disbelief', a theory which has ancient roots in Horace but was most famously propounded by Coleridge to explain how introducing the everyday could persuade readers to accept the fantastic. It works just as well for building a historical novel.

Interestingly, it also works for creating a false alibi after a crime: the more truth a statement contains, the easier it is to conceal holes in the story from a sceptical investigator.

Routinely, I omit bibliographies. Novels should stand unsupported. If they happen to lead people to deeper study, there are experts to provide reading lists. *But* you have asked me to suggest good books.

My earliest Roman encounters were in Rosemary Sutcliff, and a copy of *The Golden* Ass by Apuleius, which I suspect my dad had acquired because of the sex – my first sight of sex too. Thirty years on (when I had mastered sex), Richard gave me Peter Salway's *Roman Britain*. There I discovered Vespasian (more sex? I've never forgotten a BBC interviewer who broke down in front of a statue and could not continue when I said, *Well, look at him – he was obviously good in bed*).

While I was at school, someone clearing a house thought of me and I was given a two-volume *Dictionary of Greek and Roman Antiquities* by Smith, Wayte and Marindin, which I still use, though it dates from 1890 and there are modern versions. My vision of imperial Rome was grounded in Carcopino's famous *Daily Life in Ancient Rome* – 1941, but it still works because its literary examples are culled from Latin authors. I read many classical authors, usually in the Penguin Classics translations: Suetonius' *Twelve Caesars* (which just fell apart as I wrote this); the satirical works of Juvenal, Martial and Horace; the *Histories* of Tacitus and Josephus; Petronius' *Satyricon;* the *Letters* of Pliny the Younger and of Seneca (much more palatable than Pliny, though he was famous for not practising what he preached) – then plays, poems, essays and recipes. For our first trips to Rome and Naples I had the Blue Guides, the *Rome City Guide* and *Southern Italy,* which cover monuments and art for all periods and remind me Rome had a history outside the Empire …

If, today, I had to snatch a suitcase of Roman books from my own shelves to save from rising flood waters, I would grab:

Rome and Her Empire, Barry Cunliffe (McGraw-Hill)

Daily Life in Ancient Rome, Jérôme Carcopino (Taylor
    & Francis)

Ancient Inventions, Peter James and Nick Thorpe
    (Michael O'Mara)

Oxford Archaeological Guide to Rome, Amanda Claridge
    (Oxford University Press)

Houses and Society in Pompeii and Herculaneum, Andrew
    Wallace-Hadrill (Princeton University Press)

The Making of the Roman Army, Lawrence Keppie,
    (Batsford)

Ancient Rome, City Planning and Administration, O. F.
    Robinson (Routledge)

Imperial Inquisitions, Steven Rutledge (Routledge)

Satires of Juvenal (Penguin Classics)

Apicius, Christopher Grocock and Sally Grainger
    (Prospect)

Travel in the Ancient World, Lionel Casson (Johns
    Hopkins)

Handbook to Life in Ancient Rome, Lesley Adkins and
    Roy A. Adkins (Facts on File)

The Oxford Classical Dictionary, Simon Hornblower
    and Antony Spawforth (OxfordUniversity Press)

The Barrington Atlas of the Greek and Roman World, ed.
    Richard J.A. Talbert (Princeton University Press)

But – and for me this is a big but – if bailiffs took everything except the tools of my trade, *those* would be: *The Shorter Oxford English Dictionary*; *A Dictionary of the Underworld* by Eric Partridge; Roget's *Thesaurus*; and John Woodforde's absolutely indispensable *The Strange Story of False Teeth.*

I won't recommend Internet sites, which change so often and are so variable in quality, but you will now find virtual tours of Rome. For its reliable scholarship, I use the University of Virginia's *Rome Reborn.* I still think imagination is the best virtual tool, but I'm so old-fashioned I know how to make my own entertainment.

When in trouble, I shove in a smell. I believe I am famous for my smells … How do you research an odour? Site visits, perhaps – or that other vital author tool: memory.

People were nonplussed when I claimed that for *One Virgin Too Many,* I researched virginity from memory too.

Sometimes you have a lucky break. Richard paced out the bridge at Cordoba for me, enabling Falco to say it was *three hundred and sixty-five paces, one for every day of the year.*

Experts

I am bolder now, but for years I was very shy of asking people for help and information. I did everything myself. By *Last Act in Palmyra,* I needed to contact the Reptile House at London Zoo about pythons. Have I imagined that Richard dialled the number, announced 'A young lady wants to ask about snakes' then passed over the handset sternly? It proved wise, because the Reptile House staff begged that I did not show a python killing a person, even by constriction, since pythons are loath to do it. I later heard a lovely piece on the radio about keeping snakes, including a pet python who was so lonely and upset when left alone in the house, he spitefully destroyed a stereo set ...

Now, if I know who to approach and I really need more information, I ask.

Archaeology

My Latin teacher Elys Varney (who probably taught me more than she thinks – or more than she thought at the time) ran an archaeological society. We all joined because, as a 'minority' subject, it was joint with the Boys' School; it produced some career archaeologists and left me with a lifelong interest. I was too nesh to like crouching on my knees in the earth, out of doors, but I nonetheless ended up making a career from my fascination. Elys can be proud of that.

Scholarship has changed in the past twenty years: a British tribe in the Midlands, once the Coritani, are now the Corieltauvi. King Cogidumnus, I've learned, should be Togidubnus. I do make fun of this in *A Body in the Bath House,* hoping that might indicate to people that <u>I may know something</u> ... It doesn't stop those frosty letters: *Miss Davis! I seem to remember that fifty years ago my teacher told us that the king was called Cogi!*

At least when you are writing a series you can adapt. In *Venus in Copper* Falco's cheese grater poignantly survives his apartment collapse; it was modelled on one in a case of First Century domestic implements at the British Museum. For their exhibition *Vases* and *Volcanoes,* they reassessed it as Etruscan and centuries older. Hence: *The cheesegrater had a curious history. I had swiped it at Pa's warehouse, thinking it looked like an ordinary product of a house clearance. When Pa noticed it at our apartment one day, he told me it had in fact come from an Etruscan tomb. Whether he was himself the tomb robber remained vague as usual. He reckoned it might be five hundred years old.* [TFL]

In writing about the First Century I have a vivid heritage from Vesuvius to assist – I couldn't have chosen better!

Archaeology is my starting point, where so many other novelists have begun with Latin literature, often fawningly. Even the best archaeologists are prone to hanker after a grand Forum dig – but they do cover the workshops and houses too; I think this gives a wider spectrum than relying on texts. (Ideally you need both, it goes without saying.) My own interest is not just in the remains and what they tell us, but in the history of archaeology as a discipline; problems of conservation and presentation to the public; and funding. All these issues are live in Rome and the Bay of Naples sites particularly.

And what could be better to fire up the creative furnace than sitting on a lump of fallen stone, in sun or shade, letting ideas just drift into your brain? So let's talk about where it's taken me …

The Novels

The Course of Honour

First published 1997
Shortlisted for the Georgette Heyer Historical Novel
    Prize 1986

I remember the wolfhound, howling. When his owners went on holiday, he stayed with my neighbours, desolately homesick. He howled every night, all night. I worked late on my portable typewriter, with the dog mournfully serenading a new moon over the slate rooftops of south London, a Mars Bar to sustain me. I was living in my first flat, all I had been able to afford as a government employee. This maisonette would one day inspire Falco's bachelor apartment, but it first informed the rented room where Caenis lives. Her landlord came from older memories: one Bryan in Croydon, when I first worked in London. I felt good, finally nailing that creep Bryan, he of the mouse, the remark about blouse buttons, the professed liking for single lady tenants, the habit of entering a girl's room without knocking, as he hoped for a glimpse of underwear ...

    I was nailing a lot of other things, too. I had found my writing 'voice'; I became brave enough to speak my mind about people and life, back when I tended to be rude, bitter or pessimistic. I had known tragedy, loneliness and disappointment, so there is much of me in Caenis, and vice versa – yet we always were distinct. Mrs Thatcher's Britain was depressing for people of my tastes and background, but it was hardly the Rome of Tiberius, Caligula or Nero. The Iron Lady and her fawning grey henchmen were more akin to Augustans, stamping down the masses with platitudes while diligently accruing cash and covering up hypocrisy. This is relevant; it shows why I found Vespasian so good-hearted and intelligent as a man and a ruler.

    Until *The Course of Honour*, I tried to write novels set in the Seventeenth Century. After a few feints, I was

Head of Vespasian

changing to this love story about the ancient Romans. Even I suspected publishers would baulk, but I knew it was the right time for me.

I looked at Roman Britain because that seemed less worrying for British publishers. I grasped that they only liked the familiar, but they did know Robert Graves' *I, Claudius* which had gripped the nation on TV. Descriptions of the Claudian invasion of Britain always mentioned 'the future emperor Vespasian' bopping the Dorset hill forts. I discovered his biography by the Roman historian Suetonius. Vespasian's background and public service ethic, his talent and modesty were attractive, especially after the weirdness and extravagance of the more famous – that is, infamous – Julio-Claudians. Suetonius clearly wants to sneer and sensationalise, but with the Flavians he cannot find much scandal; after Livia, Messalina and Agrippina, he is brief with Caenis. A sentence which is primarily about Vespasian's wife and children dispatches my heroine fast: *he then took up again with Caenis, his former mistress and one of Antonia's freedwomen and secretaries, who remained his wife in all but name even after he became Emperor.* Caenis can be glimpsed elsewhere, including in the anecdote about Antonia's letter to Tiberius given by the historian Dio Cassius, but generally I built my whole novel on that first statement. The more I explored, the more I was amazed that apparently this wonderful personal story had been ignored by historians and novelists.

Bust, thought to represent Antonia

Part of the reason is that Roman snobbery towards the non-patrician Vespasian has subtly persisted down the centuries. So many historical novels concentrate on men: heroes and aristocrats, never frugal jokers who can get a job done while still seeming surprised at their own capability. Because Caenis had been a slave, *she* rated even less attention. It left me a clear field, a challenge in which I revelled. I could make my own rules.

As with all historical figures I had genuine diffidence, respect and reluctance to get Caenis and Vespasian wrong. Their story is glorious, but covers forty years, much longer than the scope of most novels, with many a tricky hiatus when the couple lived apart. Long periods passed where, even if we now know what happened to her lover, Caenis can have had little idea.

None of the historians bother to say what she herself was up to in the Year of the Four Emperors. It's my own guess that *Caenis* sorted out Nero when he turned up at Vespasian's house in the chariot of Jupiter.

Primarily, I had to illuminate her background. First I used the times in which she lived, retold from a woman's and a slave's perspective. Robert Graves made these extraordinary events familiar, but I could take the story forwards, making it my own. My civil service career was unexpectedly useful for government behind the scenes, rule through imperial freedmen. My own experiences of love and loss resonated. My deep fondness for social and political satire must be obvious on every page. I am proud of how I handled that – how the grim jokes zing and the narrative surges through often-ridiculous episodes. But I am proudest of the way I considered what it meant to be a Roman slave.

As the property of the imperial family, Caenis was relatively fortunate. In a secretarial position, she lived in an elegant home and her work was not physically oner-ous; she must have been given education; we know she enjoyed trust, with its associated benefits. As a freed-woman, she became part of the Claudian extended family, the imperial *familia* – as high as anyone could go. Vespasian realises she has to some extent outstripped him, even though he is a senator. To illustrate the per-manent damage inflicted on a slave, I also had to find telling details such as the fact that Caenis never knows her birthday. Crucially, Vespasian could never marry her; it was illegal under Roman law. The fact that he was a deep traditionalist makes his response to this situation the more admirable, and that he stayed true points up just how special Antonia Caenis must have been.

I made my Caenis uncertain of her parentage – though I have since been told that in Istria, in the former Yugoslavia, inscriptions record she originated there. She eventually visited the province. Vespasian endowed buildings in her honour; I would like to have shown him doing this after he became sufficiently influential to have palace records unearthed – or per-haps Narcissus would have found her birth records ... Too late now. That's the trouble with history. New facts will pop up after you compose your big work. It is all the more maddening because in my teens I went to

Pula, visited the amphitheatre and may have seen those inscriptions, long before they held any significance for me. Now I just have to smile to myself and imagine some wry quip from Caenis at the impossibility of creating perfect work, however hard you strive.

Strive at it I did. The roof was leaking, my savings were fast running out and the howling wolfhound seemed all too apt as night music. Had not the research for this book inspired Falco, it would have been the grim path back to 'real' work for me. Falco, who sprang out of the Rome I described in this book, saved me in the nick of time.

When I wrote *The Course of Honour* it was the best thing I had ever produced. Perhaps it still is. Even so, nobody would publish it for ten years; a love story set so long ago was seen as too difficult for readers in the 1980s. Only after I had established the lighter-hearted Falco series as a selling genre, once archaeology regularly featured on TV, reconstructions of ancient equipment and re-enactions of ancient life began to grip documentary-makers, and Latin was even taught in primary school lunch clubs, did a publisher risk it. I was able to revise the text, with ten years as a professional writer behind me, though it needed little editing; I did add details I had discovered in the interim, particularly in the passages about Antonia, and I had discovered the real name of Caenis' steward, Aglaeus (who put up a memorial to her near her house – now under the Italian Ministry of Transport ...). The English edition has remained permanently in print, delighting many readers with this strong true story where moral strength, sanity and devotion manage to endure through appalling times. In the dark world we have now, it may be even more of a beacon.

When I re-read *The Course of Honour*, I confess I am startled at what I achieved. If I had written nothing else, this book would justify that long-ago change of careers. It is a story that reminds us in the West of a moment in the past when much of our present social structure was formed. Set at the dawn of the Golden Age of the Roman Empire, it holds apt lessons about imperialism, of course. Madness, extravagance, perversion and ambition will always be entertaining, but against the dangerous glamour of power gone wrong, the steady tale of

Vespasian and Caenis has much to tell us. We see how fragile 'civilisation' can be, but we also see how human decency can doggedly survive.

The Falco Novels

I was in correspondence with an agent. She (Heather) couldn't sell *The Course of Honour* at that time, but said to carry on with the Roman detective I mentioned, making sure I paid attention to the plot ...

The Silver Pigs

First published 1989
Shortlisted for the Georgette Heyer Historical Novel
*   Prize 1988*
Winner of the Authors' Club Best First Novel Prize 1989

There were no prototypes, or none that I knew. For me, that was the point. I innocently thought a new writer should be original.

In order to ground my historical figure, this book has references to the 'real' detective genre: *I was wearing my powder blue suit, with dark shirt, tie and display handkerchief, black brogues, black wool socks with dark blue clocks on them. I was neat, clean, shaved and sober, and I didn't care who knew it. I was everything the well-dressed private detective ought to be. I was calling on four million dollars* [CHANDLER]. So in Falco: *Since I was visiting a million sesterces I risked my throat under a barber's razor. I wore a worn white toga with the holes folded out of sight, a short clean tunic, my best belt with the Celtic buckle, and brown boots.* [SP]

I had to balance familiar elements and my own new ideas: *I went to the funeral. In my line of work, it is traditional.* [SP] But it is a specifically ancient Roman cremation. I had fixed my creed: I would use classics and archaeology. I would care about them. I would not alter or pervert what we know, or believe we know.

However, I would overturn stereotypes merrily. The big one is what happens to Sosia Camillina: *I rarely know the victim; I don't meet the victim until after the crime. That order of events is what I recommend.* [SP] Theft from the Treasury and a plot to dethrone an emperor wouldn't make a 'crime' novel. I had to produce a murder. I took a startling decision: I killed off the ingénue. Apart from letting me escape the dilemma of whether the hot-blooded Falco would seduce the willing Sosia, this made a valid point. In traditional plots, the victim is a naked blonde. Her role is merely to kick-start the action. We learn little about such women and certainly don't feel affection for them. But Falco has fallen for the girl, and readers are invited to feel her bright attraction too. Killing her is a thump in the guts.

It was the first time I had devised a murder (those in *The Course of Honour* came ready-made). I gave the death a direct source in history: *At the beginning of his reign Domitian would spend hours alone every day doing nothing but catch flies and stabbing them with a needle-sharp pen* [SUETONIUS].

Losing Sosia would set the melancholy tone for Falco's experiences in Roman Britain – which I introduced to reassure publishers. Britain was ours. (At that time, I had no thought of Falco being read elsewhere.) Britain was also a gloomy, uncivilised place to write about – always a pleasure to do. So I established a tradition: Falco travels; has a horrible time so complains morosely; he despises the places and their people; he is homesick for Rome.

Archaeologically, I made Roman Britain as accurate as possible, yet ran into problems that were to dog me. For Roman London, for instance, I learned the probable site of the Governor's Palace, with hints of layout, but centuries of rebuilding meant there wasn't enough detail – and I felt scared of inventing. I took Falco to Bath, such a famous and well-preserved archaeological site now – only to read that in AD70 this was just a small Celtic shrine. At least that lined up poor Falco as the man who gets the future hilariously wrong: *Rome had replaced some basic native equipment with a proper lead-lined reservoir, yet I could not believe that anything could ever be made of the place. Oh there were plans, but there were always plans. We sat in the reservoir, which was full of sand thrown up by the spring, drank flat tepid water laden with foul-tasting minerals* [ever been to the Pump Room, people?] *and watched red-nosed building surveyors clambering about the cliffs, trying to convince themselves there was scope for a vibrant leisure spa.* [SP]

I can never use real murder victims. If human remains from Roman times are excavated, clearly hidden under floorboards or knifed and thrown into ditches (as has happened), then Falco may not discover and remove them; they must stay for the archaeologists. But the fabled silver pigs were one wonderful exception. Four Roman ingots, apparently from the right period, had been found in the Mendips. I think I saw one at Dorchester Museum. They had been hidden under a cairn and abandoned; their strange stamps implied dodgy deals. These were perfect. My plot speculates on their criminal history, then Falco hides them for safety; he is in too poor condition to go back to fetch them.

By the end of this book, I had established the Falco genre: a mix of 'gumshoe' pavement-pounding and overseas adventure, glances at 'police procedure', occasional set pieces from history, archaeologically

A Vespasianic ingot

authentic Roman life, nods to more modern concepts, the love between Falco and Helena, the importance of family, and the tussle between a pragmatic establishment and one man's dogged morality. I had also established that all of this could be – *should* be – funny.

My agent managed to sell the book; Oliver, my farsighted editor, took a second one as well. The Falco books were a series. My life would never be the same again. What a lucky girl I was.

Shadows in Bronze

First published 1990

I started this book before *The Silver Pigs* found a publisher. That may explain the rambly synopsis. (At least now I did complete a synopsis!) No other book in the series would be so closely linked with what had gone before. Afterwards I deliberately tried to write each book so it could be picked up by a new reader and read in its own right; I just hoped people would be so intrigued they would go back to the beginning. Some do; others happily read the series in a haphazard order.

Mystery novels leave unfinished business: usually it's the murderer, who is so often killed off to save the bother of writing a trial. I am more tidy. So I provided a horrific introductory scene where, ten days after the chief plotter has been left dead in a hot warehouse, his maggot-ridden remains must be secretly cleared up. Needless to say, this ghastly job falls to Falco. I have always been proud of the nauseous description, much of which is achieved by colourful metaphor and your nervous imagination, rather than explicit detail. A pathologist's memoirs helped.

After Publius drops down the drain, what of the other plotters, by now all fugitives? Faustus Ferentinus went abroad to stay with his auntie in Lycia; will he *ever* reappear to be dealt with? If he does, will Falco or any of the rest of us even remember who he is? Such a lovely name, with those onomatopoeical Fs ... That left two brothers and an ambitious senator, all of whom Vespasian wants to salvage if possible, plus a mystery man I couldn't bear to abandon. Falco has to track them down.

At the heart of the book is the Bay of Naples with its glorious archaeological sites. We visit the best known: Pompeii, Herculaneum, Oplontis. (*I* visited them – oh bliss!) As Falco strolls around, hindsight tells

Pompeii street, with stepping stones and Vesuvius

us that Mount Vesuvius is just waiting to explode. He calls Pompeii *a place that intended to last*, perhaps with ironical hindsight himself. Some of my favourite scenes take place in Herculaneum, which has always been to me the Solihull of Roman Naples, though you may need to be a Midlander to understand that. It is where the much-loved episode occurs when Nero the ox tries to rape a donkey, so Falco and his endearing nephew Larius are arrested for blasphemy.

Although there are 'proper' murders, starting with a death by arson at the (invented) Little Temple of Hercules Gaditanus, this story is primarily told through the developing love between Falco and Helena. I knew not to resolve that too soon (it would take several more novels, and perhaps neither character will ever feel entirely secure). Here, each misunderstands the other's intentions, they both wrongly decide that social class is a barrier, they fail to talk openly about their feelings and there is a serious breakdown of communication over Helena's pregnancy. NB: I was determined that actions should have consequences. Unprotected sex will bring babies. Contraception is so rarely used by heroes in fiction, yet those 'girl in every book' action men are never pulled up by paternity suits. My boy was to be different.

On the other hand, it was too early for Falco and Helena to be parents.

Subplots explore other kinds of human love: the hormonal teenaged Larius; the tetchy, realistic, yet romantic marriage of Petronius Longus and Arria Silvia; the homosexual leanings of Aemilius Rufus Clemens, which come as such as a surprise to Falco; the piteously lovelorn Aemilia Fausta, who – after empowerment through Falco's cithara lessons? – sorts herself out rather briskly; even the ambitious barmaid Tullia, who will bury the man who betrayed her, in gratitude for independence and funds.

A confused donkey got over-friendly with a spectator at an agricultural show. The jack donkey rushed towards a large man displaying a 'builder's crack' from his trousers as he leant over railings. Towing his woman owner behind him, the donkey mounted the terrified man at the Great Yorkshire Show. A witness said: 'The man was pinned by the donkey's forelegs and it started to bite his neck. His mates were in heaps of laughter.' The donkey's owner lashed out with a long cart whip, crying 'Git orf, Piglet!' Earlier the victim called a judge, who asked him to move off the railings, 'A toffee-nosed twit in a bowler hat'.
METRO

We explore Helena Justina's previous marriage. Two characters who will become significant appear for the first time: Geminus and Anacrites. The golden magistrate, Aemilius Rufus, is my first exercise in the over-promoted high-flyer. Owing everything to money and rank, his presumed talent is a sham, his judgement hasty, and power makes him dangerous.

Triremes on the Bay of Naples

A big theme is political. Falco advises the plotters to make their peace with Vespasian, on practical grounds: *It's clear the Flavian circus is here to stay.* Gordianus is convinced, and so saved, by Falco. Among those who resist, Atius Pertinax has no moral core but is a jumped-up young man with a grossly inflated idea of his worth, supported by a deluded patron; we know that his shallow treatment of Helena foreshadows how badly he would act in a public position.

Aufidius Crispus is most telling. Falco sees his quality; I myself half admire him. He has genuine leadership qualities; he is clever, tough, resourceful, persuasive, even likeable. He says: *After Nero died, we saw Galba, Otho, Vitellius, Vespasian – and the only thing which made any of them better than anybody else – for instance better than me! – was that they had the simple luck at the time to be holding public positions which provided armed support.* It is cynical, but irrefutable. Falco responds – to us – *The man had talent. He had shown over the problem of Fausta that he had some compassion, which is rare. He also had good sense, a cheerful humour, the ability to organise, and an approachable style. Vespasian's family had years of public service behind them, yet they continued to seem small-minded and provincial in a way this urbane, likeable character never would. I did like him. Mainly because at bottom he refused to take himself seriously.* [SB] Crispus refuses to reach an accommodation with the Flavians. Historically, of course, he has to.

The problem Aufidius Crispus poses still seems to me one of the most interesting I've covered. It gives real poignancy to this story of misplaced ambition and failed effort. Meanwhile Falco will go forward into other books, accepting his own uneasy alliance with Vespasian – not swayed by uncritical devotion to the man, but believing this is as good as Rome can hope to get.

Venus in Copper

First published 1991

I had to survive a period of anxiety: my editor, Oliver, lost his job at Sidgwick & Jackson in a reorganisation. The replacement editor fouled up, so I was free to follow Oliver. Random House UK offered me a super three-book contract. My agent still has the letter she wrote to my bank manager to explain why a person on the breadline was about to become rich enough to buy a new house.

It had its own study. I was a real author.

Second study (airing cupboard not shown)

With *Venus in Copper* I portrayed Falco as a freelance investigator. He is formally engaged by private clients – who later, in the traditional manner, dismiss him; he, in the traditional manner, then continues with the case independently. We see him in his own city, among the rich and the poor. We watch him on surveillance, interviewing witnesses, investigating obvious murders both past and present, then to the best of his ability solving them.

I tried hard to have the three occupations and murders of Severina's husbands specifically Roman in character: the bead-seller who dies of sunstroke in the arena, the apothecary whose death is caused by the kind of Roman medicinal pastilles that archaeologists really find, and the wild-animal trainer who is eaten by a panther. Central to the story is property fraud; the scene where a developer buys a burning house cheaply reflects the practices of the Roman millionaire, Crassus. Although Severina is never tried, she will marry the legal clerk who knows her crimes and who can prevent her killing again because of evidence he has planted in a particularly Roman place: on a will deposited with the Vestal Virgins.

Moreover, observing how extremely subject the city was to fire and falling down of houses, by reason of their height and their standing so near together, he bought slaves that were builders and architects, and when he had collected these to the number of more than five hundred, he made it his practice to buy houses that were on fire, and those in the neighbourhood, which, in the immediate danger and uncertainty the proprietors were willing to part with for little or nothing, so that the greatest part of Rome, at one time or other, came into his hands.
PLUTARCH, trans. DRYDEN

In this story Falco meets Thalia the exotic dancer and Jason the python. Both were such good value and so popular they would reappear in later books. It wasn't planned. I just enjoyed them.

During the investigation Falco and Helena are settling their private lives. Like me, Falco obtains better accommodation (apparently). In a key scene Helena Justina then chooses to come to live with him – arriving just as he is cooking the enormous turbot, his gift from Titus. Turbots frequently appear in Latin literature as the ultimate luxury. In Juvenal one is presented to Domitian, with a long satirical description of attempts to cook the thing – 'oven-bake by committee'. For research, I too cooked a turbot. This was one of my

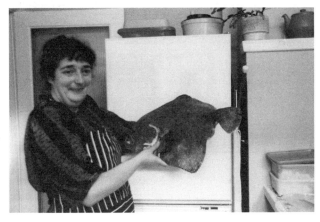

most intriguing research efforts. Selfridges provided a whole fish – they called it a baby, though it seemed big enough and unexpectedly deep and sturdy, so its snout and tail had to be bent up in the pan. Many details in the iconic scene are based on our experiences (though my mother did not come to grab the skeleton for stock). But Petronius having his arms burned by the shield represents Oliver my editor who was holding the fish on a fast-conducting stainless-steel tray.

Another key scene is the collapse of the apartment building. We know such disasters happened – often some deliberate ploy by landlords so they could re-develop and charge higher rents. My description owes a lot to TV films of the demolition expert Fred Dibnah neatly bringing down redundant industrial chimneys. The property plot involves themes dear to my heart: hatred of landlords, shoddy builders – and it can be no

We live in a city shored up, for the most part, with gimcrack
Stays and props; that's how our landlords arrest
The collapse of their property, papering over great cracks
In the ramshackle fabric, reassuring the tenants
They can sleep secure, when all the time the building
Is poised like a house of cards.
I prefer to live where
Fires and midnight alarms are not quite such common events.

HORACE

Parrot in the House of the Birds, Alexandria

coincidence that an estate agent is killed by a mob, in a book I wrote while selling my flat ...

But let's be clear: I have never owned a parrot.

The Iron Hand of Mars

First published 1992

Other novelists take Latin writing and Roman history as their starting point, but I generally use archaeology more. However, in this book I used historical events, relying heavily on Tacitus and Josephus. The plot this time is a 'quest' adventure. Falco must solve the two real mysteries of what happened to the colourful German rebel leaders, Civilis and Veleda. I came across a third question, too: what was the fate of Munius Lupercus, commander of the fort at Vetera, who was sent as a 'gift' to Veleda?

It was to be a novel with a heavy military background. I feared this might trouble readers, though it turned out to be among the most popular books in the series. The plot concerns recent chaos and restoring normality. Rebels have to be contained; rogue legions are tamed; fractured industry is restored. Ethics are re-established too, we hope. Love and loyalty also have their moments.

Unravelling the complex events of the Year of the Four Emperors was a challenge. I particularly dealt with that most stroppy of legions, the Fourteenth Gemina Martia Victrix; they had been part of the Claudian invasion force, helped establish Roman Britain in the early days, and were one of the legions – unlike Falco's – that defeated Queen Boudicca. So I felt affection for them, enlivened by what I knew of their later ups and downs from Graham Webster's magisterial *The Roman Imperial Army*.

Writing about Germany brings to mind the Varus disaster of AD9. A newspaper article alerted me to the now well-known story of Captain Tony Clunn, a British officer fascinated by the 'lost' battle site, which he discovered near Kalkriese. I decided that Roman soldiers would be equally fascinated by their fellows' fate – from which sprang some haunting scenes. Writing my book pre-dated the new museum at Kalkriese, but we visited Mainz, which has a fine Roman collection in the Landesmuseum – not many surviving remains, but we obviously found a Jupiter Column because here's our photo.

Nobody knows how the historical mysteries ended, or they wouldn't be mysteries … Veleda's ultimate fate, though sometimes referred to as conjectural, is probably known. I hint that her tribe, the Bructeri, eventually turned against her (perhaps because she was unsuccessful; isn't that always the way?). The Bructeri were wiped out later by rivals. I would be able to cover Veleda's personal history in *Saturnalia* – though at this stage it was not planned.

Her 'gift', Munius Lupercus, had been in command of the huge double fort at Vetera, which fell to the rebels in terrible circumstances. Lupercus was dispatched to Veleda, but executed before he reached her. I guessed at the kind of tribal tensions involved and suggested the manner of his death. This alludes to the 'bog bodies' found in various parts of Europe. The most famous in Britain, the wonderfully nicknamed 'Pete Marsh' (Lindow Man), had been unearthed in 1984. Now in the British Museum, Pete is one of the most poignant archaeological relics. Scientific tests suggest this young

Mainz, Jupiter Column

man of twenty-five, who lived in Falco's period
between AD20–90, suffered a very violent ritualistic
death, perhaps a victim of human sacrifice: he was probably struck twice on the head with a heavy object like an
axe and kneed in the back so hard it broke a rib; a narrow
cord around his neck may have been used to strangle
him and break his neck; though probably dead, his
throat was cut, and he was placed face down in a pool.
Other bog bodies have shown evidence of being pinned
down under hurdles. Ötzi the Ice Man, that other iconic
ancient body, was found in September 1991, which
must have been just when I was finishing this novel.

We don't know if Civilis lived or died, but I decided
he might have been persuaded to live under house
arrest, like another rebel, Classicus, who lived in Trier.
Civilis claimed a friendly relationship with Vespasian, so
must have been a candidate for pardon. Xanthus is all
my own (you guessed!). You may think I must have
invented him specifically to deal with Civilis. I can't
fully remember, but I am fairly sure that the idea of
controlling the rebel through *barbering* came as a last-
minute flash. That's writing!

The much-loved Little Mess Tin Song perhaps owes
something to Rosemary Sutcliff.

> *But the girl I kissed at Clusium*
> *Kissed and left at Clusium,*
> *The girl I kissed at Clusium*
> *I remember best of all.*
> *A long march, a long march, and twenty years behind,*
> *But the girl I kissed at Clusium comes easy to my mind.*

Poseidon's Gold

First published 1993

By the fifth story I realised that what readers wanted,
and what I enjoyed writing, was picaresque Roman
soap opera.

The rampant Didii came about to overturn the
stereotype that 'gumshoe' detectives are solitary men
without families or true friends; so I conceived Falco as
a member of a huge, raucous Italian clan who push him
about. In *The Silver Pigs,* he enumerates his siblings and

their offspring, but they are merely numbers. Moving on, I needed to colour in individuals: give them names and personal characteristics, show why Falco moans about them. This was the book where I accepted that as my main responsibility.

It hinges on Festus. The crux is ambiguity about whether Falco's dead brother was a national hero or a trickster. This puts Falco in the classic position of the investigator who comes under suspicion of murder; he is even arrested by his best friend Petronius. While he works to exonerate himself, his mother hires him to clear his brother's name. Later his father hires him as well. A typical Falco quandary. Even if he settles one question, he will still be in trouble …

I really tore into this, and in the course of the story I introduced his Didius relatives in detail. Falco is forced to work with his father too; he discovers he quite enjoys being one of the fighting 'Didius boys'. Eventually he unbends sufficiently to ask Pa for a loan in order to achieve the middle rank. His hopes to settle down with Helena go wrong of course. He and Pa are bankrupted – until twists and turns in the plot, of which I am proud, rescue the situation.

The theme of family runs throughout the whole series, but is very strong here. It suits a Roman setting, and suits my satirical bent. The more we learn about Falco's chaotic background, the more ironic is the struggle of Marcus and Helena to set up their own household, fondly believing – as we all do – that *their* family will be liberal, sensible and different. *They* will not make the mistakes of the past – mistakes which we see in lurid colour as Falco investigates exactly what did occur on his brother's last night in Rome. As he tentatively explores his childhood, we go right back to his primary school – which doesn't happen in much detective fiction.

References to army life in the Judaean desert remind us of the Empire at large, while obsessed art dealers and their murky world of import/export stand for peacetime preoccupations. Arising very slowly from a giant hole in the Forum, we see the Flavian Amphitheatre – that symbol of Flavian regeneration. Falco scoffs, but we know it will be Rome's most iconic emblem. Building it are the Jewish prisoners taken at the Fall of Jerusalem. They give us one of my cross-genre jokes, pleading with Falco to accept Harrison Ford's job in *Raiders of the Lost Ark*. He turns it down. He says it needs a real hero.

The book's conclusion tackles the vexed issue of whether Falco and Helena are married/can legally get married/ will ever be married. Readers seemed obsessed by the question. By now I had looked into Roman Law, where marriage is defined as two people agreeing to live together. My passage about Marcus and Helena is three pages long, yet many readers miss this, or perhaps they want doubt to linger ...

Soldiers with Jewish treasures, on the Arch of Titus

What is marriage but the voluntary union of two souls? asks Helena. *Ceremony is irrelevant ... I gave you my heart a long time ago, so I may as well add my pledge.*

She turned towards me, grasping my right hand in hers. Her left hand lay upon my shoulder, as always with that plain band of British silver that she wore on her third finger to mark her love for me. Helena made a good stab at adoring submissiveness, though I am not sure whether I quite pulled off the frozen look of caution which is often seen in married men on tombstones. But there we were, on that April night on the Embankment, with nobody to see us, yet the whole city assembled around us, had we wanted the presence of witnesses. We were standing in the formal Roman matrimonial pose. And whatever communing in silence entails, we were doing it ... [PG]

Of course I knew I had to do *somebody's* wedding. So two books later, Lenia and Smaractus copped the grand treatment.

Last Act in Palmyra

First published 1994

Being brought up in Birmingham, I was extremely fortunate. I loved the theatre and we were surrounded by the best: the Birmingham Repertory Theatre was a world leader, a magnet for aspiring young actors. As season-ticket holders, my friend Rosalie and I saw many who went on to be very famous, headed up by Derek Jacobi, Ian Richardson, Brian Cox, Julie Christie ... We saw David Warner's nose broken on stage in a play called *Little Malcolm and His Struggle against the Eunuchs*. We saw Jacobi's Troilus several times, as he was young, blond and spoke verse extremely well. The actors were all really hoping to be recruited for the Royal Shakespeare Theatre, Stratford-upon-Avon, which was but a twenty-minute drive from my house; with my parents, I went to almost every production in the Sixties, including the memorable Hollow Crown history series, then later the legendary Peter Brook *Midsummer Night's Dream*. In Birmingham, too, we had the Crescent where amateurs/semi-professionals often did avant-garde plays; the Belgrade at Coventry and the Nottingham Playhouse were also within reach. I went to a school where Shakespeare was specially studied under a fine team of women led by the redoubtable Kate Flint. I also studied plays in Latin and Greek.

So, I was thinking about a novel set in the Roman theatre, when my university friend Helen, an intrepid traveller, uttered the fateful words, *I've always wanted to go to Syria*. I am not intrepid, but a very worried little traveller, therefore I seized the chance to visit a country I might not even have been allowed to see when I was a civil servant, with a fearless companion and on an organised tour with an expert to explain the archaeological sites.

I was determined not to write about Petra; it seemed a cliché. That lasted only until Day 1 of the tour and our walk up to the High Place. The first scene was born, giving rise to the theme of 'water'. I had written the Heliodorus drowning and its immediate discovery by Falco and Helena; having read the draft, Richard was struck by one of those middle-of-the-night blinding insights authors can do without: *Drowned people sink straight to the bottom – that's why they are not noticed in swimming pools!* A rapid check of *The Crime Writers' Practical Handbook* (which I am not supposed to tell you exists, in case you get hold of it to plan murders) confirmed this, while also providing useful technical information about froth, etc. Hence the slightly unconvincing 'buoyed up by inflated goatskin tangled in cloak' feature ...

The Decapolis offered a challenge: could I take my characters to all the ten towns? Some lists give different sets of ten, while not all towns can be located with certainty, yet I was undeterred. There is, perhaps, a superfluity of towns, but attagirl!

By now my work was well enough known for us to meet fellow-travellers who had read the books; when our Syrian guide heard, he took to buying an extra ticket 'for Falco' at archaeological sites. There, I faced a tricky dilemma: the stone-built Roman theatres, which were absolutely marvellous, often date from too late a period. I couldn't use them as they stand today; nor will they ever be dug up to see what lies underneath them. (I dread thermal imaging, I'm afraid …) Anyway, I claimed they have all replaced wooden theatres that previously stood on the same spots. This is a reasonable guess. I am writing fiction; it is my right – perhaps my *duty* – to invent.

The theatrical 'stuff' needs no comment. I revelled in it, particularly revisiting Aristophanes' *The Birds*, which I had studied at school as part of an ill-advised foray into ancient Greek. I read the whole play again, safely in translation; there, I rediscovered the informer, who flies about Greek islands delivering subpoenas. This enabled the joyful joke when Falco has to act the part: *Just be yourself, Falco!* The play, Tranio tells Falco and Helena, only won second prize in the festival for which it was written, being beaten by *The Revellers*, now lost; perhaps I take a sidelong glance there to myself as three-times runner-up for the Georgette Heyer Prize.

This is the novel where I clarified for myself my views on putting my heroine in danger. Yes, Helena is bitten by the scorpion, but I loathe 'woman in peril' suspense. For one thing, it is usually the character's own damn fault for going alone to the haunted house or the villain's lair. And why does she *always* drop the torch/mobile phone/map and never take a good packed lunch? … I had doubts about that scorpion, but Helena is soon rescued and saved by Thalia, riding out of the desert with her vial of *mithridatium*. I was given practical details from the father of a bookshop manager; Bill Tyson had been bitten by a scorpion in North Africa during the war and agreed to tell me about it.

INFORMER: *Now if you can fit me out with a nice light pair of wings I can summon the islanders to court, give evidence against them on the mainland, and fly back to the islands –*

PEISTHETAERUS: *So that the case will be all settled and the fine imposed before the defendant can even arrive –*

INFORMER: *You've got it exactly.*

PEISTHETAERUS: *And while he's still on his way to Athens you're already back on the island, distraining his goods.* [Both laugh heartily at the idea.]

INFORMER: [through his laughter] *I shall have to whiz back and forth like a top!*

PEISTHETAERUS: [through his laughter] *Like a top – that gives me an idea. Yes, I think I've got a pair of wings here that'll set you spinning all right.* [He takes a whip from the basket.]

INFORMER: *But that's a whip you've got there!*

PEISTHETAERUS: *Yes. For a whipping top. I'll give you wings!* [He whips the ground close to the INFORMER's ankles.]

INFORMER: *O! O! Help!* [He leaps away, and continues to skip and revolve as PEISTHETAERUS chases him round the stage, aiming whip strokes at his ankles.]

PEISTHETAERUS: *Bzz! Bzz! I'll make you whiz, you nasty little twister, you! Go on! Fly! Right away from here! And I hope this'll teach you a lesson.* [Exit INFORMER.]

ARISTOPHANES

Production: the Chremes and Phrygia Touring Company
Played at Scythopolis and Hippos, July AD 72
With Philocrates as Peisthetaerus
And introducing Falco as the Informer

A collection of jokes serves as the McGuffin; such collections were real. I don't see myself as a teller of jokes, so to illustrate the clowns I had to rely on what English students call 'close allusion'. The punnet joke affectionately recalls Les Dawson and Roy Barraclough who, in a sketch in a museum, gaze at a statue we can't see frontally, and comment, *You don't get many of those to a punnet!* My editor asked his friend Dave for help, whence evolved the camel joke.

The camel joke

In the interests of research, I asked Oliver to ask his friend Dave to repeat the original joke for this *Companion*. Sadly, neither my editor nor his pal can remember, so they looked up 'camel jokes' on the Internet (thinking to bluff me?). The first results were unsuitable. Reminded that I had adapted their Wild West setting for ancient Syria, they then found two versions of what appears to be the generic joke.

Oliver thinks the original included some reward for making the animals talk and as an editor he notes: *The joke lies somewhat in the TACTILE relationship between the farmer and the animals.* Dave has a different technical approach: *The Internet is quite interesting as a sort of reverse oral-formulaic medium. So when jokes and stories got handed down orally they were gradually refined, but when a joke does the rounds on the Internet it goes the other way and gets watered down, over-complexified and festooned with superfluous comments.*

Well folks, you see how *thoroughly* we go into things. So, it's either a farmer and a ventriloquist or a rancher and a cowboy, and the best hybrid goes:

COWBOY: Hey, cool dog! May I speak to him?

RANCHER: This dog don't talk!

COWBOY: We'll see. Hey, dog, how does your owner treat you?

DOG: Real good. He throws a stick for me, scratches my belly, and I just love him.

[RANCHER looks dumbfounded.]

COWBOY: Mind if I talk to your horse?

RANCHER: Horses don't talk.

COWBOY: You'd be surprised what he might tell you. Say, horse, how does he treat you?

HORSE: Pretty good. He rides me regularly, brushes me down, and keeps me warm in the barn. I love him.

[RANCHER is totally amazed.]

COWBOY: Mind if I talk to your sheep about you?

RANCHER [stuttering anxiously]: Th-th-them sheep ain't nothing but liars!

This rebounded on Oliver unfairly when I received a complaint that my writing had deteriorated until my books could no longer be recommended to members of a church circle; that was ascribed to me being badly influenced by some sensation-seeking editor.

Some time towards the end of writing the manuscript, my mother died unexpectedly. I don't think you can tell exactly where I was in the story when it happened. I managed to finish the book only two weeks late on my deadline, which in one way seemed cold, but was what she would have told me to do.

Time to Depart

First published 1995

By the time I reached this, the eighth book, I had learned that the vigiles were established by the Emperor Augustus to prevent and douse the fires that always threatened Rome. This was news to me. No matter. Fiction is bluff. I could put it right. I would write not just a 'police procedural', but perhaps the first and only 'fire brigade procedural'. Excellent!

Falco will always take the lead in this series, but now I experimented with a station-house story. I like modern ensemble mysteries, set in metropolitan police stations, Ed McBain's 87th Precinct stories being favourites. (Perhaps my deaf baby is a vague nod to the deaf man.)

The setting works for ancient Rome, with a little imagination. We know just enough about the vigiles' structure; so we have the downtrodden cohorts doing a dangerous job, insufficiently appreciated. They moan about the work, the conditions, the public, and their superiors, who are seen as idle, inept and disloyal. The men pride themselves on their efficiency. We don't know much about crime investigation procedures, though I presume these were rough and ready; the Fourth Cohort have a man whose designated job is beating up suspects until they talk. When an old lady reports the loss of her bedspread, the complaint Fusculus takes down is based on a real ancient text.

My starting point is a genuine Roman phenomenon. This is what makes a true historical novel, not just a novel in fancy dress. Capital crimes in Rome were punished by execution: the nobility died by the sword, preferably at their own hands, which was cheap and could have legal advantages for their heirs. Lower orders were sent to the arena; in the Roman ideal of liberty, to be sent to the beasts was so degrading that even if a free citizen had committed a terrible crime, he was allowed an alternative: the time to depart of my title. He was 'deprived of fire and salt', life's staples, but could leave the Empire. He was supposed never to come back, the ancient equivalent of exile on the Costa del Crime. I have given Balbinus a typical crook's yearning to return, if possible to continue his life of crime.

Evidence for organised crime in the ancient world is sparse. It must have existed, as it does in other societies where there are brothels, where gambling is illegal, where small businesses can be made vulnerable, where large amounts of money can be made by the unscrupulous from the frightened. So long as there are accountants there will always be bent ones; where there are doctors, there must be doctors whose diagnosis can be bought; whenever a force of law and order exists, officers will be bought off by those they are supposed to apprehend. This seems cynical but it is reality, particularly in large cities where much can happen out of sight and where if commerce is flourishing the potential profits are so great.

However, it is axiomatic in crime fiction that there also exist incorruptible men who will struggle to eliminate the filth. That is such novels' purpose, even though realistic ones say the cleansing can never work permanently: there will always be a Florius, newly arising. But for us, there is solace and relief when we read about men like Falco and Petronius, tirelessly attempting to do right even when wrong is so widely accepted and seems impossible to combat. If we thought they could never win, it would be too depressing. They represent a glimmer of encouragement, not just for their society but for ours.

A Dying Light in Corduba

First published 1996

A Dying Light in Corduba is a compliment to my readers and my publisher in Spain. Edhasa, based in Barcelona, are a highly unusual company: they specialise in historical novels – something I have never come across anywhere else. They were the first publisher who ever invited me to promote my work abroad, which I have done regularly ever since, making very dear friends of my Spanish literary agent and everyone at Edhasa, while gaining a great love for that country.

Hispania came early into the Roman Empire and was vital to the careers of many famous Romans. It was time for Falco to visit and I wanted my plot to relate to Spain in his period. Unfortunately for Edhasa, that meant olive oil – which was produced in the south. From the moment I set the first scene at the banquet for the Society of Olive Oil Producers of Baetica, I knew I must compensate my dear publishers, who live in the Catalan north. That is why poor Helena Justina is forced to drive two hundred miles at the end of her pregnancy: so Julia Junilla Laeitana can be born in the city for which I had gained such great affection.

The plot involves two fascinations of mine: first, corruption, with its ally nepotism; second, high-level administrative power struggles. Olive oil was the equivalent of the oil/gas industry today, just as critical for every country that depended upon it. I had fun researching its production and its many uses. Better still, I could consider the moral and financial pressures when a dependent province was being eyed up by various factors in central government; when traditional landowners came under threat from mightier moguls and even faced the possibility of what we call nationalisation. As Falco unravels the complicated situation, he finds many ambiguities – not least how the Emperor will want to proceed, given the potential for huge personal profits. Falco's mission will not simply be to prove the existence of an olive oil cartel; he has to decide whether his masters genuinely want him to bust it. He must pick his way, right from the first scenes where he finds himself with responsibility for the suddenly helpless Anacrites.

His one serious fault was avarice. Not content with restoring the duties remitted by Galba he levied new and heavier ones ... and openly engaged in business dealings which would have disgraced even a private citizen – such as cornering the stocks of certain commodities and then putting them back on the market at inflated prices.
SUETONIUS

The spy's plight may have been engineered by Laeta; Laeta will definitely exploit his rival's misadventure.

Of course Falco takes the humane course. He knows he will regret saving Anacrites' life – though even he can't foresee just how much future trouble will result. I didn't know myself!

In selecting my killer I returned, like any crabby Roman satirist, to a hobby horse. I wanted to lambaste the kind of booby who sails into high positions without common sense or experience and probably without real talent. This member of the false élite, favoured by a fast-track management system, creates havoc but is moved on to a new office before the havoc becomes visible; he leaves hard-working underprivileged staff who do have common sense, experience and almost certainly talent, to pick up the pieces because *their* ethics demand that they should. Falco says of Quinctius Quadratus: *This was the rotten side of government. Enormous power was placed at the disposal of an untried, over-confident young man ... As I expected, he had been educated by the best tutors – and he knew nothing. He'd be a magistrate one day, laying down laws he had never heard of to people whose lives in the real world he would never understand. That's Rome. City of glorious tradition – including the one that if the landed élite can bugger up the little man, they will.* [DLC]

I had a lot of fun with it.

Then, unexpectedly, came neat revenge on Cornix – one of those little links back that suggests itself quite late in a story.

This book is set in the home of Spanish dance, as famous in ancient times as it is today, so we have my tentative introduction of Perella, the unlikely middle-aged female assassin and spy – who will be developed further later.

The Archimedes hodometer never fails to elicit curiosity. While it is not certain if these were really constructed in ancient times, the technology existed and there have certainly been modern reconstructions.

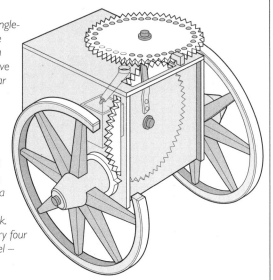

Hodometer, or milometer
The wheel-hub had been fitted with a single-tooth gear. Every rotation of the carriage wheel caused this gear to engage with a flat disc set vertically at right angles above it, which was cut into numerous triangular teeth. Each wheel rotation moved the disc on by a notch, eventually operating a second gear, which in turn moved on a second disc. That one, which was horizontal, had been drilled with small holes, upon each of which was balanced a smooth pebble. Every operation of the top disc moved up a new hole, allowing a pebble to drop into a box below, which Stertius had secured with a huge padlock.
'The top disc rotates one hole for every four hundred revolutions of the carriage wheel – which takes one Roman mile!' [DLC]

The 'Partners Trilogy'

I decided to experiment: it has always been important to me to vary the approach and style of the novels, as well as their content and settings. I want regular readers to be comforted by familiar elements, but without the books becoming dismally formulaic. I cherish variety myself and I believe that will keep readers coming back.

Now Falco will try to improve his social standing and add to his caseload with the help of partners. The *Three ..., Two ..., One ...* trio was the only time I consciously planned ahead by more than one book – at least to the extent of announcing the general theme to my publisher in a one-page proposal for the three books. Even so, one of the intended partners subsequently changed.

All I knew for sure in advance was that none of these partnerships would be easy. Falco's true partner in life and work is Helena Justina. He makes a poor subordinate and is never happy supervising staff. He imagines it will be thrilling to work with his best friend Petronius Longus, but they are soon at loggerheads in a way that jeopardises their investigation; in an irritating contrast, great achievements come out of his loathed stint alongside his rival, Anacrites. To Falco's annoyance, that is what wins him a social position and some wealth.

Three Hands in the Fountain

First published 1997

Set against the background of Roman water supply, this was to be my 'serial killer' book. They were all the rage, fuelled by 'offender profiling' (which theoretically I couldn't use as it was such a new science, though I fearlessly had a go). I felt that if I was to have credit as a modern crime-writer, I had to pack in a serial killer. I did not enjoy it. This book was my most gruesome, with the highest terror/suspense quotient. A killer who preys on women, abducting and torturing them before sexual deviance and death, was unpleasant to write about – and because he *was* a serial killer, it had to happen repeatedly. Also, by tradition, I was supposed to threaten one of my known characters …

That said, I did enjoy the various 'watery' locations. I plundered one textbook much more than usual – Trevor Hodge's *Roman Aqueducts and Water Supply* (fortunately Trevor is a really nice man, and a devotee of crime novels). There was other research, however. Sally Bowden, the fiction editor at *Woman's Realm* who gave me my 'first break' as a published author, has a son, Dr William Bowden, who was then studying at the British School in Rome. Will had already helped me visit the Domus Aurea, Nero's Golden House, before it was formally opened to the public. Now he came up trumps again. He obtained passes to look at an aqueduct, the Aqua Virgo which runs above street level; I wimped out, having no head for heights (or depths), so Richard went down inside to photograph the interior for me. When it came to the sewers, the Cloaca Maxima under the Forum of Nerva, Richard said no – having already suffered a serious eye infection after accompanying me down the sewers in Paris. So I had no choice.

The Cloaca Maxima is still in use, at least for storm water. It is looked after by both a water board and a heritage agency; one would allow us access, but the other said it was too dangerous. Presumably they relented, because I was sorry to learn that permits had arrived. Will and I kitted ourselves out with wellingtons from a market stall and rubber washing-up gloves from a hardware store; we had written instructions to be covered head to foot, as a precaution against Weil's disease. That is carried in rats' pee and is frequently fatal … As a good Englishwoman I take rainwear even to Rome in July, so I had a decent plastic mac, with a hood, which Richard fastened firmly under my chin with a large safety pin.

Ladders arrived, slung down from the Via dei Fori Imperiali, where curious Romans at street cafés paused in mid-cappuccino to look over at the strange goings-on. A manhole was thrown back. I could hear distant water rushing. Two ladders were tied together and put down, so steeply that a man had to be stationed at the top with a safety rope. One by one we launched ourselves on to the ladder and descended. I was squeaking with terror, though encouraged by Richard shouting, *Whatever you do, darling, don't let go!* and Will urging, *Lindsey, you are upholding the honour of British womanhood!* You can tell his mum worked for *Woman's Realm*.

We walked up and down admiring the Etruscan brickwork. What it was like appears in the novel.

Climbing out, with wet wellies, my legs were trembling so much, I almost stuck helplessly at the big gap where the ladders were tied together. And the most useful research? As Falco reports: *When you have walked through a sewer, you have to pull off your own boots.* [THF]

A new length of ladder soon arrived, which was lashed on to the first with cords. The whole cockeyed artefact was dangled down the dark hole. It just reached the bottom, leaving no spare at the top. It looked almost vertical. Anyone who deals with ladders will tell you that's fatal. A large man was posted on top to hang on with a piece of ragged rope. He seemed happy; he knew he had the best job. [THF]

On a bowing ladder, with narrow treads, in wet footwear, going up was even worse than coming down. [THF]

Lindsey and Will in their wellies

The story develops around the ill-fated partnership of Falco and Petro as they investigate a long series of murders which, in classic style, the authorities prefer to ignore. When body-parts emerging from the aqueducts cause public panic, they are given the job formally, under supervision of the real Julius Frontinus, who would later be the author of the seminal *De aquaeductu;* we can kid ourselves his interest was kindled by working with Falco. Anacrites, the Chief Spy, tries to snatch the kudos of solving the mystery, a new step in his slow-burning feud with Falco and a further incentive for the partners who want to beat him to it.

Although Petronius is on suspension for his daft affair with Balbina Milvia, there is all the 'police procedure' I could devise, as the pals try to trace the villain in the dense crowds emerging from the Circus Maximus Games. I very much enjoyed re-using the hard-bitten vigiles.

We all find grisly serial killings fascinating. Anxious to avoid voyeurism, I kept most of the victims anonymous and their deaths 'off-stage'. Only one is identified deliberately: the young wife, Asinia. Through her, I wanted to stress the enormous private misery that results from such killings.

The denouement involves a red herring I am proud of. It has a ghastly humour, yet it should be salutary because this victim – initially an unsympathetic character – is rescued, yet has been permanently traumatised and reduced to a shadow of herself. I remain ambivalent about using psychopathic death for entertainment. This is one way to remind us again of the terrible consequences.

Two for the Lions

First published 1998
Winner of the Crime Writers' Association Ellis Peters
Historical Dagger 1999

I sometimes define my role as a historical novelist as showing where people in the past were the same as us – and where they were very different. So, the Romans had democracy (for men) and central heating. The two main aspects in which their society differed from ours

were slavery and the arena. In this book I gritted my teeth and took on another subject I viewed unsympathetically: gladiatorial combat. I would deal not just with humans fighting, but with the wide-scale killing of animals, to get the worst possible side of it out of the way.

Raising wild beasts to the arena

We start with the unexplained death of a lion. Falco is drawn in as if it was a standard murder investigation, looking for paw prints, investigating the locked cage, asking, *Who saw him last? How did he spend his last evening? Who were his associates? What did he eat last? Whom did he eat, in fact?* [TFL] For Falco (and me) the state executioner counts as a civil servant – a joke, but one which provides a reason to track down his killer.

My take on gladiators was influenced by a TV documentary about young men in the East End of London who want to be boxers; it is something they can do, something that just may bring the fortunate few both money and fame. We know that Roman gladiators were adored like modern celebrities: Sergius, for whom the senator's wife Eppia gave up everything, was pretty run-down, says Juvenal:

Was I eccentric to care? Was my obsession with Leonidas unhealthy and pointless? Or was I right and the noble beast's fate should be as significant to a civilised man as any unexplained killing of a fellow human being? [TFL]

... no chicken, forty at least, with a dud arm that
*   held promise*
Of early retirement. Besides, his face looked a
*   proper mess —*
Helmet-scarred, a great wen on his nose, an
*   unpleasant*
Discharge from one constantly weeping eye.
*   What of it?*
<u>*He was a gladiator.*</u>

While fighting clearly equated to modern football, its bloodshed was occasionally criticised; Seneca denounced the indiscriminate hacking of criminals and said: *What is the point of armour? Or of skill? All that sort of thing just makes the death slower in coming. In the morning men are thrown to the lions and the bears: but it is the specta-tors they are thrown to in the lunch hour. The spectators insist that each on killing his man shall be thrown against another to be killed in his turn; and the eventual victor is reserved by them for some other form of butchery; the only exit for the contest-ants is death ... 'But he was a highway robber, he killed a man.' And what of it? Granted that as a murderer he deserves this punishment, what have you done, you wretched fellow, to deserve to watch it?*

This was a minority view, however.

In my story the Colosseum, not yet built, is already a catalyst for the suppliers whose greed and ambition form the main plot. I turned to Libya for arena action. Once again, my dauntless friend Helen lured me on a guided trip, led by the late John Dore – an archaeologist who not only gave us wonderful insights into the Latin and Greek remains, but stirred me to obtain Internet connectivity, which enabled my website. That's another story – though from this point on my writing life was heightened and occasionally hampered, my horizons and contacts very much expanded.

The structure of the book came about because Helen got married. David, her new husband, was teaching in Canada, so at Easter she went to visit him; this meant her passport was not available for obtaining a visa to Libya in the spring. It must be clear that my plot is heading to Lepcis Magna, Sabratha, Cyrene and Apollonia, but we could only travel in the last two weeks of September. So it takes Falco a long time to get on that Tripolitanean boat – and it took me a very short time to write the last half of the book: 50,000 words in October. Ever since, I have wished I never discovered such deadline-diddling was possible!

Lindsey and Helen in Libya (NB: feet haven't changed since aged ten)

By now, fired by sympathy for Helena, I had decided that Falco must at last obtain some funds. So, he works on Vespasian's Census with his new partner Anacrites. I could find out very little about how a census worked in practice. However, I had been a designated 'small business' since I began writing; then I could not afford an accountant so I grapple with taxation myself. In Britain it is an offence to fiddle your income tax, though you are allowed to order your affairs so you pay as little as possible; when you register for VAT (Value Added Tax), the regime is much more rigorous. If HMRC decide you are lying, they can say what tax you *ought* to pay, and you must cough up, with no appeal. I gave Falco and Anacrites these draconian powers. There is no doubt that Vespasian, that tax collector's son, raked in enough from his census to rebuild the Empire and Rome. His helpers must have been fierce.

He named himself and his elder son Titus as Censors, then called up the rest of us to give an account of ourselves and of everything we owned. Then we were swingeingly taxed on the latter, which was the real point of the exercise. Some heads of household found themselves excited by the challenge; foolish fellows tried to minimise the figures when declaring the value of their property ... [TFL]

So, at the end of this book, Marcus Didius Falco not only solves a series of deaths but earns a decent amount of money, is bumped up to the middle rank, and acquires a sinecure in public life. He does it by working as a tax official. This gave me simple pleasure – and is not inappropriate in the Roman world.

Also important are events which affect the fortunes of other regular characters. Justinus and Claudia are committed to one another. The death of Famia cruelly frees up Maia for new plots; as she struggles as a widow and single parent, she will be available for romantic adventures of all types.

Equally important is our study of Anacrites. We see he does have professional talent, which makes him a dangerous enemy. We watch his contorted relationship with Falco until he shows that his jealousy makes him actually want to *be* Falco. The hold Falco gains over him is both good and bad – bad, because posing a threat to Anacrites is not a good idea. It will be the bedrock of much fiercer rivalry, which builds to its fateful climax in *Nemesis.*

He seemed to have brightened when he joined me in partnership; he gave the peculiar impression he was looking forward to his new active life … [TFL]

A Flamen

A Vestal

One Virgin Too Many

First published 1999

I had realised tension between Falco and his opposite number was good, so in the third book of the 'trilogy' Helena's 'nice' brother Justinus was ditched in order to exploit Falco's scratchier relationship with Aelianus.

When I decided to tackle religion as a theme, I felt almost as squeamish as I had over gladiators. Luckily the Romans offered me a wide choice, and in my usual way I sought out the less familiar. Avoiding the Olympian pantheon, I explored aspects of Roman religious life that originated in rural Italy in the remote past: the Vestal Virgins and the Arval Brothers. The Arvals, one of the ancient priestly colleges, soon led me to the highly superior Flamen Dialis. My choice of theme brings us face to face with Roman social climbing and snobbery.

We start with an unusual twist on the 'client seeking a private eye' situation: Gaia Laelia is a frightened child, whose hidebound family – some crazy, perhaps due to inbreeding – form the circle of suspects. She is due to become a Vestal Virgin, if she 'wins' the coming lottery; I had no evidence that lottery fiddling happened, but I am as convinced of it as Falco. Dramatic suspense is provided when Gaia is trapped in a well; for this, I was inspired by several modern accidents involving infants.

Falco has a desperate race to find her, battling against her family's suspicion of his status, motives and methods.

I owe two great incidents to my friend, fellow-writer Deryn Lake. First, after we had been to the theatre in London, she was harassed by horrible football fans who tried to hijack her car in a lonely station car park. Her response was to land a straight hook to one of the louts, then speed off through the 'No Exit'. This inspired Terentia Paula: *The furious ex-Vestal let fly at her nephew with a straight-armed, right-handed punch that came all the way from the shoulder. I heard his jaw crack. His head jerked back. Scaurus looked at the ceiling abruptly. Then he went down.* [OVTM]

After I discussed my plans for the well rescue, Deryn asked: *Did the Romans wear underpants?* – an issue of moment which had to be addressed (see FAQs).

I believe the scene where Falco is lowered upside down into the crumbling well is the most terrifying I have written. The great journalist Katharine Whitehorn pointed out that I inflict dark enclosed spaces on Falco as a frequent horror. Is the fear mine, she wonders? I once had claustrophobia briefly in an underground dungeon, but my fear would be that I'd lack the physical stamina to carry off such an exploit when needed.

Richard helped me with technical aspects, for instance, *This is a bearer and brattice job.* But the scene and its writing are mine, and I am proud of it. Apart from the suspense – will little Gaia be brought out alive? – my intention was to round off the three 'Partners' books with a very special incident. Falco's descent is only possible with aid from his three partners. Helpless on those dangerous, stretching ropes, he has to trust them absolutely; meanwhile, they have to draw on all their loyalty and physical strength to keep him safe. Even Anacrites is moved by the situation and counts as a friend. Petronius and Aelianus are indispensable.

So these four very different men work as a team, on a task they dread will be hopeless. The focus is a child, always representative of hope for the future. At risk are not just her life, but the stability of her mother and other relations, plus the life of Falco and all who care for him – including his helpers. The scene is about absolute courage and indestructible morality. *We have to try – is that agreed?* No other option for them – and for me, of course, their success is the only option too.

Although I know the result, when they collapse exhausted on the turf together, even I have to wipe away a tear.

Ode to a Banker

First published 2000

This book is indeed about banking. It was written when I finally earned enough money to care very much how my bank might handle or mishandle it. I have been both severely poor and newly cash-rich; my views on banking had firmed up sternly. In the following decade people would suffer much more from the greed and incompetence of financiers, but I already had plenty to go on.

However, the main theme of the book is patronage, such a big feature of Roman life, particularly in the literary field. This enabled me to examine ancient authorship and publishing, a wonderful subject. *If you listen to people who commission material, they have a lively stable of writers and are expecting shortly to ruin their competitors. The competitors, however, will accuse them of teetering on the brink of bankruptcy. If you ask the scroll shops, life is a long struggle; manuscripts are hard to come by at reasonable prices and customers don't want to know. If you look around, people are nonetheless reading – although probably not reading what the critics are praising.* [OB]

Uniquely, this time I knew from the start who would die: a publisher. And who would do it: a disappointed author. I am afraid it is a savage killing too!

I managed to discuss why people write, why so many wannabes are failures, and why the talented few should continue despite all setbacks. *Ode* was my thirteenth published book; I no longer felt like a lucky interloper but was beginning to speak boldly about my craft and the life it had brought me. I am particularly fond of the scene where Falco and Rutilius give their public reading. The terrible sentence 'I have not read any of her work; I don't suppose any of you here have'

You will finally read this stuff
From a public platform,
  carefully combed, in a new
  white toga,
Flashing a gem on your finger,
  rinsing your supple throat
With a clear preparatory
  warble, your eyes swooning
  in ecstasy.
PERSIUS

was actually said once by a man (not sober) who was introducing me as an after-dinner speaker.

Despite the cynical tone throughout, a potential bestseller is discovered, *Gondomon, King of Traximene. A shining new talent. A breathtaking story, written with mystical intensity. An author who will sell and sell* ... [OB] Every writer needs to believe this is possible.

The scene where Avienus is found hanging under the Probus Bridge alludes to the strange death of Roberto Calvi, the Vatican banker who was discovered beneath Blackfriars Bridge in London after apparently committing suicide. I knew Blackfriars well; it was my train terminus for years, so I had always felt a particular interest. Of course the Banco Ambrosiano should not be identified with the Aurelian Bank of Chrysippus, any more than my own bank.

'He's the first suicide I ever saw who climbed under a bridge – when most desperate people jump off the top. Then he not only tied himself to the stonework in a very awkward position, but roped a massive bundle of roof tiles to himself. Now it could be in case his nerve failed and he suddenly wanted to climb back up –'
'Or not.' [OB]

Structurally, this book shadows Agatha Christie, with a 'body in the library'. (*Would that be his Greek or his Latin Library?*) At the end, there is an epic scene where Falco gathers all the suspects together, back in that library (he and Fusculus have discussed tips for cleaning the blood off the marble floor mosaic). With everyone assembled, Falco and Helena talk through the clues until, after an inevitable false confession, they identify the murderer. I found this scene tricky to write and frankly I wouldn't do it again without a good reason. But the body in the library motif would recur. There is something about the contrast between violence and the hushed atmosphere that is classical in every sense.

A Body in the Bath House

First published 2001

Two great loves of mine feature here: archaeology and public administration.

Model reconstruction of Fishbourne Roman Palace (showing Togi's trees)

I first heard of Fishbourne Roman Palace at school. How it was unearthed by a mechanical digger during water-main construction and how the mosaics were preserved through a local benefactor's generosity is a great story in the development of archaeology. The main excavation began in 1961 and it must have been fairly soon afterwards that my teacher Elys Varney persuaded the then young Barry Cunliffe to come and talk to our school archaeological society. I remember him saying he *believed* it could be an enormous palace, although he was still reticent. Even now there are many questions about why such a wonderful building was built in that position.

I am allowed to be positive; well, in a novel you have to be. To me, there is no doubt that this was a reward to King Togidubnus for giving the Romans a foothold for invading Britain. Other people still debate whether the troops sent by Claudius landed at Fishbourne or at Richborough on the Isle of Thanet. In my opinion they probably came to both, but a friendly king, in a place where evidence says there already was a Roman base, would have been a logistical godsend.

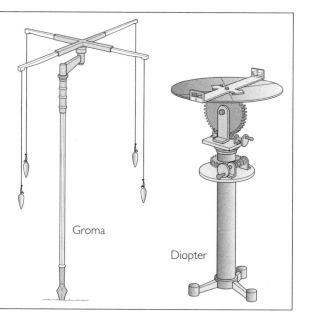

We found Magnus, the surveyor, pottering. His groma was plunged in the ground, a long metal-tipped stave with four plumb bobs hung from two metal-cased wooden bars; it was used for measuring out straight lines and squares …

… A sturdy post supported a revolving rod set in a circular table, marked out with detailed angles. The whole circle could be tilted using cogged wheels. Magnus was underneath, tinkering with the cogs and worm screws that set it. Some distance away another assistant waited patiently beside a twenty foot high sighting rod with a sliding bar, ready to measure a slope. [BBH]

Groma

Diopter

The various stages of the palace had been studied enough for me to be confident that around AD75 a major redevelopment occurred. This chimed perfectly with my experiences as a home-owner and the age of TV home-makeover programmes! As Fishbourne was expanded to the plan we know so well today, craftsmen and materials were sent from all over the Empire. It must have been organised from Rome, the equivalent of projects I had dealt with in the civil service:

Feasibility: the client proposes a project, which everyone can see will never happen. Work is held in abeyance. Some disciplines do carry out independent preliminary work, failing to inform the project manager that they are doing so. The scheme then revives unexpectedly, and is thrown into the formal programme with inadequate planning … [BBH]

All the problems Falco faces were hideously familiar – going over budget and over time, restraining the client's extravagance and even the frauds, like those which beset my own department.

Archaeologists don't speculate in print about why a Roman villa at nearby Angmering should have been built with identical materials and similar techniques to Fishbourne, but I was strongly reminded of a certain senior architect who was notorious for using expensive materials to adorn his own house … Like other 'bent' staff and contractors, he was never charged; I speculate that the problems and diplomatic excuses have not altered for two thousand years.

This was another novel where I relied heavily on just one book for research, Barry Cunliffe's *Fishbourne Roman Palace*. It supplied many details, including the fact that some fragments of wall painting resemble famous finds from Stabiae, which was destroyed when Vesuvius erupted (this was where Pliny the Elder died on the beach). So I brought over nephew Larius, no longer a dream-struck fourteen-year-old but holding his own with the two Camillus brothers as they fling themselves into bad behaviour. A favourite moment is when the three lads are getting ready for a night on the town.

This is where we see Perella, the dangerous but no-longer-young agent, perform her mesmerising dance. My inspiration came from flamenco troupes, where of course the spotlight falls on the beautiful young women, though often one or more older dancer belongs to the group.

She was aware of her maturity and challenging us to notice too. She was the queen of the room because she had lived more than most of us. If her joints creaked, nobody would notice. And unlike the crude offers purveyed by younger artists, Perella was giving us – because she had nothing else to give – the erotic, ecstatic, uplifting, imaginative glory of hope and possibility. [BBH]

I had visited Fishbourne when I first began writing Roman stories, long before I conceived Falco. I revisited to research this book, sneaking around shyly incognito. Luckily the novel was well received. I've been back many times; I have given readings, and watched progress with exemplary new facilities. This was the first time I devoted a whole book to a single site; I am thrilled, and very proud, that a wonderful warm relationship came out of it.

The Jupiter Myth

First published 2002

> *'This place should never have been rebuilt.'*
> *'Disaster has that effect, man. Volcanoes, floods, avalanches — bloody massacres. They bury the dead, then rush to reconstruct in the danger area …'*
> *'The end of the road! It's a bugger to police. This place is a draw to scum, Falco.'* [JM]

In February 2001 I was a Guest of Honour at the Left Coast Crime mystery convention, which was being held in Anchorage, Alaska. It took me three planes and nearly twenty-four hours to get there (the same back!) and, curiously, it left an impression that helped form this book. Even today Alaska sees itself as different, off-side on maps, still an outsider among the US states because of its remote location and its unique social make-up. Was this how Britain was regarded by the Romans, and perhaps regarded itself? In my conference 'goodie-bag' was the biography of a mobster in early Anchorage, when its frontier nature encouraged gangsters and the sex trade. It was an easy step to seeing Londinium as similar: turned into the capital after the Boudiccan Revolt, it is rapidly expanding, benefiting from two-way trade and the assets of 'civilisation', yet a magnet for all types: not just entrepreneurs like innkeepers and lawyers, but bad men who want to exploit it. Fun to give them the very latest hand-held weaponry!

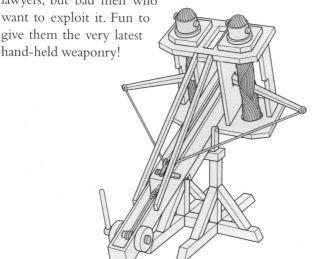

They had an armoury none of us expected: two full-sized ballistae which they pushed quickly over the threshold, and set up to guard the entrance, plus several rare, hand-held crossbows. I heard soldiers gasp. This was staggering firepower. Most legionary footsloggers had seldom been so close to artillery, and never when it was in opposition hands …

… Maia had found and raised the ready-primed crossbow. Then she lifted the safety claw, snapped up the trigger pin, and shot Norbanus in the back. [JM]

Coincidentally, before I began there had been significant new archaeological finds, supervised by the Museum of London where curators and archaeologists are Falco-friendly. Not all archaeology was helpful; the history of the Roman bridge (by modern London Bridge) was so involved I wrestled to make sense of it via the sustained 'permanent/temporary' joke. Finding the Roman amphitheatre (at the Guildhall) was super for me; then, while I was actually writing, redevelopment of a site in Gresham Street in September 2001 brought to light the fabulous waterwheels that feature, trundled by Myron. My details were taken from the very first press release. Later a working model was built at the Museum and theories of how the wheel worked were adjusted; with a deadline at the end of October, I couldn't wait for rethinks! Most significant to the plot was a re-used giant wine barrel in which the first body is found drowned. It was inspired by an exhibition called High Street Londinium, where a row of Roman shops was reconstructed, including this kind of cask, probably imported from Germany, used to line a well.

Another fascinating discovery in 2001, in Southwark, was a woman's grave containing items that *might* mean she was a gladiatrix, or at least interested in the sport; there are doubts, so I had my Chloris buried elsewhere (in the Roman cemetery that's now under the Old Bailey) rather than support an idea that may be untrue. Chloris is that old Tripolitanian girlfriend Falco has always harped on about; her role is not simple sensationalism but to make him muse on his own development, by now crucial to my series: *I had moved on — way, way into another life. Face to face with what was expected of my old self, I felt awkward. I had loyalties nowadays; I had standards. As Petronius had said to Maia earlier, once you make huge decisions, you cannot go back. The shock is the way other people fail to see how much you have altered.* [JM]

I never forget that people are reading for what happens to my characters. Yes, this is a book about a city, the city that has become important to me personally, but against that background, we want to learn of Gaius, Camilla and Frontinus in their diplomatic work; Petronius pursuing his gangster; Petronius pursuing

Not to mention our lady fencers —
We've all seen them, stabbing the stump with a foil,
Shield well advanced, going through the proper motions
...
JUVENAL

Maia; and Falco pitting himself against the demands of work and family – enjoying both, balancing them, even risking them when it is morally essential to do so.

The Accusers

First published 2003

Fifteen books in, I wanted to do a 'courtroom drama'. By chance, I had just found Steven Rutledge's book on Roman informers, which suggested aspects of my plot. First, as Falco says right at the beginning, the story treats of what informers do: *In popular thought we were all parasites, bent on destroying respectable men.* It appears that the 'respectable' Metellus family are politically corrupt; they have been convicted of abuse of office but their prosecutor may lose his compensation because Metellus senior seems to have killed himself. Rutledge gave me this idea: *In the very next year we find two prosecutors complaining to the consul when Cremutius Cordus committed suicide before his prosecution ended, asserting that it was a deliberate attempt to deprive them of their reward.* I did enjoy the concept of a lawyer whose best advice to his client is to die!

I had further fun with the theme of 'ambulance-chasing' for bequests: *delatores … were notorious for trying to lay claim to the legacies of others,* says Rutledge. And it's instructive to know just how big the rewards could be: *Justice has a price. In the informing community the price is at least twenty-five per cent; that is, twenty-five per cent of all the condemned man's seaside villas, city property, farms, and other investment holdings … Since the minimum estate of a senator is a million sesterces – and that's poverty for the élite – this can be a nice number of town houses and olive groves.* [AC]

As the complex plot develops, Roman Law provides a delicious series of legal twists, before eventually Falco exposes the conniving senatorial informers, Silius Italicus and Paccius Africanus; they have chillingly set up the Metelli in a vicious series of scams, planned for years. At the heart is a secret about birth that can only come from Roman social snobbery. It is a sad situation, where a man who has everything loses it and becomes a non-person, through no fault of his own.

*His father
Breaks promises, mis-spends
His business partner's capital,
   hoodwinks his friends
And busily puts by
Money for an unworthy heir.*
HORACE, bewailing the decline in modern morals

As the informers manoeuvre, Falco himself acts as a courtroom prosecutor. He has previous experience, though not at this level. I am proud of the Ciceronian debate (I had read part of Cicero's *Pro Sexto Roscio* as a set text at school; intriguingly, it is about a son accused of murdering his father). Falco has to cast doubt on the character of his opponent, Paccius Africanus, a real-life orator who had become notorious under Nero. Helped by his father-in-law, Falco is able to remind the jury of the incident that, for me, not only colours Paccius but illustrates the public's low opinion of informers. Rutledge writes that *The senate now drew up an oath, which fellow senators were forced to take, swearing that they had imperilled no man's safety under Nero and received no reward nor office from any man's misfortune. Known* delatores *who attempted to take the oath were convicted of perjury.* In the book Paccius, being powerful and skilled, is bound to fight back nastily. It was fascinating to relate what *we* know of Falco's own professional and personal history, putting the worst possible gloss on each aspect (see Appendix).

Personally, in this book Falco is as settled as he has ever been, making him all the more vulnerable to the crippling financial risks involved in making a false allegation or even abandoning a case. He and Helena have their house at the foot of the Aventine; he and the Camillus brothers are working together as Falco and Associates – *a little-known firm of private informers who specialised in background investigations of the family type (bridegrooms, widows, and other cheating, lying, money-grubbing swine just like your own relatives).* [AC] Falco is trying to train the brothers, who generally disagree with one another over anything that matters. The position is complicated when Honorius, a Grishamite young lawyer, temporarily joins them, a cause of distrust and friction until he allows himself to be bought off. This is the book where Camillus Aelianus acquires an interest in law. It causes him to be parcelled off to Athens, if only because the more the brothers are involved in a story, the more Helena gets shoved aside.

So many touchy lawyers complained about their treatment that I had to add a disclaimer for the paperback version!

Scandal Takes a Holiday

First published 2004

This had two main starting points. First was the wonderful archaeological site at Ostia Antica, which Richard and I loved on our annual trips to Rome. Our visit for this particular book coincided with the state funeral for nineteen Italian military personnel who had been killed by a suicide bomber in Iraq. We saw the gun-carriage cortège from our hotel and after such a close connection with Italy and Rome for so many years, I was extremely moved. It still makes an odd, unexpected memory of my writing life.

Ostia had been discovered when Fiumicino airport was built; the remains were silted up by the Tiber as the coastline shifted, which preserved the archaeology. We always thought Ostia better than Pompeii. Not so dramatic a history, perhaps, but a less crowded site, while many ancient buildings survive to first-storey level, so you can wander about feeling you are in real ancient streets.

Much was built by Domitian and Hadrian, but I could create a picture of life there under Vespasian. Future imperial redevelopment even suggested the theme of ambitious building contractors; records exist of this ancient trade union, with their aggressive 'booted ranks' and traceable links to tame town councillors. Falco and I are preoccupied with civic corruption. I explored the abuse of local power, embroidering it with fancy details such as the fake vigiles office; I must have read one of those perennial news items about bogus policemen. Some of the buildings I used are real: the builder's house, the gatehouse, the cistern where the final body is discovered, and of course the vigiles' station-house which you can wander round and envisage in great detail. It is set slightly back from the main route into the heart of the site, and was a late discovery for us. We also took photos of temples Falco is forced to visit. The same happy day, we explored the sanctuary of Cybele and the necropolis where the lively funeral takes place.

Hercules Invictus
'And by the way – nice arse!'

Temple of Augustus, Ostia

Entrance to underground chamber

Statue of Cybele, Ostia

Helena Justina's father always sent along his secretary in time to bury himself in his copy over breakfast. This, I was sure, had nothing to do with Decimus Camillus wanting to avoid conversation with his noble wife as he blearily ate his nice white morning rolls. [STH]

The second feature I was eager to develop was the *Daily Gazette*; I had frequently mentioned it and people often queried the reference. Sadly, we don't have relics of the Forum inscriptions, but the *Acta Diurna*'s flavour comes from a passage in Petronius' *Satyricon*. The ghastly nouveau riche freedman Trimalchio shows off throughout a dinner party, telling his hapless guests more than they want to know about his own wealth:

What really interrupted was his accountant, who sounded as though he was reading out a copy of the Gazette: *26 July: Births on the estate at Cumae: male 30, female 40. Wheat threshed and stored: 500,000 pecks. Oxen broken in: 500 … The official edicts were read out and the wills of certain game-keepers. In specific codicils they said they were leaving Trimalchio nothing. Then the names of some bailiffs; the divorce of a freedwoman, the wife of a watchman, on the grounds of adultery with a bath-attendant; the demotion of a hall-porter to a job at Baiae; the prosecution of a steward; and the result of an action between some bedroom attendants.* This suggests the *Acta Diurna,* which was established to record the doings of the Senate, included official decrees plus a court circular about the imperial family, a tally of births and deaths in Rome, equivalents of the finance pages in a good daily newspaper (money paid into the Treasury, corn supply statistics, progress on major public buildings), and general daily news: prodigies and marvels, fires, funerals and marriage notices, sacrifices, public games (the sports pages) – and a scandal column. No commentator says that Vespasian tried to manipulate news coverage to make his regime look good – but I bet he did!

As always, I enjoyed 'police procedure' at the outstation, concentrating on rivalries between cohorts and between the vigiles and the navy. Pirates, still a problem on the high seas, were good to include; they allowed me to touch on Rome's recent past, to mention dangers to trade, and to introduce poignant personal relationships. I liked the elderly pirate who wanted a ghost writer for his memoirs!

We see the Camilli together at unusually close quarters, especially enjoying a barbecue before seeing off Aulus on his ship. Julia Justa perhaps tipples too much hot toddy while shopping with Helena; we see Helena at ease with her mother. Decimus lets himself enjoy his tiny granddaughters touchingly: *Once they were let out of their town house on a spree, they knew how to throw themselves into a country feast. We could have been at an olive harvest. We were loud, we ate heartily, we laughed and talked until it grew so dark we had to light oil lamps and start batting at insects.* [STH]

Just a nice reminder that these books are about traditional Mediterranean life.

See Delphi and Die

First published 2005

> *Devotees of physical culture have to put up with a lot of nuisances. There are the exercises in the first place, the toil involved in which drains the vitality and renders it unfit for concentration or the more demanding sort of studies. Next there is the heavy feeding, which dulls mental acuteness. Then there is the taking on as coaches of the worst brand of slave, persons who divide their time between putting on lotion and putting down liquor, whose idea of a well spent day consists of getting up a good sweat and then replacing the fluid lost with plenty of drink ...*
> SENECA

2004 was the Athens Olympics, and in April that year the Classical Association's Annual Conference had the ancient Games as a theme. I generally attend that conference and sometimes pick up ideas. Now I decided to 'do' Greece and athletics for the next Falco novel. Personally I shrink from sport; to coincide with the modern Games there were a lot of new books on the subject, handily. Only after I became fixed on the idea did I work out that AD76 was not the right year. However, I convinced myself I could make a joke of this. From what I learned of the hazards, it would be much more feasible for Falco, Helena and their party to move around Olympia if there were no crowds – and much more hygienic!

My second theme would be travel. I had enjoyed organised tours of ancient monuments since long before I began writing. I could tell of many a terrifying coach journey on mountain roads, deadly moussakas, and over-friendly hotel porters in fleapits provided by the 'low-end' kind of holiday company. The Romans invented heritage touring, carving their names on ancient temple pillars as they took advantage of their own roads and the comparative safety of the seas under the Pax Romana. They must have had entrepreneurs to facilitate journeys; so was born the Seven Sights Travel company, an operation to avoid unless you are a novelist wanting colourful material.

I have fond memories of the *in situ* research. Time was short; I can't remember why. Richard and I both loved Greece, though oddly we had never been there together; this year we went twice. It was almost the last time we were able to travel abroad because he became ill not long afterwards; my memories are poignant. First I arranged a very brief escorted trip to take in Athens and Corinth. Our hired car reached Olympia after midnight (it's quite remote even now), after travelling through a storm that showed just why Zeus was the god of thunder; I am still sorry I didn't manage to fit in a version of the incident when we gratefully took to our room: the hotel had kindly supplied a big tray of cold food. Tired and starving, we fell on it, but just as I was about to plunge in a fork, the electricity failed and we were in complete darkness …

As darkness fell, all the hills around us were lit by ever more intense bursts of sheet and forked lightning … A long, heavy rainfall then lasted all night, until any among us who believed in divinities must have believed that our presence had angered the all-knowing gods. [SDD]

Things were better in the morning, though at the ancient site I was disappointed to find that because of the coming modern Games, the museum had been stripped of ancient athletic equipment. It was neither the first time nor the last that I was thwarted by a closed museum. It just gave us an excuse to fix a second trip to Athens, to see the special exhibition. Even that was due to close shortly … With only days to go before my deadline, we slipped in just in time. There I saw the special jumping weight in the form of a wild boar that was my murder weapon. It was in a case, so my photo isn't good.

Boar jumping weights (poor quality photo as in an exhibition case)

I did acquire interest in ancient sports, and particularly enjoyed a television documentary where modern students recreated ancient athletics, finding with computerised reconstruction that there was little difference between what could be achieved then and now in jumping, running and discus. The novel's scene where the wrestling champion, Milo of Dodona, nearly kills first Cornelius and then Falco was picked up by reviewers as particularly terrifying.

There are two unexplained deaths in the book; one drew on several real cases in my lifetime where daughters had died mysteriously abroad, with the local authorities slow to investigate; dogged fathers kept up

the pressure to discover the truth, often for years. In my version, the death is an accident. I wanted to show how difficult it must have been two thousand years ago to decide the facts, especially after time had passed.

The murder is one of a series linked horrifically to certain Greek legends. The outcome is signalled all the way through the book, but for reasons I still don't entirely understand, some readers felt I had not resolved the mystery. Strangely, I think part of the problem was the print layout; the story ended at the bottom of a page and people expected more overleaf ... Rereading it now, I explained very clearly what had happened, who was responsible, and of course where the latest corpse was. By Helena's anguished cry after she sees that Nux has discovered the missing body, it ought to be no surprise at all, merely an unusually dramatic way to end a book. And really gruesome!

There is a strong theme of exploring famous sites, a keen hobby of Helena's, which Falco loyally tries to further whenever his investigations allow. I took special delight in discussing the people on the tour, which is like any disparate group in transit: the ones you avoid

Caryatids on the Erechtheion, the Acropolis, Athens

I kissed Helena beside the caryatid porch of the Erechtheion. Informers are not complete worms. I enjoyed the day too. [SDD]

with good reason – and the others you think you don't care for, but come to like unexpectedly. Against the enjoyable background of family travel, a bonus is seeing Aelianus at the university in Athens, as he tries to be studious despite the efforts of his partygoing tutor. Minas of Karystos is based on what was said of academics at the time.

Since Greece had been a major donor to Roman civilisation, a rival power that Rome had brutally destroyed, I portrayed many a moment of unease. I reprised my fascination with empire and its administration (there is yet another young high-flyer, covering up for the governor, though we are allowed to end up liking this one). It was a pleasure to revisit the country itself and the culture I had studied, albeit it ham-fistedly, when I was at school.

Ironically, I didn't see Delphi – though I had been there before.

Cleonymus had spotted the stone money box for donations; he dropped a silver coin in the slot. 'Show willing.'
[SDD]

Saturnalia

First published 2007

> *It is the month of December, and yet the whole city is in a sweat! Festivity at state expense is given unrestricted licence. Everywhere there echoes the noise of preparations on a massive scale ... The man who said that December used to be a month but is now a year was not far off the mark.*
> SENECA

Family feast

I have to admit, Christmas was an unhappy time in my family. For some years I have spent it much more cheerily with friends in Wiltshire and London, but I knew enough about seasonal tensions to write this book about festivities among the Didii from the heart! Even the great ridiculous set piece of the Fourth Cohort's Saturnalia drinks party is resonant of office parties long ago – though I never went to any that were subsidised as gloriously as this one is by Marcus Rubella.

The plot links back to *The Iron Hand of Mars,* of course. From the moment I discovered that Rutilius Gallicus captured Veleda, I had been mulling over how Justinus could meet up again with his lost love. In the meantime I had given him a wife I am fond of, as he may be himself. There can be no possibility of a happy resolution for anyone. Good stuff! I adore a challenge like this, needing to keep true to my romantic spirit yet to impose an unsentimental story where weedy authors (and some of my readers) just hanker for a happy ending. The Falco novels may be historical but they have never been simplistic costume dramas. The demands of history meant Veleda must either be executed or sent to a temple exile – and I don't mess with events.

One thing that made the situation easier was that I realised she might no longer be a girl. I think myself perpetually thirty-five, but somewhere during my writing career I had passed the menopause and acquired arthritis; I easily reasoned that a young man in his twenties, a decent man with a wife to whom he was loyal and a new baby he adored, would start to see Veleda in a new light. Veleda was going to lose Quintus. Readers have asked why she doesn't fight back. As I see it, she is a woman who from the start recognises total defeat, both political and personal.

Themes revolve around Saturnalia, that time of enforced jollity and upset, over-indulgence and over-excited children. Saturnalia flavours every scene and unwinds through innumerable official and family feasts: the good, the bad and the ugly of celebration and catering, with a constant risk of fire.

Then comes medicine. Medicine was enthralling to cover in detail, even though for me it was not the best time to be satirical, because Richard had just narrowly escaped death; gratitude to medical science might have been more seemly. But we were sardonic. I decided that the various ancient medical systems would be represented by individual doctors. Clearly one of the motley group must be murdered; I could pick him out at some point, like selecting a Saturnalia magic bean. Once again, the primary death occurs accidentally – though since I had once had a narrow brush with an ENT surgeon who wanted to remove a gland just because it was a cordon bleu operation, I don't stint my disapproval of the treatment involved. The medical background enabled me to discuss how in the Roman world post-mortems were illegal – making a crime novel set in that period very different from a plot about modern policing.

While Falco hunts for Veleda, who has gone missing due to several kinds of official incompetence, the two themes combine in one particular very dark scene. As with Christmas now, Saturnalia then would have been a disastrous time for anyone outside normal society. So I devised a meeting with runaway slaves. Their lives as fugitives are desperate – desperate even without being preyed on by a killer whose madness takes the form of believing it his role to remove perceived 'filth' from the streets. Falco, ever compassionate, encounters the down-and-out slaves with dark introspection. His mood becomes so black, I had to lighten it with a comic ghost and witches. Falco's gloom over the runaways is heightened because domestic needs have forced him to own slaves himself, with predictably complex results.

Scene of prisoners in a Triumph

There was one very happy piece of research; Richard and I went to Italy for the last time together. Through the kindness of Andrew Wallace-Hadrill, then Director of the British School at Rome, we spent a wonderful day at Lake Nemi where I have Veleda seek refuge at the Sanctuary of Diana. There we also saw the brutalist museum Mussolini built for the enormous raised ships that Caligula had had on the lake. They were sunk by the Romans, to efface memories of Caligula's extravagance, so in theory Falco could have

Fire-damaged remains of one of Caligula's boats, museum at Nemi

View of Lake Nemi from the modern road above

Mr Mischief, in his element

nothing to do with them when he and Helena visit the shrine. But it was too good to miss. Falco is told about the sunken boats (using what we know from archaeology), before the scene at the lakeside becomes an atmospheric meeting place with the prophetess.

The day after we visited Nemi, Andrew took us down to Herculaneum where an Amazon's head had emerged from the mud at the site of the unexcavated basilica. We had a chance to talk to conservators, something that does not happen when I creep around sites incognito. Richard, whose background was in historic building conservation, strode around Herculaneum for three hours entranced, though he had barely recovered from surgery and it was pouring with rain. For us it was the last of so many enthralling visits to such wonderful sites, our gift from Falco and Helena over those long years.

So although I am not keen on Christmas, *Saturnalia* will always be for me a very happy book.

Alexandria

First published in 2009

During *Saturnalia* and *Alexandria* I was secretly writing a very different novel, my enormous English Civil War story, *Rebels and Traitors*. I have never used libraries much for Falco, but the British Library was invaluable for my Seventeenth Century research. I felt I was a student again, though doing rather more work this time. It was, pleasingly, double research once I started this book, because I used my experience of what very grand libraries are like to work in.

Reconstruction of interior of Trajan's Library, Rome

The book was to be set in Egypt, examining not the world of pharaohs and pyramids on which most novelists dwell, but the relatively unexplored Roman-administrated province that was the personal treasure house of emperors from Augustus on. For Falco and Helena, as for my modern readers, the story of Cleopatra and Mark Antony would resonate, but I wanted to show a country where very ancient traditions are now coloured by Roman masters. It is not an unhappy world, but when a dead librarian is discovered in the Great Library (unavoidable, really!) solving the case is a diplomatic problem. Incidentally, I made it a locked-room mystery (something I never have much patience with) but my solution derives from what I know of public building maintenance.

Enter Falco, who has really come to Egypt so Helena can add more of the Seven Wonders of the

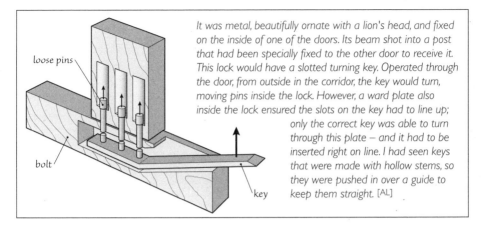

loose pins

bolt

key

It was metal, beautifully ornate with a lion's head, and fixed on the inside of one of the doors. Its beam shot into a post that had been specially fixed to the other door to receive it. This lock would have a slotted turning key. Operated through the door, from outside in the corridor, the key would turn, moving pins inside the lock. However, a ward plate also inside the lock ensured the slots on the key had to line up; only the correct key was able to turn through this plate – and it had to be inserted right on line. I had seen keys that were made with hollow stems, so they were pushed in over a guide to keep them straight. [AL]

Ancient World to her collection. In fact she has seen the Colossus of Rhodes off-stage on their journey from Rome, which may have been a waste on my part. Such are the riches of the ancient world, I can toss away in a paragraph a scene that could have developed into a whole book …

The Nilotic scene

Of all the difficult projects I have tackled, describing Roman Alexandria would be the worst. All the famous ancient monuments were lost to an earthquake and disappeared into the sea; although the underwater archaeology exploring the muddy harbour is fascinating, it has not yet told us much about such buildings as the royal palaces, the Library, the tomb of Alexander … Even the locations of these famous old buildings remain uncertain. At least we know where the Lighthouse was, and

Lindsey and Michelle find some remains (at last) in Alexandria

have descriptions. A desperate dramatic scene takes place there.

I went to Alexandria briefly with my friend Michelle, and it was not my best piece of organising. We glimpsed Cairo too, in case we never had a chance to revisit; we saw the Pyramids and Sphinx – in a driving sandstorm, just as Falco and his family do. At Alexandria we were mobbed by eager schoolgirls at the Fort, which stands where the Lighthouse was. We had hoped to visit the Romano-Hellenic Museum – only to discover it was closed indefinitely for renovation, so thoroughly removed from sight that we never even found it. This was not the first time I had promised Michelle a museum treat only to be thwarted by administrators who don't even tell you on their websites that an amenity is closed ... She took it stoically.

Despite all that, I managed to find enough to write about. The themes concern books: why we collect them, how we store, catalogue and discard them. Arising from it are considerations about knowledge – how we value that:

> Doctrines swotted to the small hours by bug-eyed,
>   crew-cut
> Students sustained by lentil soup and thick porridge.
> PERSIUS

That scholars are layabouts, other-worldly, lustful for women or highly peculiar, is a running joke, though eventually students come good: Aelianus, who has crossed over from Greece, makes an amiable assistant, while a group of young men set to and help combat a fire using the latest technology.

Once the Librarian dies, by fair means or foul, a race begins to succeed him. Appointments are a matter of Roman interest, so Falco witnesses the seedy contest at close quarters (besides, someone who coveted the job may well be the murderer – if there was a murder). The in-fighting and jealousy which ensue are, of course, no reflection on my father's old department which, being stuffed with people teaching political subjects, was a hotbed of intrigue. (They all wanted to go into politics so much that at least three became Members of Parliament.) Nor does it reflect my own experience as a civil servant, where machinations were marginalised by out-manoeuvring the real opposition: members of the public and our generally defective ministerial masters.

I did this time produce an ancient autopsy; it was fascinating to write and quite moving. I also had a daft scene with a gigantic crocodile, using one piece of research Michelle and I managed; we had paced out a mummified croc at the Cairo museum. And although his dates may be a bit too close for comfort, I introduced Heron, the inventor whose work had been mentioned in my previous books: *Not for nothing was Heron known as the Machine Man. We already knew of him from his work with automata, famous devices he made for theatres and temples: noises like thunder, automatic opening doors using fire and water, moving statues. He had produced a magic theatre, which could roll itself out before an audience, self-powered, then create a miniature three-dimensional performance, before trundling away to resounding applause. As we sat enthralled, he told us how he once made another that staged a Dionysian mystery rite; it had leaping flames, thunder and automatic Bacchantes who whirled in a mad dance around the wine god on a pulley-driven turntable.* [AL] It is Heron who solves the locked-room puzzle.

Although the setting is so far from Rome, regular characters are present. Falco and Helena stay conveniently with Fulvius and Cassius, to whom I gave rather short

The most fascinating gadget Heron told us about was his aeolipile, which he modestly translated as a 'wind ball'. His design for it used a sealed cauldron of water, which was placed over a heat source. As the water boiled, steam rose into pipes and into the hollow sphere. As I understood it, this resulted in rotation of the ball.

'So what could it be used for?' asked Helena intently. 'Some kind of propulsion? Might it move vehicles?'

Heron laughed. 'I do not consider this invention to be useful, merely intriguing. It is a novelty, a remarkable toy. The difficulty of creating sufficiently strong metal chambers makes it unsuitable for everyday applications – but who would need it?' [AL]

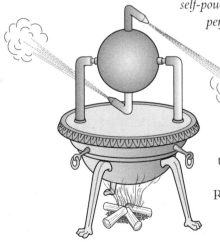

shrift before. I play with ambiguity about their social role, especially after Geminus joins the party, to Falco's intense annoyance. Thalia appears, since the plot involves exotic species; her presence will have unexpected and very far-reaching consequences.

The decisions made by the appointments board are probably as cynical as anything I've written. But I must be mellowing; so too my protagonists, who view it almost optimistically: *'There are men,'* says Helena, after the worst candidate succeeds, *'men with limitations at the outset, who nonetheless defy opinion and grow into a new position.'* To which Falco responds with resignation, *He might come good. In the terrible satire that is public life, you have to have some hope.*

Nemesis

First published 2010

> *Soon farewell town house, country estate by the*
> *Brown Tiber washed, chain-acres of pasture-land,*
> *Farewell the sky-high piles of treasure*
> *Left with the rest for an heir's enjoyment ...*
> HORACE

From time to time in a series, an author has to be ruthless, to maintain the dynamism. The start of *Nemesis* will be shocking to some; stark events occur for Falco and Helena. From this moment, their lives will change utterly. What will never change, I promise, are their characters.

I intended that book twenty would gather up strands; towards the end several plot-lines actually offer possibilities for the future if I choose to continue. As always, I wanted to write so new readers can just begin here; they shouldn't feel left out. I hope references back are done with a light hand. Despite a self-imposed challenge to include a subliminal reference to each previous book, I never forced that and I haven't ticked them off.

An Etruscan altar

The first chapters cover extremely sad events, though lightened by dry moments. Out of this situation, a murder plot unexpectedly grows.

Geminus has been selling statues to adorn the nearly completed Flavian Amphitheatre. (Oliver thinks it profligate that I only toss in this idea in passing – 'wasting' what could have been the foundation for a whole book!) This storyline takes Falco to the coast, where he learns of the strange disappearance of his father's husband-and-wife suppliers. Soon the man is found cruelly murdered near Rome, his corpse laid out in a strange ritualistic fashion (I had never done strange ritualistic corpses!). So Petronius becomes involved.

The chief suspects are named almost immediately: a family of imperial ex-slaves, who live in the dangerous Pontine Marshes. They have become a social menace which the authorities seem impotent to tackle. They thieve, get drunk, beat people up, have quarrels with neighbours, batter their own wives, collect knives and live with vicious dogs. Few hold down long-term jobs or manage decent family life. Nothing is done about the situation (or so it seems initially). The freedmen claim immunity; they have protection high up in Rome. Astonishingly, their protector is identified by Falco and Petro as Anacrites, the Chief Spy. Soon the vigiles are pulled off the case while Anacrites threatens Falco and Petro to make them drop their interest. Even his colleagues – Laeta, Momus and Perella – seem afraid to address his plainly corrupt involvement. They, too, warn off the two friends – thereby ensuring they will never let go.

It can be no surprise to regular readers that we are heading towards a deadly confrontation with Anacrites. Falco and Petro see dealing with the spy as their personal responsibility, enflamed by the antagonistic history we have followed for so long. The spy goads them; they try to out-manoeuvre him. After his past dark affair with Maia, he now starts hovering around the apparently vulnerable Albia. A showdown is inevitable. (Surely *nobody* thinks the book's title only refers to the winged goddess of equitable fortune?)

While Anacrites dogs them, often literally putting them under surveillance, Falco and his team tackle the serial killers. I dislike overt sadism in escapist novels; however, it has to be known that the deeds are dreadful. My depiction of the killings is informed by cases many people know about, which I hope lessens the need for lurid details of abuse, torture and death; for a long time many murders are only suspected, while all happen well 'off-stage' until, almost at the end, a character we have met is killed. I had to distinguish carefully between these serial killers and Thurius in *Three Hands in the Fountain*. The stress here is not so much on the crimes but the family involved and their increasingly relevant background. Of course the killers are psychopaths and there must be no sympathy for Anacrites when he associates with them. He tolerates them, shields them, and gives them work. How can such people pressurise or blackmail him? Is he just as cruel as they are?

The horrid answer emerges slowly. As Anacrites manoeuvres, he makes awkward social overtures. He throws a dinner party, a crazy set piece which draws upon clichés of Roman entertainment. There is a Trojan Hog, something known from Petronius' *Satyricon: The chef took up a knife and with a nervous hand cut open the pig's belly left and right. Suddenly, as the slit widened with the pressure, out poured sausages and blood puddings. The staff applauded this piece of ingenuity and let out a concerted cheer …* It is during this episode that Albia takes it upon herself to tackle Anacrites; betrayed by Aulus, she has become depressed and fatalistic. She risks her safety in a brave scenario that could easily become tragic; the mere possibility that the spy will harm her, or has already harmed her, is enough to give Falco motivation for extreme action.

During the book we see just how tough Falco and Petronius can be. In one striking scene they are questioning someone, the situation is desperate, their methods become brutal and an angry Helena points out that their behaviour comes very close to that of the criminals with their victims. In the present climate of distaste for how intelligence services obtain information through tortures like waterboarding, this is highly topical and an extremely dark moment. The two friends are shocked (which I hope redeems them); I am shocked too.

At the end of the book we see the ghastly unearthing of numerous bodies. My knowledge of the area where it happens came about by a lucky chance. While appearing at the Edinburgh International Book Festival, I had dinner with Donald and Susan Adamson.

The son of my first principal in the civil service, a man I much admired, Donald is a keen amateur archaeologist. He had been investigating sites from the Second World War landings at Anzio, Roman Antium – not far from the Pontine Marshes. Our discussion of the striking terrain suggested the forest where corpses are discovered and the frightening ravine where the main criminal is confronted.

Falco and his comrades have put a stop to the killing spree. Unfinished business remains, however, and for political reasons it will need a brave solution. The sheer number of corpses found at Antium is meant to prepare us for an unavoidable final scene.

Helena calls a family council; this was the ultimate Roman device, when a deadly situation affecting family members arose, especially if legal recourse was unavailable. During this story, Helena and Falco have more than one dreadful decision to take, some personal. They must cope with death and birth, acquisition and loss. Grief, good fortune and unwelcome responsibilities have all been dumped on them. People close to them have had their lives jolted, with repercussions I have not even begun to explore. I devised turns of fate that even startled me; for instance, the old apartment in Fountain Court will have an occupant again. And we finally learn just why Anacrites has in so many ways envied, snuggled up to, and yet preyed upon the Didius family.

One previously open-ended issue has to be resolved. In keeping with much of the series, this will have Falco, aided by Petronius, acting outside the law – not just from personal motivation but for the health of the Empire. Ultimately, their role as heroes requires them to pursue justice even if they have to go solo.

It's short and sweet. I quite enjoyed it. Like an informer, sometimes an author has to be ruthless.

The Characters

Falco and Helena, with Their Household

Marcus Didius Falco

I know him now without thinking. His birthday is 23 March. He has no luck, talks too much, supports the Blues, reads, loves plants, is a republican at heart, can't swim and gets seasick. Though worldly-wise, he can be a soft touch. As a series author I can even play at viewing him from new perspectives, such as that of Paccius Africanus in *The Accusers* or a young relative who has overheard her parents' comments: *That man is Marcus Didius, who married our cousin. His manner can be abrupt, but that is because he has plebeian origins. It makes him uncomfortable in ornate surroundings. He is more intelligent than he lets on, and he makes jokes that you don't realise until half an hour afterwards. He does work that is valued by the highest people, and is thought to have as-yet under-explored qualities.* [JM]

Appearance and personal character

Falco began as a voice; people don't describe their own looks. In *Shadows in Bronze* I provided the dark, wild curly black hair, brown eyes, and that overwhelming grin. They were qualified by Helena's teasing: *one of those long, straight, superior noses off an Etruscan tomb painting; eyes that keep moving, in a face that never reveals what they have seen; good teeth; dimples!* (Who, I wonder, thinks of Falco with dimples?)

He is always conscious of clothes, regarding it as a professional duty to have good gear – boots, belt, weapons, etc. He takes against tunics' colour, views askance his embroidered Palmyrene outfit, and is embarrassed when a bad cold sees him wrapped up *like some little hunchbacked Celtic forest god* [TFL] in his hooded Gallic coat (reminiscent of duffle coats). However clothes, he says, are just surface adornments: *I came with*

He is a relatively poor man, or he would not be a detective at all. He is a common man or he could not go among common people. He has a sense of character or he would not know his job. He will take no man's money dishonestly and no man's insolence without a due and dispassionate revenge. He is a lonely man and his pride is that you will treat him as a proud man or be very sorry you ever saw him. He talks as the man of his age talks – that is, with rude wit, a lively sense of the grotesque, a disgust for sham, and a contempt for pettiness.
CHANDLER

I hammered loose studs back into my best boots ... I wiped the oil from my sword ... I checked the blade and sharpened it with my sharkskin buffer ... Then I filed my dagger with pumice ... 'Aulus Camillus said, if there was to be any action, I should watch you getting ready. He said it always impressed him to see you change from a clown to a soldier ... He said, "When the eyes stop smiling, you can feel safe".' [STH]

more subtle trappings, skills which no slippery businessman should take for granted. I had been around; I hoped it showed. I sported an Aventine haircut and an Aventine stare. I was ready for anything and would take no nonsense. [SDD]

Though his trade is low, his qualities are noble. *He's entertaining and affectionate. He tells the truth. He doesn't make promises unless he can keep them – though sometimes he keeps promises he never even made. What I like most,* says Helena Justina, *is his loyalty.* [LAP] He also has enormous physical courage, alien to me, so I admire it greatly. Not only can he hold his own in a fight, but when he works in the silver mines we learn just how much punishment Falco can endure, in an environment so terrible that even he will be haunted by it permanently: *dirt, vermin, beatings, starvation, exhaustion, the filthy overseer whose kindest punishment was to strangle the culprit while his only notion of reward was an hour of enforced buggery.* [DLC]

I insist he carries forward the results of physical damage. So his trainer tells him: *Your left leg's weak from when you broke it three years ago. Your old fractured ribs still ache if the wind is north-westerly, you like to fight with a dagger but your wrestling's adequate, your feet are good, your right shoulder's vulnerable, you can throw a punch but you aim too low and you have absolutely no conscience about kicking your opponent in the balls. You eat too many street caupona rissoles and you hate redheads.* [THF]

Falco is ambitious for a better life, though he wants it without handouts, patronage or obligation. He eventually obtains it: *I was now a man of substance. I had house, wife, children, dog, slaves, heirs, work, prospects, past history, public honours, roof terrace with fig tree, obligations, friends, enemies, membership of a private gymnasium – all the paraphernalia of civilisation.* [SA] Perhaps all of us can share his ambivalent feelings: *Sometimes I had no idea myself how much I had capitulated and sold my soul to keep my family, or how much I simply played along and guarded my integrity.* [AL]

Falco the informer

Blame the army. Once the legions train you to kill, any attacker gets what-for. He meant me dead. I slew him first. That's how it works. [BBH]

The urge to right wrongs is an irresistible, ethical driving force. *Somebody had just killed this man, and I was going after whoever did it ...* [LAP] He will, if there is no alternative, take away life – though he says, *Killing people has a bad effect on me* [SP]. Like a writer, Falco can't resist: *I was enjoying myself ... there were real social undesirables to unearth and convict.* [VC] Helena describes his method: *He rampages about as if the gods had him under a murderous curse – then he clears everything up. Next minute he's demanding where is dinner ...* [BBH] If ever he speculates on having a different career, he and we know it's not serious.

I could be a bakery owner's bread-oven-paddle-pusher or a butcher's offal-bucket-toter ... [AL]

Although Falco is primarily a loner, he can find allies. Apart from Petronius and Helena, these run from Vitalis and Hilaris in *The Silver Pigs,* to senators like Gallicus and Frontinus – even the occasional goat or dog. This trait greases the wheels of the plot, but I see it as professionalism that Falco knows when he needs help, and he can winkle it out.

Skills

He is often called upon to disguise himself. He is variously a priest, a lead-pipe salesman, a fountain-cleaner, a jobbing playwright, a project manager. He acts as a bodyguard. His skills include being able to catch a thrown knife by its handle (oh really?). Not a brilliant linguist, he speaks workaday Greek (though a mistake over liquorice in *Shadows in Bronze* nearly costs him his life) and has a smattering of Celtic.

He is a city boy, who both knows his way around Rome and is streetwise: *I walked steadily, keeping away from doorways and glancing down any alleys I passed. Where there was space for more than one person, I went straight up the middle of the road. When I heard anybody who must realise I was there, I made sure my tread was confident. If the other person did not appear to have noticed me, I kept quiet.* [TTD]

Falco and the Emperor

Sometimes I worked for Vespasian. A new emperor, sprung from a middle-class background and wanting to keep a canny eye on the nasty snobs of the old elite, may need the occasional favour ... I was quick and discreet, and Vespasian could trust me to tidy up loose ends. There were never repercussions from my jobs. [LAP]

Imperial missions are often overseas: *Is the mission just dangerous, or does it involve an inconvenient journey, a foul climate, a total lack of civilised amenities, and a tyrannical king who likes his Romans laced on a spit over a very hot fire?* Falco asks Anacrites over Nabataea; his mission is exploratory, to report back on this secretive and very wealthy Eastern state, which will in the long term be taken over as a Roman province: *topography, fortifications, economics, social mores, political stability and mental state of the populace.* [LAP]

He is not above boasting about his imperial work: *I've worked for the best. Don't ask me names. I've been involved in jobs I'm not allowed to discuss and I'm trained in skills you'd rather I didn't describe. I've tracked down plenty of felons and if you haven't heard about it, that just proves how discreet I am.* [LAP]

Literary dreams

Falco wants to be a writer. His Juvenilia, those odes to Aglaia which Sosia calls rather rude, must be ghastly, but his play, perhaps the prototype for *Hamlet*, is eagerly sought by those at the frontiers of literary scholarship. Like all of us who want our name in lights but who know it will be spelled wrong, Falco has no illusions: *My elegant creation* The Spook Who Spoke *received its sole performance on a hot August evening in the Palmyra garrison theatre. If you can think of worse, I'd be glad to hear it ...* [LAP] It does, however, lead to his inclusion in the catalogue of the Great Library in Alexandria: categorised as a comedian, he is *Phalko of Rome, father Phaounios, prosecutor and dramatist.* None of which I had anticipated when I began the series.

His first attempt at giving a public reading fails when nobody comes. Next, he and Rutilius Gallicus hire the Auditorium of Maecenas for the night of embarrassment that opens *Ode to a Banker.* Believe me, I feel for them.

Helena Justina

Single-minded girls are always dangerous. A man can float along for years being cynical and flippant, then some fierce tyrant (who happens to have the advantages of a sweet mind, a delicious expression and a body that is crying out to be entwined with his) sneaks under his defences ... [DLC]

Although Falco is generally drawn to a woman's appearance, he falls for Helena's character, only later noticing that: *Once they worked her over with the manicure prodders and eyebrow tweezers, curling tongs and earwax scoops, left her fermenting all afternoon in a mealy flour face mask then finished her off with a delicate sponging of red ochre across the cheekbones and a fine gleam of antimony above the eyes, Helena Justina was bound to be presentable enough, even to me ... The effect was of a cool, tall, distinctly superior naiad.* [SP]

At home, she wore very little jewellery, and looked none the worse for it. In company she was shy; even alone with a close friend like me she might pass for modest until she piped up with an opinion – at which point wild dogs broke pack and ran for cover all along the street ... [VC]

She acquires a cross-shaped scar on her left arm where she was bitten by a scorpion in *Last Act in Palmyra;* afterwards she wears a row of silver bangles to hide it, which tend to jingle expressively under stress.

I gave Helena a birthday in September, then forgot, and could find no evidence – which led to the joke that Falco thinks it is in October.

We first meet her abroad. She is very keen on travel, developing a yen to see all the Seven Wonders of the World (which I am not sure I can emulate). Inconvenience does not faze her, and she has a bravery I envy: *Most women of her status would have frizzled up in horror at the thought of stepping into the public hubbub of a loud, lewd foreign metropolis ... Many citizens of Damascus eyed her with obvious suspicion for doing so. For a senator's daughter Helena had always had a strange sense of propriety. If I was there that satisfied her. She was neither embarrassed nor afraid ...* [LAP]

A Roman matron in her chair (after a long day?)

Her character seems too modern to some people. I suspect there were always women like Helena. *She was a true Roman matron. Her father had tried to create in her a meek, modest partner to some all-knowing male. But her mother's example of quiet contempt for the opposite species was just as traditional, so Helena had grown up forthright and doing just as she liked.* [DLC] She is my kind of girl: *she was eccentric; she knew it; she did not want to change.* [JM] People constantly ask, would a woman of Helena's status choose to live in a grotty apartment with a man of Falco's low birth? Read Juvenal's famous Sixth Satire, where he rails against Rome's uppity upper-class women, and cites Eppia, a senator's wife (not even divorced) who ran off with a gladiator.

Helena has been given a free run of her father's library and education from her brothers' tutors. In *Ode to a Banker* she assesses the contentious scrolls of novels and in *Last Act in Palmyra* she adapts *The Birds* for Falco, then scandalously acts in the performance (as the dabchick). She is a good mother – but frankly would prefer to have her nose in a scroll. When Falco has to

When that senator's wife, Eppia, eloped with her fancy swordsman ...
Husband, family, sister, all were jettisoned, not
One single thought for her country; shamelessly she forsook
Her tearful children, as well as – this will really surprise you –
The public games, and her favourite matinee star.
JUVENAL

write formal reports for the Emperor, Helena Justina takes over; she is quicker and knows what he needs to say. She does his accounts too.

In her personal life, she shows great self-determination: she issues a divorce note to Pertinax; she decides when to come and live with Falco. Hilaris explains what went wrong in her first marriage: *She found that a high position and good manners were not enough. She would rather he had picked his nose and goosed the kitchen maids – then at least talked to her!* [SP] To Falco's amusement, she tells him the moment of truth finally came to her during a quarrel about politics.

In work, she helps whenever a woman can. Approaching strangers can be dangerous; when in doubt, Helena may take Maia with her, for instance looking for Tertulla in Lalage's brothel, or trying to visit the gladiator Rumex. However, I loathe the 'woman in jeopardy' situation and indeed mock its clichés in *Three Hands in the Fountain*.

In the first book, Helena not only has the idea of sending Falco to the lead mines, but saves his life several times. She encourages their dive into a brothel to escape pursuit and is an excited companion in the subsequent chase. In less extreme situations, Falco often takes her along: *'Wear a plain dress and no necklaces. Bring a stylus, and don't interrupt. I hate a secretary who talks smart.' Some might imagine her a slave. I tried to view her as a highly trained freedwoman inherited from an aunt. Helena herself seemed quite at ease, without being explained away.* [TTD] Later, she helps orchestrate the gathering of suspects in *Ode to a Banker;* she has spotted the potential bestselling author. She organises the family council at the end of *Nemesis*.

More mundanely, Helena holds the fort at home. She doesn't enjoy that so much; neither do I.

Helena sometimes solves the crimes: she spots the room-size discrepancy at Flora's in *Poseidon's Gold,* for instance. Her motivation matches Falco's own: *That young lady could never resist a mystery.* [LAP] She also works behind the scenes for Falco, introducing him to Caenis, in *Two for the Lions,* hoping for imperial patronage.

It is probably important to Falco's self-esteem that he feels Helena is attractive to other men. *Her devotees came from some strange walks of life. The very top too. A quiet,*

I had no doubt she had spoken to the man with authority in my absence; he may not have believed how much I respected her judgement. [OB]

competent girl who listened to people, she attracted both the vulnerable and those with taste; men liked to think they had privately discovered her ... [LAP] He is hugely, ridiculously jealous (this probably increases Helena's own self-esteem, so dented by Pertinax).

Helena is a romantic, though less so than Falco. She is enthusiastic about sex, overturning gender stereotypes from *The Silver Pigs* where she seduces Falco. This may be me teasing, but it fits Latin authors' horror of threatening women.

Falco and Helena's relationship

'Interesting partnership!'
'Interesting girl,' I said. [LAP]

They don't immediately gel, naturally. *To say our eyes met would imply too much. What happened was that I looked at her because when a man is left alone with a woman in a quiet room it is the natural thing for him to do. She stared back at me. I had no idea why she was doing that ...* [SP] The sparkiness of their relationship endures, and I think it healthy; they retain enough independence to keep one another's respect. By *Time to Depart,* when they are established together, Falco says: *Sometimes we did fight. Sometimes, because she wanted me too badly to use reason, I could make her quarrel bitterly. Other times, the intelligence with which she handled me was breathtaking. She set trust between us like a plank, and I just walked straight across.*

This relationship is not traditional in crime novels. *I think he will always have a shabby office, a lonely house, a number of affairs but no permanent connection,* said Chandler, of Philip Marlowe. Maybe Falco and Helena owe more to Nick and Nora Charles, in Dashiell Hammett's 'Thin Man' books – or simply to my past experience with romantic novels.

Helena can read Falco's thoughts. Sharing every confidence is for them, as it was for the Romans, the ideal definition of a good marriage. Even when Falco is working with Petronius, in *Three Hands in the Fountain,* Falco tells Helena he will always keep a modicum of reserve, something he will only share when he comes home to her (starting with his opinion there that Petro is behaving like an idiot).

It is important to them, as it is to me, that they do things together, whatever the rules say. They never lose the excitement of dashing off to follow up a clue: *I had already grabbed her hand as we hurried along. This was the kind of moment we both enjoyed together – rushing through the evening streets to an unexpected rendezvous where we might witness something material.* [AC]

They keep a good house and are good parents; both are pleased by their success in this.

Falco and Helena's household

A whole house has been bought for me, without anybody telling me the street or the locality, showing me the site plan, or even, if I may be so coarse as to raise this, Helena, mentioning the price. [OVTM]

As the series proceeds, the couple acquire children, property – both real estate and chattels, a dog, and eventually even slaves. It makes their lives more comfortable (when it's not causing domestic problems), though it changes the dynamic from Falco the scruffy bachelor at Fountain Court. Readers fear he may grow staid, but for me adjustments keep the books fresh. But having too many characters makes life awkward for an author. Children tie down a hero who needs to keep mobile. In *Three Hands in the Fountain,* I forgot about the baby, so poor Falco also forgets, hoofs off to tail suspects – and leaves his three-month-old daughter alone in an empty house … In *See Delphi and Die,* the young children are left behind (but not Nux, who has a role to play); Falco and Helena miss them so much that in *Alexandria* Julia and Favonia travel too (but not Nux).

In order to control the cast list, regular characters must sometimes be culled; fortunately ancient childbirth was frequently fatal and many children died very young. Despite a miscarriage and a technical stillbirth, by the end of *Nemesis* Falco and Helena have:

Julia Junilla Laeitana

Born in Barcino, Hispania Baetia, at the end of *A Dying Light in Corduba* and destined to dominate any household she graces, simply by looking cute. Her unusual third name celebrates a wine from the Barcelona region.

She is a child of character: *'No!' Dear little poppet; it had been one of her first words* … [BBH] By three, she is learning her alphabet (from the senator) – and she is naughty; she scribbles on evidence tablets – though that's really because the author needs to kick up the plot …

Julia's many toys are based on archaeological finds. *I won't say my daughter was spoiled but she was fortunate. Four grandparents doted on their dark-eyed toddler. Aunts vied with one another for her love. If a new toy was created in any corner of the Empire, Julia somehow acquired it. You wonder why we had brought every one on a thousand-mile journey? Sheer terror of her reaction if she discovered we had left any treasure behind.* [BBH] So carefully does Julia audit her possessions, her parents prophesy she will become an accountant.

Sosia Favonia

Born at the beginning of *A Body in the Bath House*, Favonia nearly fails to survive. She becomes another cutey, though a more gruff and private individual than her sister. In *Scandal Takes a Holiday*, Falco describes her as *a sombre thug*; we see her doggedness as she begs for treats from her grandfather and when her deaf cousin calls, Falco comments: *she loved anyone eccentric.* Later, however, she charms the people of Ostia as she practises toddling, in her clean white tunic and tiny bead necklace.

Flavia Albia

Discovered running wild on the streets of Londinium, a casualty of the Boudiccan Revolt, Albia comes to Helena's notice and is rescued. *She was little more than a skeleton, her features unformed. She had blue eyes. They could be British …* [JM] Helena takes the decision, but even Falco is sympathetic: *She was childishly slight, and if her life had been as hard as I suspected, she was young enough to deserve a chance, young enough to be capable of being saved …* [JM] Early tantrums lead to her running away and being taken up by Florius, who evidently rapes her.

Her origins will never be known. That's definite: to show the consequences of disaster is my aim. It does not suit Albia or me to have a sugary solution.

By *The Accusers* Albia has a place in the family and is developing a personality: *a quiet, calm, tolerant teenager. She watched the decadent world into which we had dragged her with those British blue eyes, so full of reserve; they seemed to*

If Helena took her in, we would be infected with fleas and diseases, lied to, betrayed on every possible occasion, then robbed blind when the skinny scrap finally upped and fled … [JM]

appreciate our special Roman madness, while keeping her own, much more civilised, restraint. I had seen her sometimes shake her head over us, very slightly. But around this time, her position begins to rub. In *Scandal Takes a Holiday* she has a tomboy relationship with Aelianus, but Falco is already disturbed; he hopes, *soon Albia would pass for a freedwoman and the questions would stop. With any luck we could find her a husband with a good trade and she might even end up happy. Well, the husband might be happy.* Albia had lost her childhood to isolation and neglect; that would always show. She herself questions her position: *'You never told me I was merely to look after your children, saving you the price of a slave!'* Albia was adept at throwing the sympathy dice; she always knew she could make us scared our goodwill gesture would go bad. [SDD]

Sweetheart, it seems our work is done with Albia. She is the complete Roman woman — wheedling, devious and brutal when she wants something. [SDD]

Albia absorbs what being a Roman entails; she struggles to learn Greek. She gains professional insights from Falco and Helena; by *See Delphi and Die* she starts asking the right questions, for instance about the death of Cleonymus. Falco later notices, *There were many things I had never explained or discussed with her, yet she had picked them up from fragments of conversation, almost from facts Helena and I had left unsaid.* [SA] It will have its benefits. Always streetwise, at the end of *Nemesis* she decides a way to evade the unfair limitations on her future. Her choice is a surprise to Falco, who has previously told Thalia: *my foster daughter is never going to run away to the circus. Albia has already had enough adventure. She wants to learn secretarial Greek and book-keeping.* [AL] But she finds a different way out for herself. *You gave me a chance; I am grateful. I want to stay in Rome. But I am going to make myself a life, a life that is suitable and sustainable. Don't tell me I cannot try …* [NM]

Marcus Didius Alexander Postumus

Conceived in *Alexandria*, foetal in *Nemesis*. Not even born yet, this infant of questionable parentage is absolutely, archetypically a cuckoo in Falco and Helena's nest.

Nux

We meet this very important dog (her opinion) in *Time to Depart*, where the scruffy Aventine stray decides

Falco should adopt her. *She was a tufty mongrel in several colours, with limpidly soulful eyes. Something about her big furry paws and her whiskery face had a dangerous appeal.*

A tenacious defender of her adopted family, she gets her way and joins the household after helping save Falco from a thug in a fight at the apartment. Thereafter she behaves like my brother's two dogs, Nicky the Lakeland terrier and Samantha. *Nux was a crazy, friendly, frowsty little mutt, always keen to give visitors a guided tour of rooms where we kept valuables.* [SA] *Walking Nux was always a good excuse to get out of the house.* [NM]

I can't squeeze Nux into every book, but she appears regularly – otherwise readers complain. Although her skills as a sniffer dog are derided, it is she who finds the missing child in *One Virgin Too Many*. A tricky moment comes at the end of *See Delphi and Die*, where in an incident I don't regret, Nux nearly eats the missing body. In *Nemesis* her passion for a piece of rope nearly lands Falco in trouble with Anacrites.

Nux had become anxious and clinging after an episode on the Capitol where she was arrested by priestly acolytes who were looking for doggies to crucify. In addition to that, a succession of nasty male curs had occupied our front porch recently, suggesting Nux was on heat ... [OVTM]

Slaves

> *I bought slaves who were obviously useless because I loathed the idea of owning them and I could not bring myself to bargain as hard as you had to for anyone with real skills.* [AC]

Falco comes late to ownership; then his slaves come and go fast. In *The Jupiter Myth* he fails to buy a nursemaid. In *The Accusers,* his Camillus relatives have fun over the useless cook **Genius**, who becomes a celebrity chef. *'It's a new kind of investment commodity,'* the senator joined in. *'Genius never needs to visit a real kitchen – which is just as well, if I may tactfully mention the after-effects of that pork marinade ... '*

By *Saturnalia* there are **Galene**, a nursemaid who wants to be a cook, and **Jacinthus**, a cook who wants to be anything else; luckily ten billeted soldiers do the chores instead. Here, Falco does impose his authority surprisingly, when the slaves try to take over his house.

Two books later a nervous Falco has a slave bonanza but Helena takes charge.

Falco brings home from Egypt a secretary, **Katutis**; he is free and just very grateful for what he believes to be a high-class job. They rub along, insofar as Falco is prepared to toe the line. Perhaps Katutis copies out the memoirs that form these novels.

Falco's Relatives

Falco's Parents

Junilla Tacita, Ma

My mother could wop three naughty children back in line while stirring a pot of tunic dye, discussing the weather, chewing a rough fingernail and passing on gossip in a thrilling undertone. And she knew how to ignore what she did not want to hear. [OB]

She operates on the principle that if you want anything doing, do it yourself. She claims she never interferes. She wants to know everyone's business. *She had a way of saying nothing which was worth three scrolls of rhetoric.* [OVTM] She sees no reason to let go after Falco leaves home; she invades his apartment to clean it, leave him a nice bit of dinner, and sweep out his female conquests. Obviously she cannot be based on *my* mother, or I would be scared to write such things.

Ma lives in a flaky grey building on the Aventine, behind the Emporium, near the Temple of Minerva. This is where she brought up her children; Falco's affection for the place, where he retains rights to return home to Mother, suggests that the cramped apartment Geminus walked out of was somewhere different. Falco pays his mother's rent. Geminus sends her an annuity through the Auctioneers' Guild, but we can imagine the distaste with which the indomitable Junilla Tacita refuses to spend this cash on herself; she uses it to educate her grandchildren.

Her front door opens into the kitchen, which tends to be full of visitors who feel easily at home. When Sosia is there, Falco says, *I suppose she had never been anywhere where there was so much going on in such good-humoured chaos ...* [SP] Many scenes in subsequent books occur there. It becomes a haunt of Anacrites, then hosts Ma's

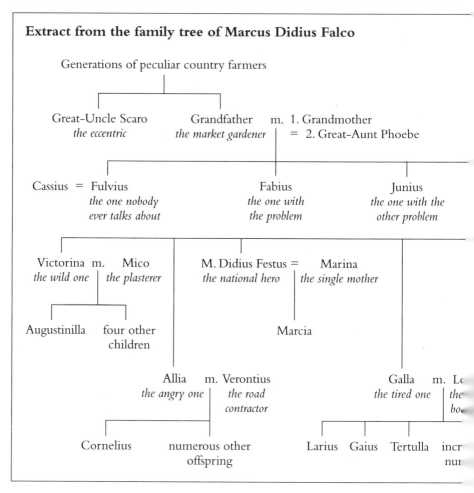

Extract from the family tree of Marcus Didius Falco

Generations of peculiar country farmers

Great-Uncle Scaro — *the eccentric*

Grandfather — *the market gardener* — m. 1. Grandmother = 2. Great-Aunt Phoebe

Cassius = Fulvius
*the one nobody
ever talks about*

Fabius
*the one with
the problem*

Junius
*the one with the
other problem*

Victorina m.   Mico
the wild one | *the plasterer*

M. Didius Festus = Marina
the national hero | *the single mother*

Augustinilla   four other
children

Marcia

Allia   m. Verontius
the angry one | *the road
contractor*

Galla   m. L⊂
the tired one | *the
bo⊂*

Cornelius   numerous other
offspring

Larius   Gaius   Tertulla   incr
nur

eighty-year-old follower, **Aristagoras**. *Despite his age,
the papery swain was agile on his walking sticks. She brushed
aside his adulation but let him into her apartment sometimes
and gave him a panfried sardine as a reward for his faithfulness.
On my arrival she always sent him packing.* [SA]

Early on, Ma seems to have no faith in Falco, appearing unfairly biased towards Festus. Falco complains, *She
treats me like a hopeless case. She speaks to me as if I were a
delinquent child. The loss of my great-hearted brother burns
between us like wormwood in the throat, a perpetual reproach.
I don't even know what she reproaches me for. I suspect
she doesn't know herself* ... [SP] Generally, Ma remains
sceptical: *Faced with a son who had noble motives, Ma lost
interest.* [AC]

Even as early as *The Silver Pigs,* Ma is a little old lady.
My mother's face would never age. Only her skin had grown

Not to be trifled with: an
elderly Roman lady

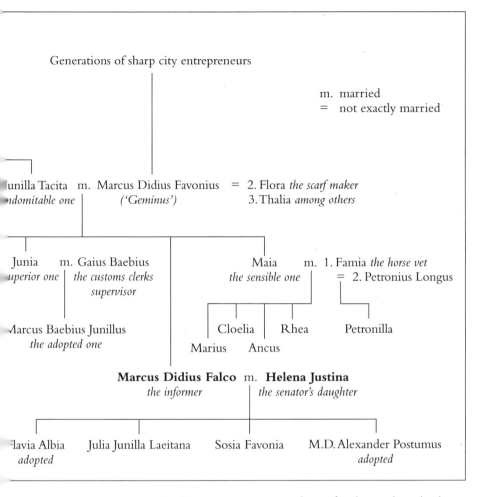

Generations of sharp city entrepreneurs

m. married
= not exactly married

Junilla Tacita   m. Marcus Didius Favonius   = 2. Flora *the scarf maker*
indomitable one   ('*Geminus*')   3. Thalia *among others*

Junia   m. Gaius Baebius   Maia   m. 1. Famia *the horse vet*
superior one | *the customs clerks*   *the sensible one* | = 2. Petronius Longus
                supervisor

Marcus Baebius Junillus   Cloelia   Rhea   Petronilla
   the adopted one   Marius   Ancus

Marcus Didius Falco m. **Helena Justina**
   the informer | *the senator's daughter*

Flavia Albia   Julia Junilla Laeitana   Sosia Favonia   M.D. Alexander Postumus
adopted   *adopted*

tired in recent years, so it no longer fitted properly on her bones. (Easy to write that at forty, incidentally – I might think twice now!) She keeps going through bustle and bossiness: *a tiny, black-eyed old bundle who could rampage through a market like a barbarian army.* [THF]. Love for her children and grandchildren, grumpily expressed but immoveable, and her endless determination to best Geminus, provide her motivation. Characteristically, *Most days, Ma was either out, whirling about the Aventine on errands and causing annoyance, or else she was in, scrubbing away at pots or chopping like fury in her cooking area.* [OB] In *Saturnalia* her daughters pay for her to have a cataract operation, which she endures with stoicism.

In *Nemesis*, she claims her position as a wife, and I believe readers will cheer her at this moment.

Marcus Didius Favonius (aka Geminus), Pa

You might as well
Accept the title – and income – of an auctioneer,
  join in
The saleroom battles, flog lots under the hammer
To a crowd of bidders – winejars, three-legged stools,
Bookcases, cupboards, remaindered plays by
  nonentities …
JUVENAL

I devised Geminus for *Shadows in Bronze* after my own father asked piteously why Falco didn't have a dad? Perhaps Falco's Pa owes something to my father.

Geminus is insidious. Outsiders think him a lovable rogue and can't see why Falco barely tolerates him, whereas Falco knows the damage Geminus can inflict. In fairness, his children do remember their infancy with occasional affection; to his grandchildren, who don't resent him, he becomes an attractive figure with a hint of mystery. Helena, who takes to him, tries to reconcile Falco to him; she says his father may stand back, yet watches his offspring and worries over them. He even bops Anacrites, for hanging around Ma – though that is macho jealousy: '*Whether it's true doesn't matter,*' roared Pa. '*People should not be saying these terrible things about your mother … *' [OB]

In *Poseidon's Gold*, we learn that Pa abandoned his family as much because of pressures caused by over-crowding as because he was pursuing his redhead. Poverty forced Ma to take in a lodger, the childless **Melitan moneylender** who paid for Falco and Maia to attend school; his plea to adopt them caused Pa wild indignation. Junilla Tacita says of the family break-up: *too many people crammed in too small a space. Too many quarrels and too many mouths to feed. Then people give up on each other sometimes …* [PG] Years later, Falco notices with a start that his father still wears his wedding ring.

Geminus lived for over twenty years with Flora. It may be significant that they had no children. The town house on the banks of the Tiber to which they return after an exile in Capua is clearly a quiet haven. Flora is by no means his only flirtation; he even cosies up to Thalia in *Alexandria*.

'I am not unaware of your sister's position … Leave this to me,' declared my incorrigible parent, throwing himself into being magnanimous as eagerly as he had once fled the family coop. [OVTM]

Physically, Geminus is *a stocky, secretive, moody man, about sixty years old, with rampant grey hair, all curls. He was good-looking (though not as good-looking as he thought). His profile swooped in one strong line without a ledge between the eyes – a real Etruscan nose. He had a nose for a scandal and an eye for a woman that made him a legend even in the Saepta Julia where the antique dealers congregate.* [SB] *Not tall, he was still a commanding presence; people who wanted to annoy me* (says Falco) *said we looked alike. In fact he was heavier and shiftier.* [TTD]

As a businessman Pa is a mixture. *He would sooner lie than tell the truth. He had sold more fake Athenian blackware vases than any other auctioneer in Italy. A potter turned them out for him specially.* [TFL] He cheats mercilessly, even attempting a fraudulent compensation claim against the government in *Time to Depart*; he certainly avoids paying taxes. But he has taste, and a genuine love for art and antiques; a fine art and furniture man, he sometimes dabbles in scrolls or statues. Falco comments that both his stock and his staff turn out to be better quality than you expect. However, *Any collector who wants twenty identical statuettes of a Muse on Mount Helicon – one or two with chipped noses – will come rushing straight here!* [TTD] Apart from the house on the Embankment and his even larger spread on the coast, he has the trappings of wealth to make his life easy: *He was travelling back tonight in his normal quiet style – a lordly litter with six massive bearers, a gaudy troop of torchmen and two private bodyguards.* [SB]

He has made himself rich. In *Poseidon's Gold*, Falco taunts Geminus, '*Go ahead – disinherit me!*' This is satirical because he suspects his father has never even made a will. In *Nemesis* we will discover just what lies behind the shifty pause that follows his taunt. Meanwhile, when Geminus offers a loan to help Falco join the middle class, they are thwarted by Domitian.

Falco's attitude to his father varies from outright hostility to uneasy tolerance. Geminus gets on well with Helena from the start and makes friendly overtures. Only in *Poseidon's Gold*, with their inherited trouble from Festus, do he and his son make a fist of working together. It can't be perfect because Falco can't forget. *My father was shocked to find anyone criticising his past behaviour. He really had convinced himself that abandoning a wife and infant children was fine. Now he was hurt and I was angry. Some things don't change.* [STH]

There is an ironical outcome, and it happens in *Nemesis*.

Flora

For a long time all we know is that Flora was a red-headed scarf-maker. Geminus buys her the **Caupona**, perhaps as a source of pin money, or to stop her nosing into his own business.

Falco meets Flora briefly at the end of *Poseidon's Gold*, where he spots that she looks very like his mother. She dies during *Ode to a Banker*; Geminus is devastated – even Ma tells Falco to look after him.

Her Caupona has a unique style: *an eatery so unpretentious it barely rated attention from the local protection rackets ... Its customers were doggedly loyal – sad idlers who tolerated the unwashed bowls of lukewarm broth. The surly clientele at Flora's wanted to sit where there were other antisocial types whom they could steadfastly ignore.* [OB]

'Go to the baths and the barber, Pa.'
'Sod off – And don't tell me that was what Flora would have wanted, because Flora had one great advantage – she left me alone!' [OB]

Falco's Other Relations

Most of my family were offensive and all of them lacked tact. You couldn't hope to find a bigger crowd of loud, self-opinionated, squabbling idiots anywhere. [THF]

I came from a family who saw it as life's greatest challenge to be the first to interfere in any problem. [OB]

Victorina

It takes four books before we learn the lowdown on Falco's sister Victorina: *the eldest in our family, the bane of my childhood and my worst social embarrassment since then,* says Falco. *As a child she had been a tough little tyke with a constant runny nose and her loincloth at half-mast around her scabby knees. All the other mothers warned their children not to play with us because Victorina was so violent; Victorina made them play with her anyway. When she grew up she played only with the boys. There were plenty. I could never*

understand why. [IHM] One of the boys was Petronius Longus; in the one scene where she appears, she calls him Primrose, to his discomfiture.

Falco's view is unchanging: *She had a terrible reputation: an eye for the boys, a saucy green parasol, and the side-seams of her tunic always revealingly unstitched. When she visited the Circus, the men who held her parasol for her were always repugnant types.* [PG] In *Saturnalia*, Falco says she once organised a nymphs-and-satyrs party but inadvertently let out the secret so all the family aunts turned up.

Married to Mico, she has five children but dies of a 'female problem' during *The Iron Hand of Mars*. We never see very much of her.

Mico

Mico's name sends even hard-bitten foremen with thirty years' experience rushing off to the nearest public fountain to drown themselves. [SB] Even when contractors are desperate, Falco sneers, Mico – with his famously bumpy scrim – is the last plasterer they call in.

Mico is a lot of fun to write about – so I had to give him a good side. Left a widower, he is bringing up five fractious children single-handed, without complaint. His mother comes to stay, but doesn't help. His nature is gloomy and his luck is worse. *If Mico tripped over a bag of gold bits on his way to the baker's, the bag would split open, the aurei would scatter – and he would watch every one of them drop down a manhole into a sewer at full flood ...* [PG] Falco, on the up himself, helps out with work: *He left plaster floats in doorways and tramped fine dust everywhere; he made me feel I owed him something because he was poor and his children were motherless. Really, Mico was only poor because his bad work was notorious.* [BBH]

Augustinilla

While Victorina is fatally ill, Augustinilla goes to Germany with Falco and Helena. He describes her as having *an elaborate name but a very straightforward personality – dumb insolence.* [IHM]

At eight years old in this story, Augustinilla has *a plain face and a petulant expression, with five or six thin little plaits tied together with a skinny rag on the top of her head ...*

She was hip-high, wearing a tunic that ought to have been decent, though she had managed to have it hitched up so her bottom showed. This unfortunate child does triumph when, following a toothache, she and her German friend Arminia encounter the son of Civilis at Augusta Treverorum, then report to Falco where the rebel is.

Valentinianus

Another of Mico's absurdly named children. In *A Body in the Bath House* the infant eats too many gherkins and, while trying to humiliate Falco, strives to be sick on Nux.

Marcus Didius Festus

A very significant character.

I am still waiting for a message to say, Festus has landed back in Ostia so will I please bring him a wagon and some wineskins because he's run out of cash but has met some lads on the boat that he would like to entertain ... [SP]

Killed at Bethel in Judaea, aged thirty-five, Falco's brother probably died heroically – though there will always be a question mark. Supposedly, he was first man over the battlements and died as he turned back to encourage his men. For this he won the Palisaded Crown. The sculptor Orontes thinks Festus chose to die in battle because he was under pressure; but Orontes embodies unreliability.

Everything we know about Festus is said by other people. We never see him. (We never will; I mean that.)

He is the antithesis of what I like in a man, representing the untrustworthy side of Falco himself. His importance is as a bad influence and as a personal loss that darkens the early books. Falco, eight years younger, is both fascinated by and envious of his brother's charisma: *He was shorter and more thickset. More athletic and with a sweeter temperament. More gifted in business, luckier with women, smarter, sharper, more easily accepted as a treasure by the family ...* [PG]

Festus was a cynical soldier; he *saw the chance to eat, drink and fart at the Empire's expense, while using its unrivalled travel opportunities ...* [PG] His legion is the Fifteenth Apollinaris, commanded by Titus, so Titus knows of the Didius family – a connection that may explain why Vespasian and Titus first trust Falco.

Clearly he had a good side: *Festus could always be relied on to throw crumbs to a stranded fledgling or pat a three-legged dog.* [PG] Marina wanted to marry him; Falco thinks Festus had other ideas, though if presented with baby Marcia, his brother would have accepted her (which traps Falco with the problem).

As a businessman, Festus had all the good and the bad traits of Geminus; his complex web of deals unravels posthumously, landing his father and brother in deep trouble.

Festus was a dedicated womaniser, a massive drinker, a feckless, elusive relative who would bring home a stream of tiresome new friends and spongers. *My brother Festus could walk into any tavern in any province of the Empire and some wart in a spotty tunic would rise from a bench with open arms to greet him as an old and honoured friend … What's more, if our lad then progressed into the back room where the cheap whores were entertaining, equally delighted shrieks would arise as girls who should have known better all rushed up adoringly …* [PG]

Maia disliked him, and although their mother grieves, there are indications that she may have seen through Festus.

So was he a hero? Falco believes the Jewish prisoner who says an arrow squeezed in between Festus' helmet and his head. So let Falco have the last word on the brother he envied and loved:

Helmet not strapped properly. Trust him. Always unlaced, unhooked, half belted. He hated feeling trapped.

He was bloody good. Our Festus, with even only half his mind on a problem, could outstrip most of the dull plodders he was up against. Festus was the charismatic kind who soars to the top on talent that is genuine, easy and abundant. He was made for the army; the army knew its man. Stupid enough to show he did have that talent. Placid enough not to offend the establishment. Bright enough, once he was in position, to hold his own against anyone … [PG]

Marina

Originally a braid-maker, Festus' exquisite girlfriend has a hard streak of self-preservation. *She might have gone off and married, but why should she bother when she had me paying the bills? Her conquests were getting a voluptuous shape allied to a free and easy manner, attractive goods even before they discovered the lien on my bankbox.* [PG]

Marina lives almost at the foot of the Caelian, in the Street of Honour and Virtue. *A short, dark, sultry vision with immense wide-set eyes. She manoeuvred those eyes constantly, to nerve-racking effect. A cracker to look at, but she had been born common and was making a brave attempt to remain completely faithful to her origins.* [PG] *Only when she spoke did the mystique fade; she had the voice of a winkle-seller.* [THF]

She is not very bright (apart from rooking Falco). A fond but vague mother, she is given to farming out Marcia with unsuitable neighbours (**Statia** and husband, the ex-priest of Isis). Helena tries to discourage this wanton, but from time to time Marina pops up, when she can tear herself from her social life. After the early books she becomes more remote, but she sees her chance again in *Nemesis* and briskly reappears to claim any booty that's going.

Marcia

Marcia, Falco's favourite niece during his Fountain Court days, is a good-looking child of character. It is possible that Falco is himself her father. As he says, *For various reasons, a few of them noble, I tried to take his place.* [THF]

We first meet her as a handful at three: *Marcia flopped like a sack in her arms looking thoughtful, gazed up at her, deliberately dribbled, then blew bubbles in the spit ...* [SP] She improves but is still a worry: *She was a frank, open-hearted child. Maybe that was why I worried about her. She would be a frank, open-hearted woman one day.* [PG]

She can be uncooperative and knows how to make her mother look like a monster with well-timed wails. By *Nemesis*, when she must be around eleven, she has developed an attractive straight-talking style. It is clear she and Falco have kept their good relationship – and she has the capacity to wind him around her little finger.

Allia

Falco's second-eldest sister is a close ally of Victorina and sometimes has a spiteful attitude to him. She is famous for borrowing (and not returning) items. Falco calls her big-boned and somehow slightly awkward, as if she might have been damaged in the birth process.

Married to the ghastly Verontius, she has various children of whom we know Cornelius. *All Allia ever taught her children was how to borrow from relatives.* [SDD]

Verontius

A shifty, untrustworthy road contractor who smelt of fish pickle and unwashed armpits … The lengths he went to defraud the government were tortuous. A glance at Verontius looking half asleep and guilty was enough to explain half the potholes on the Via Appia … [TTD]

He first appears when Falco's client has been an aedile in charge of road maintenance contracts. Falco visits this charmer, who *could bend figures better than a conjurer stuffing doves up his fundament … He was colourless, bald, squinty and half deaf. He stank of armpits and feet … I won't say he and Allia lived in squalor. We all knew they had money. It was squirrelled away somewhere. Hoarded meanly, never spent. They would both die early, worn-out victims of a life they need not have had.* Falco knows too much to be palmed off. Verontius has a secret second job selling squid, which involves an intriguing slave girl … *Verontius still fooled around with the girl, and he knew I knew.* [AC]

In *Scandal Takes a Holiday*, Falco makes direct allegations: *Petronius had a serious down on Verontius, whom he once tried to arrest for bribery on official contracts; Verontius got off without a stain on his character (he bribed his way out of the charge).*

Domestically, *Verontius thought being a good father meant bringing home a fruit pie once a week; when he wanted to be a very good father, he bought two.* [SDD]

Cornelius

Taken to Greece to help guard baggage, etc., Cornelius (filled out with the fruit pies) is *one of those large, chubby lads who is constantly taken for older than his real age; he might be only about eleven.* [SDD] He does become horribly homesick, so Falco takes him to the gymnasium where Cornelius nearly comes to grief when he is seized by the wrestler Milo of Dodona.

Galla

Falco's third sister is married to the absentee Lollius: *Sometimes he left her; more often Galla threw him out. Occasionally she relented 'for the sake of the children' (that tired old myth); the family's father stayed with her a month if she was lucky, then he drifted off after the next short-sighted garland-seller, my sister produced another unhappy baby, and the whole brood were left on their own again; when they were stuck, the poor things were sent to me.* [SB] In this sorry situation, Falco is repeatedly put upon to assist. It facilitates new characters as he nurtures the neglected children.

Galla, who *cannot be called a deft budget manager,* [OVTM] does know how to get free food at Saturnalia. She lives in a rented doss by the Trigeminal Gate, with her offspring, who include Larius, Gaius and Tertulla, except when they escape from home on occasions when their father briefly reappears.

Lollius

My sister Galla's husband was a lazy river boatman whose main advantage was the fact he was never at home. He was a hopeless womaniser. We could all have coped if my sister had not minded but Galla was unusually fastidious and she did. Not even Galla ever expected any support from Lollius ... In *Time to Depart*, when all the other brothers-in-law rally to try to find Tertulla, Lollius is the only one who fails to turn up.

· Lollius is introduced properly when Falco seeks his advice. *He was lazy, deceitful and brutal – ugly too, yet so cocky that he somehow convinced women he was vitally attractive. Galla fell for it – every time he came back to her from the others.* [THF] Falco describes Lollius as probably drunk, always walking with a serious limp, and looking as if he smells; about fifty, he is short, stout, ugly, toothless, and has one eye permanently closed after Galla hit him with a solid-bottomed pancake pan.

He is a joy to write about.

A foul bubble of riverbank scum [OVTM]

Larius

Falco's favourite nephew is a troubled fourteen-year-old when we meet him first. Something of my brother Max in his last year informs this picture of Larius, though they are not the same.

He was half my age and twice as despondent, but when he stopped being miserable he had a wonderful sense of fun. I was very fond of Larius … He had an intelligent brow under an unkempt swath of hair that drooped into solemn deep brown eyes. His body had stretched so fast it had left his brain behind. His feet, and ears, and the parts he was suddenly too shy to talk about, were those of a man half a foot taller than me. While he was expanding into them, Larius had convinced himself he looked ridiculous, and in all honesty he did. [SB]

Delightfully aware of the 'difficult phase' he is going through, Larius reads Catullus, despite which he comes good when he saves Falco from drowning then also saves Milo and actually sinks the villains' ship. He decides to become a wall painter and to marry **Ollia**, the daft lump who is nursemaid to the Petronius children.

We next meet him in *A Body in the Bath House*, eleven books and four years later. Larius has reached another difficult phase. Parted from his wife, he is among the experts working on the King's palace. He has become reprehensible and laddish, but skilled. *He was a big lad. I could see one protruding ear, half covered by unkempt dark curls that would have been improved by a serious trim and work with a teasing comb. His clothes were covered with multicoloured paint splashes, though the rest of him looked clean enough, given that he was about eighteen and a thousand miles from home. He worked steadily, adept and confident.* [BBH] He teams up with the Camillus brothers, egging them on into bad behaviour, but he is useful when the going gets rough: *Larius had grown up in the toughest neighbourhood in the Empire; he knew nasty tricks with feet and fists.* [BBH]

He is left behind a second time, in Britain. Perhaps I wanted to save him from Vesuvius. But Larius has talent; he could go anywhere.

Randy little beggars, the lot of them. Why do you think they become painters? They go into people's houses, with access to the women! [BBH]

Gaius

An urchin of some character, small for his age. He had the gravity of a patriarch and the manners of a lout. He liked to wear boots that were too big for him. He had tattooed his name on his arm in Greek lettering with something that passed for blue woad; some of the letters were festering. He never washed. [PG] This ragamuffin grew on me and became a fixture: *A shaved head, an armful of self-inflicted tattoos of sphinxes, half his teeth missing, a huge tunic belted in folds by a three-inch-wide belt with a 'stuff you' buckle and murderous studs. Hung about with scabbards, pouches, gourds and amulets. A small boy making a big man's fashion statement – and, being Gaius, getting away with it. He was a roamer. Driven on to the streets by an unbearable homelife and his own scavenging nature, he lived in his own world.* [THF] At one point, Falco arranges for Gaius to stay with Great-Auntie Phoebe on the Campagna farm, though it doesn't last.

Looking in *Poseidon's Gold* like an embryonic copy of Festus, Gaius is taken up by Geminus at the auction house, while also becoming close to Falco and Helena; they take him to Africa in *Two for the Lions*, where he is homesick and upset because people are too nice to him. In Greece he steals votive figures, so is clearly destined for the antiques world. In the absence of Geminus, without being asked he takes charge of the auction business like a born entrepreneur. *Helena had suggested his mother should donate him to some apothecary who was developing experimental medicines. But he was a sweetie underneath; we sometimes used him for babysitting.* [NM]

Tertulla

Figuring in *Time to Depart* when she is kidnapped for ransom (a mistake!), Tertulla exemplifies Falco's young relatives. She is *a grubby little girl of about seven years, with large feet and a very small nose.* She bunks off from school, though Falco's mother (who has paid the fees) determinedly tries to ensure that the child attends. Her disappearance shows the whole Didius family – except her own useless father – rallying for once to tackle the crisis.

Junia and Gaius Baebius

This house-proud, formal pair are so devoted to the idea of being a Roman couple (tending to pose as if practising for their own tombstone) that they have to be considered together. Married young, they have no natural children but throw themselves into home reconstruction, dog-owning and social ambition. Junia is regarded as a great annoyance. Helena tries, but can hardly stand her. She can be spiteful in telling tales. Although the couple are apparently prosperous, in a rare aside in *Scandal Takes a Holiday*, Falco points out that if Gaius ever lost his job they would be in trouble.

Junia was an impatient, supercilious piece. She had a thin face, a skinny frame, and a washed-out character to match. She wound her black hair into tight plaits pinned around her head, with stiff little finger-long ringlets in front of her ears and either side of her neck. This was all modelled on a statue of Cleopatra – a big joke, believe me … Life had disappointed Junia, and she was firmly convinced it could not possibly be her own fault. In fact, between her terrible cooking and her resentful attitude, most of what went wrong could be easily explained … [TTD]

Junia 'volunteers' to run Flora's Caupona as a 'little project'; like many people who insist on running bars she can't cook, she has a history of quarrelling with staff, she bosses the customers. Her big coup is the Fourth Cohort's Saturnalia drinks party where she serves *vinum primitivum* – my tribute to the house wine at the British School in Rome.

He and Junia had started saving up for ghastly furniture and an eight-bowl dinner set the minute they first held hands on a garden bench. [OB]

The boring Gaius first appealed to Junia because he was an orphan with his own apartment. He is a customs clerk supervisor, lusting for an honourable appointment as a priest of the imperial cult. Always hungry (because of Junia's awful cooking?), always slow to pick up the tab, Gaius Baebius is *about as exciting as watching a bird-bath evaporate.* [PG] He is truly devoted to Junia and an immaculate father to their adopted boy. Falco acknowledges the generosity, but still feels, *My brother-in-law was completely unsociable; people fled his company. He was a ponderous, pontificating, boring, boasting drone.* [STH]

When he and Falco take a trip to the coast looking for the pirate Damagoras, Gaius almost costs them their lives; after he is beaten up, we see him for once crushed, frightened and miserable – though he delights in his ensuing bad back. Gaius represents a specific, imperturbable kind of official. Falco imagines how he appears to traders: *A treat awaited. Gaius Baebius would be here.*

They would find him lying in wait on the quay at Portus, seated behind his customs table with his soft smile and his maddening attitude, ready to give them their first long, slow, unbearable experience of a Roman clerk. [STH]

Ajax

He was black and white, with a long snout, ferocious teeth that did occasionally sink into strangers, and a long feathered tail. [OB]

The dog Ajax is a spoilt child-substitute for Junia and Gaius, so uncontrolled he has been cited in legal actions for biting people. *'He loves children!' protested Gaius Baebius, as Ajax strained on the flimsy string on his collar and tried to reduce Mico's family to something he could bury on Gaius' home-built sun-yourself pilastered breakfast patio ...* [TTD] An attempt is made to use Ajax as a sniffer dog to find Tertulla. It fails.

Marcus Baebius Junillus

The 'skip baby' – kidnapped by brothel girls, then abandoned by his family – is adopted by Junia and Gaius. They do this, knowing he is deaf – a serious problem in the ancient world. *Whatever I thought of my sister, she and Gaius would dote on the babe. Both would make every effort to help him communicate.* [TTD] And so they do, Junia becoming an unlikely forerunner of Helen Keller. *He was a pretty boy, now showing some intelligence, and he watched Junia carefully. If anyone could do it, my sister would one day make him talk.* [OB]

Little Marcus becomes a handful: *Soon we were subjected to an hour of him running around, showing everyone his bare bottom. 'We can't stop him. He is our King for the Day!' He might be deaf and speechless, but he had a flair for misrule.* [SA]

Falco and Helena know his real parents: the unnamed **VIP magistrate**, glimpsed at Lalage's brothel, and his wife. They keep this secret. So if there is trouble in the future, which Falco might say is inevitable, then it's a long way in the future. It's a bonus of writing a series that there is scope to imply much but not cover it.

Maia Favonia

Falco's only younger sibling, the sparky Maia is his favourite; they grew up as family allies. *The sight of a normal, rather attractive fellow with spots of fish sauce down his tunic, being shoved down hard beneath his little sister's expert thumb, must have confused the poor woman. It often confused me.* [OVTM]

Maia had always been a looker. Despite four children she had kept her figure. She combed her dark tight curls in a neat frame to her round face. Her eyes were intelligent, merry and adventurous. [TFL] In character, she carries a hint of danger: *She knew how to get what she wanted, and what Maia wanted tended to be a tad different.* Yes indeed, as Norbanus finds out when she shoots him in the back.

Married to Famia, her home life becomes desperately sad: *Famia preferring to be almost always absent, and tiresome when he did appear; Famia constantly raiding the household budget for wine money; Famia proclaiming loud social jollity at unsuitable moments; Famia forcing other people either to share in his relentless habit, or making them seem tight-arsed if they tried to save him from himself. Maia would be much better off without him, but he was the father of her children, and really too far gone to abandon.* [TFL]

Like Falco, she hates their father for abandoning them, but as a widow she is forced to accept his offer of secretarial work in the auction house. At this time, she tangles briefly – but fatally – with Anacrites. *Eventually even Maia sensed a dangerous imbalance in their friendship. Anacrites was too intense for her. She told us they had parted. She would have been tactful. She was even a little upset ...* [BBH]. The spy's refusal to let go leads to him stalking her, then sending men to destroy her house. Falco and her children manoeuvre her to safety through travel to Britain, where she links up permanently with Petronius. Falco and Petro together swear revenge on Anacrites, but they know they must wait their moment. They are still waiting in *Nemesis* ...

Maia's relationship with Petronius Longus creeps up on Falco, if not us: *I wondered why my sister would be visiting Petronius.* [OVTM] Then Falco reminisces about how he introduced them: *Petro had been surprised when he met Maia, for some reason; he asked why I had never mentioned her.* [OB]

Always vibrant and attractive, she had been dangerously self-willed. Maia was the kind of young woman who seems to offer something special – special and mature. She was intelligent and though virtuous, she always seemed to know what good fun was. The kind that even experienced men can fall for very heavily and yearn for obsessively ... [OB]

Maia has five children with Famia, including her much-missed eldest daughter glimpsed in *The Silver Pigs*, who dies (mainly because I mixed myself up). The four survivors gang up with Petronius to organise their mother's life very sensibly.

Famia

Maia's darling was the best of the bunch, though I have to report Famia was a slit-eyed, red-nosed drunk who would have regularly cheated on Maia if he could have found the energy. While she brought up their children, he whiled away his time as a chariot-horse vet. He worked for the Greens. I support the Blues. Our relationship could not and did not flourish ... He had a florid face with puffy eyes. Maia fed him well and tried to keep him neat, but it was hard work. [TTD]

Sometimes Falco draws in Famia's contacts to assist a case, even though he says they tend to be *one-legged jockeys and liniment-sellers who drank too much.* Famia relishes these situations, extracting flagons as bribes.

It's clear that Maia married Famia out of desperation, probably when pregnant. *Famia had made Maia a drudge, fathered four children just to prove that he knew what his plunger was for, then gave up the struggle and set himself the easy target of an early death from drink.* [TFL] When Maia is bowed under the effort of trying to hold the family together, Falco thinks that taking Famia out of the country, to buy new horses for the Greens in Africa, is the best thing he can do for his sister. Drink takes its terrible toll: Famia makes racist comments about the Carthaginians, is charged with blasphemy and devoured by a lion in the arena at Lepcis Magna. This colourful scene was begging to be used and it was time to develop new plot-lines. Poor Famia had to go. I am afraid I liked doing it.

Marius

Marius, Maia's eldest, who actually enjoys school and plans to be a rhetoric teacher, is a well-brought-up nice little boy – which encourages Falco to believe fatherhood need not be a disaster. *He was a good-looking, extremely solemn little person, and completely self-possessed. He had the same curls as me and Pa yet somehow managed to make his look neat.* [TTD] He organises the rota for guarding Falco's rubbish skip and has been placed by his grandmother in charge of seeing that Tertulla doesn't bunk off school.

He acquires Arctos, Nux's only known pup, in *Ode to a Banker*. While organising their mother's love life, all the children try to fix up Maia with Petronius, who trains them like members of his squad when he takes them across Europe; they think Petro is wonderful.

Cloelia

Little Cloelia who had never seen her father for what he was and who doggedly worshipped him … [TFL]

Anyway it's probably best if I stay at home to help Mother. [OVTM]

She desperately wants to be a Vestal Virgin, though her father's death bars her. *She had the Didius curls and something of our stocky build, but facially she resembled Famia most. The high cheekbones that had given her father's features a tipsy slant could, in Cloelia's finer physiognomy, make her strikingly beautiful one day. Maia had probably foreseen trouble. Whether her daughter would agree to be steered on a safe course had yet to be seen.* [OVTM]

Rhea

Rhea, the pretty, funny one. [TFL]

Rhea, poor scrap, smells the body under the floor mosaic in Pa's bath house after Gloccus and Cotta leave a dead workman there.

Ancus

Ancus, with the big ears and the shy smile. [TFL]

Ancus is a quiet little soul, a bit of a mother's boy. Marius claims he is training up his little brother to work with Falco (to avoid the job himself). *'Ancus? Will he be any good?' 'He's useless.'* [TTD]

At the Market Garden

My relatives' disorganised patch of vegetable fields, where as usual the leeks and artichokes were struggling on their own, while the uncles busied themselves with lives of fervent emotional complexity … [OVTM]

Out on the Roman Campagna lies Falco's mother's family home. This represents to me, an urban girl, the nightmare of rural family life. For Falco's father, the absent Fulvius is a crony, but the other relatives are a blight: *being constantly despised by my mother's peculiar relatives must have been one of the trials that had eventually proved too dreary to endure.* [PG]

We hear little of Falco's late grandfather, apart from: *I remember him sounding off about old land 'reforms', which drove countrymen out of tenancies where they had farmed for decades. Gramps kept his farm – but we all thought he had done it by tricking someone else. All his neighbours thought so too.* [STH]

This farm is presumably where Falco flees to a grape-harvesting holiday in *The Silver Pigs*; it is where Festus had hidden blocks of marble and where Gaius is sent to be reformed. Ma regularly visits her brothers to pick up free veg.

Great-Uncle Scaro

Brother of Falco's maternal grandfather, we never meet Scaro who has died while choking on home-made false teeth – having an obsession with corrective dentistry. Phoebe keeps the teeth on the *lararium* (the family shrine).

He has been a good male influence on the young Falco: *a friendly old scallywag who had always given me the place in the world that my father had taken away.* [PG]

Scaro stood sponsor when Falco joined the army and needed a male relative's signature of release. Commenting on Scaro's one-time plan to break into silphium production, Falco says, *A noble character, a complete liability in fact. I had dearly loved the crazy experimentalist, but his schemes were ludicrous.* [TFL] *He had the knack of convincing you that when he showed you some weird piece of carved bone that looked like a pot-bellied pigeon, he had discovered the secret of flight.* [OVTM]

Great-Auntie Phoebe

The loyal freedwoman Falco's grandfather never married is a classic country matriarch who stabilises the rabble: *a small, sweet round-cheeked woman who looked as frail as grass but had more strength than three grown men. This was just as well because while the others were being introspective about their personal lives she had to harvest cabbage and turn a fork in the manure heap.* [PG] It is Phoebe who shows strangers Scaro's false teeth (model four) on the *lararium*, saying they are all that remains of the previous unwanted visitors, and threatening to set the dogs on them.

Uncles Fabius and Junius

They were men of huge passions – grafted on to absolutely mediocre personalities ... The two brothers had a lifelong feud, a feud so old neither of them could remember what it had been about, though they were comfortable loathing one another. [OVTM] In *Scandal Takes a Holiday*, Falco blames the feud on Fabius thinking Junius cheated over their father's will and Junius thinking Fabius will ruin everything through his association with a neighbour's wife. Their doings are listed flamboyantly from time to time. It is quite convenient that I only have to cover one brother at a time.

Junius is described as 'dopey'. It is Fabius we see most: *Nothing about my uncle was scientific or organised, except when he went fishing. His note-tablets of tedious data on fishes caught, variety, length, healthiness and bait used took up a whole shelf ... Otherwise, Fabius could hardly put on a pair of boots by himself.* [OVTM] Despite this, he has invented battery chicken farming (aided by Pliny).

'*Fabius, if every get-rich scheme that came out of this family had worked, we would be a legend among the Forum banking fraternity. Instead, we just go downhill from year to year – and our reputation stinks.*'

'*The trouble with you,*' said Fabius, in his maddeningly grave way, '*is that you never want to take a risk.*' [OVTM]

The One Nobody Ever Talks About (Uncle Fulvius)

'*Has he really cut off his whatsit with a piece of flint?*' '*Not as far as I know.*' *Even if Fulvius had done it, self-castration was an offence and he was still my relative. I was not going to give the navy an excuse to lift his tunic and inspect him.* [STH]

Twenty-five years before the series begins, Fulvius took himself off to Pessinus (birthplace of the goddess Cybele), but got on the wrong boat. He had intended to have a sex change, but met Cassius instead.

When they meet, Falco fails to recognise him: *overweight, flabby and hook-shouldered. He wore what must be a valuable cameo ring, vivid white glass over lapis blue, which appeared to show a miniaturised pornographic scene. It was the*

*kind of thing that appeals to men who call themselves connois-
seurs, men with cold eyes … something about him was getting
on my nerves. He gave the impression he enjoyed being contro-
versial … He had a streak of dark intelligence, plus loathing of
the social rules; he took a joy in doing people down.* [STH]

It emerges that Fulvius has been a naval intelligence
agent, under cover of being a corn factor in Dalmatia.
He is cagey about it, though at least he doesn't work for
Anacrites. Falco is not impressed with his methods.
*Fulvius was a sibling of Fabius and Junius. It followed that he
was a lunatic.* [STH]

By *Alexandria,* Falco has mellowed, perhaps because
Helena quite likes his uncle. Fulvius plays host to their
Egyptian visit (though may not have anticipated what a
large party they would bring). His situation remains
ambiguous; he could be a trader or a worse villain.
Since he colludes with Geminus, Falco knows what *he*
thinks.

Cassius

Cassius is first seen disguised as a beggar: *dirt camouflage
stripes blackening his face. What a poser … Grey-sideburned
as he was now, in the straight nose and brown eyes I could still
trace the handsome younger man for whom Fulvius had fallen.
Biceps strained against the tight sleeves of his tunic, his big
calves were muscular, and there was no fat on him.* [STH]

In *Alexandria,* he is the domestic god, throwing
himself into hospitality. Helena spots that although he is
supposed to be the muscle man, while Fulvius is
wheeler-dealing, Cassius may sit in a corner reading a
scroll. She wonders if he would have liked an intellectual career but his family could not afford it. *We just
assume Cassius was once some beautiful vacuous young boy
Uncle Fulvius picked up in a gym or a bath house – but he is
probably not that young.* So, surprisingly, it is Cassius who
gives Helena information about problems at the Great
Library. On their return to Rome, it is Cassius who cor-
responds with Helena.

Aunt Marciana

*My Aunt Marciana could zing beads along their wires on her
abacus with a verve any money-changer would envy.* [OVTM]

I have no idea who this is! I had completely forgotten her. What luxury for an author, to invent a character with neither pedigree nor provenance, just for one bit of narrative colour.

Helena's Relatives

The Camillus family were certainly patrician when viewed from my own perspective, though there were no consuls or generals in their ancestry. They were rich — though their wealth was in land. Their house was spacious and detached, a lived-in town villa with water and drainage but rather tired décor ... [TTD]

Gnaeus Atius Pertinax
Caprenius Marcellus

Helena's divorced husband is first seen as a brutal aedile: *typical of the breed, a short-haired pup, yapping up the political ladder, nagging butchers to sweep their shop-fronts and beating the hell out of me ...* [SP]

Pertinax cannot realise his ex-wife will find in Falco the dream of her life — I hadn't devised her and didn't know it myself. He shows us how the Roman marriage system, alien to the modern Western concept, sometimes worked among the aristocracy: *Helena led a solitary life. She slept alone in that beautiful room while Pertinax had his spacious quarters in a different wing, with Barnabas as his confidant. For a young, ambitious senator, taking a wife was an act of state service which he endured to win fools' votes. Having done it, Pertinax expected his marital rights, yet begrudged her his time.* [SB] After three years of sterile luxury, Helena gave up on him. That was the limit of my original intentions. Having Pertinax killed off-stage in a prison cell would remove him and release Helena from any obligation.

Reviving Pertinax as Barnabas in *Shadows in Bronze* was not my best piece of plotting, but I still think it too good to miss. Falco's fanatical jealousy, and even Helena's crisis of conscience, justify the ploy.

Pertinax was fatally flawed from birth, then dangerously encouraged after his adoption by the very rich, interfering **Caprenius Marcellus**: *an old patrician stick,*

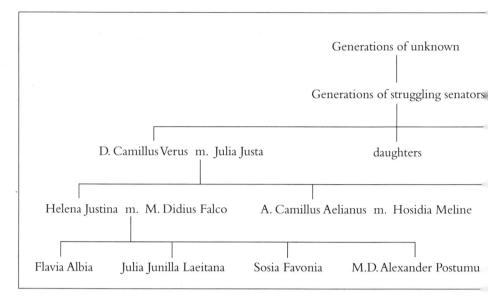

fading from the world at his country estate. [SP] *One of Rome's elderly senators, with seven previous consuls in his glorious pedigree. He had possessed an enormous fortune and no heir, until Pertinax caught his eye … Either he was very short-sighted, or being descended from consuls did not make a senator astute.* [SB]

At the luxurious Marcellus *villa rustica* on the slopes of Vesuvius, Falco sees that Pertinax, who lives a play-boy life with his racehorses, has much to be thankful for but fails to value it – just as he failed to value Helena. Steered by the indulgent Marcellus to punch far above his weight in politics, Pertinax bungles everything; he is dumped by the astute Aufidius Crispus, fails to see when to surrender, and goes crassly to his fate. Though he probably does not intend to knock Helena down the stairs at their old house, he has an undercurrent of vio-lence, the violence that is the only resort of the incom-petent. He even shows no gratitude to Marcellus, thus stranding himself alone.

It is incredible to him that Helena should even deal with a plebeian like Falco. This incomprehension pro-vided a way for me to leave Falco with clean hands (more or less). I agree with Helena that if Falco had killed Pertinax, a permanent shadow would have threatened their future. So, when he learns the truth about the lovers, he explodes in outrage and indigna-tion; Pertinax slips and effectively kills himself.

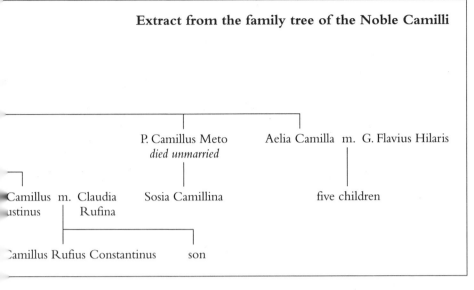

Extract from the family tree of the Noble Camilli

P. Camillus Meto
died unmarried

Aelia Camilla m. G. Flavius Hilaris

Camillus m. Claudia
ustinus   Rufina

Sosia Camillina

five children

Camillus Rufius Constantinus   son

Decimus Camillus Verus

On Falco's first visit in *The Silver Pigs*, we learn most things about the senator, Helena's father. He is not as rich as most of his rank, so shares his home plot with his brother. His side of the semi-detached pair is slightly shabby, with an unfinished look to the garden, though Falco decides it has *an approachable, easy-going smile.* [SP]

Decimus has *heavy eyebrows above decently spaced eyes that looked at me directly. His hair bristled straight up from his head, even though it was not particularly short, giving him a cheerful, boyish look.* [SP] Falco meets him in his study. He is competent, and although he seems squashy, he resists Falco's bullying and bluff.

Overlooked by statue busts and high shelves of book canisters ... Unlike many an aristocrat, I knew he read the scrolls. [SA]

'Nobody tells me anything. They just keep me to lie on one of the eating couches to prevent the dining room looking empty.' [OVTM]

Though Decimus makes out he is hen-pecked domestically, probably his marriage is happy; Falco even speculates queasily on the children's close ages: *It suggested an unnerving period of passion in their parents' marriage.* [OVTM] I loved showing the humorous side of Helena's parents at the feast in *Saturnalia*.

He makes a devoted grandfather. His sense of family and political duty shows most seriously at the climax of *The Silver Pigs*, where astonishingly, he kills his brother. We see his old-fashioned rectitude when he formally marks the arrival in Rome of Veleda, even though she so threatens his son's equanimity: *He represented the governing body of Rome and she was a national figurehead from outside the Empire. So this sturdy old pillar of noble values stomped out to the street and gave her a polite greeting. He even put his toga on to do it.* [SA]

Falco comes to have a deep respect for this man: *Camillus Verus was shrewd and intelligent, with a diffident manner. He did what was necessary and did not waste effort on the rest. I liked him. It mattered to me that he should be able to tolerate me.* [TTD] He lost his chances to flourish: *Life had made him wealthy enough to have standing yet too poor to do much with it … Just at the moment when Vespasian – with whom he had long been on friendly terms – became Emperor, family embarrassments had held Camillus back. A relation involved himself in a stupid plot and everyone was damned. Camillus Verus knew he had lost out to Fate again.* [AC]

From the start Decimus is tolerant of Falco, mainly because he sees how good Falco is for Helena. By *The Accusers,* he has Falco's interests so much at heart that he gives him the necessary steer for out-prosecuting Paccius Africanus. The plotting takes place at their gym: *I was rather impressed that Camillus brought me here, rather than contaminate either of our homes with what he had to say. He was a man of curious refinement.* [AC]

Julia Justa

She was what I expected: glossy, tense, perfect manners, jingling with gold jewellery – a well-treated woman, with an even better kept face … [SP] Julia's shrewdness shows over Sosia: *She was just the sort of sensible matron a bachelor would be lucky to find when he was presented with an illegitimate child he felt unable to ignore.* Later, it is she who spots that the skip baby is deaf.

Julia Justa is a powerful figure in the home. At first Falco thinks her hard. When they are beginning to reach an accommodation (aided by the unreliable behaviour of both her sons), she softens in his eyes: *The noble Julia had the suffering air of a woman who was doing her best even though everyone around her seemed determined to ruin her carefully planned day.* [TTD] Later he thinks she is merely impatient with hypocrisy.

In a ghastly way she trusted me. It made life very difficult. [SA]

Julia Justa has the habits of a conventional, well-placed matron; she attends Bona Dea ceremonies and is friendly with a Vestal Virgin (possibly her cousin). This works to advantage in *Saturnalia* for resolving the

Veleda problem. Although Julia's influence is subtle, it is unclear what she wants for her daughter. Would it grieve Julia, if Helena escaped the establishment, or would she envy her daughter's freedom? Maybe even Julia cannot make up her mind.

Aulus Camillus Aelianus

We hear of Aelianus, the elder Camillus son, in *The Iron Hand of Mars* where he writes a letter to Helena in wrath at her association with Falco; she is deeply upset. By *Time to Depart* he is still furious: *He looked much like his father – sprouting straight hair and slightly sloped shoulders. More chunky than Justinus and Helena and heavier-featured, he was less good-looking as a result. His abysmal manners were a patrician cliché ... Aelianus had completed his military service rather dully, then a year as a governor's unpaid aide-de-camp in Baetica had failed to give him lustre. On the other hand, none of that had been his fault,* says Falco, already hoping for good in this unpromising material. Rough edges are a social and political handicap, however: *He was of a slightly grumpy disposition, a little too self-centred and lacking the fake warmth to ingratiate him with the smelly old senators he needed to flatter.* [OVTM] Aulus admits he always rather liked his Uncle Publius, which causes concern: *Aelianus might lose patience with the rules and seek out his own solutions, unless he was handled just right in the next few years. An outsider. Latent trouble.* [OVTM] In *A Dying Light in Corduba*, Aelianus lets an important dispatch fall into the wrong hands and seems open to overtures from Anacrites. He is generally secretive about his wild time in Baetica.

His personality has contradictions: *Aelianus told this tale with rakish fluency. He could be a prude over women, but I knew that as a young tribune in Baetica he was one of the crowd. Even in Rome, with his fond parents watching, he had been known to roll home at dawn, uncertain of how he had spent the previous night ...* [BBH] Soon he can't decide: he starts a doom-laden friendship with Albia, although Falco says *he was now determined only to cast his big brown eyes on a gilt-edged virgin with a line of pickled ancestors and moneybags to match.* [STH]

We may feel a glimmer of sympathy when Claudia Rufina jilts him and wrecks his chance of standing for

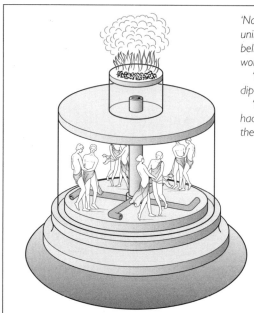

'Now we have to find some completely uninterested buyer then try to fib him into believing he needs a set of dancing nymphs worked by hot air, whose costumes fall off ... '
'Next thing you'll have one of Philo of Tyre's dip-me-in-all-ways inkwells.'
'Gimbals!' snarled Aulus. This proving that he had heard all about Philon's magic octagon, the executive toy every scribe wants ... [BBH]

the Senate. Then in *One Virgin Too Many*, I decided it would be more fun to write about an abrasive, untrained assistant for Falco than a competent, congenial one, so I let Aulus supplant his brother. He learns. He develops.

Athletic, a good rider, able to draw a plan or list suspects colourfully, Aelianus starts showing promise when he organises a rescue of Falco from jail after his offence at the Vestals' House. From *Ode to a Banker* on, Falco successfully teaches him social interaction and investigative techniques. In Britain, he is disguised as a statue-seller's assistant – bitterly complaining, yet acquitting himself well. By *See Delphi and Die* he can't resist the mystery he stumbles upon at Olympia. On tour with the travel company, he shows compassion for a bereaved husband and selflessly sits with a dying man at Epidaurus. He is genuinely upset when his new young friend Heras dies in *Alexandria*.

From *The Accusers*, his yen for law seems genuine. Study takes him away from Rome (partly to thin out characters). Falco is initially sceptical: *the unmarried son of a senator, with money in his pocket and a carefree outlook, I could not see him gravely attending jurisprudence lectures under a fig tree at an ancient university.* [STH] Aelianus sticks with his choice in Greece and Alexandria, then seems

He was arrogant, crass and snobbish, and had hurt Helena very much by criticising us. Now he stood in the street, a hot, bothered, stocky young figure, trying to bluff it out ... [THF]

reformed, until – oops! – he lets himself be pushed by his terrible tutor Minas into reversion to type socially, causing heartache for Albia. I shall punish him for that!

Quintus Camillus Justinus

The younger Camillus brother, Quintus is briefly glimpsed as a good sort in *The Silver Pigs*. Still serving in Germany, but now making his mark, in *The Iron Hand of Mars*, Falco begins to get to know him well. Their first great shared mission in Germania Libera shows his potential. Quintus acquits himself with distinction; he is brave, adaptable, popular with subordinates. He has what will clearly be the adventure of his life with Veleda.

Justinus returns to Rome marked for rapid advancement – only to be stopped by the backlash from his uncle's treason. His frustration and his lovelorn state first lead him to defy convention and work with Falco, then precipitate his elopement with his brother's fiancée. By now he is familiar: *a tall spare figure with neat, short hair, dark eyes and a striking grin. He managed to combine an apparently unassuming air with a hint of inner strength. I knew he was confident, a linguist, a man-manager, courageous and inventive in a crisis.* [TFL]

Falco never doubts his good qualities, though cynically aware that life will be hard for the young man: *Quintus has a warm personality and a fine intellect. People like him, and he's interested in everything – naturally such a man stands no chance in public life!* [TTD] Working with Falco, Quintus is winningly aware of his deficiencies: *I don't know how to live rough. I can't talk to the right sort of people. I have no experience to judge situations, no authority – in fact, no hope.* [TFL] His resistance to sharing the position with his brother is fairly short-lived.

Does he ever think he loves Claudia? Yes, though his lust for adventure blinds him to the miseries he puts her through in Libya. The poor girl will always take second place to his romantic vision of Veleda. Reluctantly, Justinus opts for Claudia's fortune and settles down to family life. He becomes a proud father. When Veleda arrives in Rome, it is tragic all round (despite the hilarious turnip incident). Justinus submits to duty; it is realistic, but terrible to watch. *He had lost the love of his*

He was too young to get married; she was much too keen on the idea. [SA]

life not once but twice. He had never got over it the first time;
he probably imagined it would be even harder now … [SA]

Claudia Rufina

We meet Claudia in her home province of Hispania
Baetica, a neat, smart, shy, very serious orphan, courted
for her money even before she becomes a major heiress
after her brother **Rufius Constans** is killed. She is tall
and has a big nose, on which Falco comments a little
too much in my opinion. Helena takes her to Rome as
a potential rich bride for Aelianus, but Claudia falls for
his handsomer brother. Justinus seems much more fun –
until the Libyan desert sours their relationship. Cobbled
together in marriage, they reach an uneasy accommodation. Her husband retains affection for her; they have
first one and then a second child.

She is a good young woman with a fine character. She has been well brought up. She is honest, direct, serious, and loyal to those she loves. [DLC]

I perceive Claudia as more than a victim. She stands
up for herself (she insults Veleda with spirit). *There was a*
spark to her sometimes that I know made Helena think the girl
deserved more. Part of the spark, the only hope of redeeming
her, was that Claudia did want better for herself. [TFL] She
understands her position with cruel clarity. She and
Quintus commit themselves too eagerly, then they are
both trapped. But as a foreign bride in Rome, Claudia
is isolated and vulnerable, her only status and power
residing in her dowry.

Claudia was a delicately reared young lady from a pampered home. Basic training for an heiress consists only of assaults on Greek novels and a gruelling small talk course. [TFL]

She was wearing a necklace of extremely large emeralds with the air of a girl who thinks she may as well flaunt the one aspect of her personality that her husband truly admires. [AC]

Consoled by her children and her material wealth,
Claudia remains thoroughly good-natured. From the
moment she inherits, she wants to make endowments
and benefit the community, specifically in Corduba, her
birthplace – to which she can always threaten to return
if Justinus upsets her fatally. But in *Nemesis*, she acquires
a seniority that helps her feel reconciled to her lot.

Gaius Camillus Rufius Constantinus

The centre of his parents' world – though he hasn't
actually appeared. At least he has a name, unlike his
even more invisible little brother.

Aelia Camilla

Youngest and favourite sister of Camillus Verus, Aelia
Camilla may be a prototype for Helena Justina. In *The*

Silver Pigs, Falco meets *a slender, rather ordinary woman, slightly uneasy within her elegant attire,* whom he mentally dismisses as *a good, plain woman who could serve sweetmeats to the governor from the proper shape of dish, or be polite to a tribal king for three hours at a time, then remove the royal paw from her knee without giving offence.* [SP] Immediately, he realises his mistake. *She had vividly eloquent eyes. It would be a brave king – or governor – who took liberties with her.* He takes to her, smitten by her good sense and tact, before her easy-going, comfortable household upends his deep prejudice against the middle class. This, without him knowing it, starts his own grumpy progress towards joining that rank.

Aelia Camilla has a sparky side; she had a fondness for her rebellious brother Publius, who taught her to drive – *too fast.* (A feat she passes on to Helena). But even when he knows her better, she has the mastery of Falco: *Her great dark eyes were impossible to avoid. I had always found it difficult to play the hard man in her presence. While seeming gentle and bashful, she screwed all kinds of answers out of me ...* [JM]

Gaius Flavius Hilaris

I wanted Gaius to represent a *good* civil servant. I knew if I ever got to write a series, I would spend a lot of time satirising bureaucracy, but Roman bureaucracy clearly worked; the Empire ran smoothly under good emperors and even under bad ones, thanks to their staff. I left my own civil service job with happy memories of good colleagues I admired, people who had taught me much, people whose affection for me I appreciated, people I still see twenty years later.

Gaius is an equestrian, son of a Roman tax collector, born in Narona (*a one-ox town in Dalmatia*); he came to Britain with the Second Augusta when the legion was commanded by the young Vespasian (which gives him unexpected influence). Unusually, he never left. He has knowledge of mining but we see him as the influential Procurator of Finance, living in London, with a 'second home' in Dorchester, to which he may retire. *A winsome, vigorous man ... He had crisp brown hair cut to outline a neat head, and lean, firm hands with straight-cut clean fingernails ... from the start I thought the man was excellent.*

His mistake was that he did a thorough job and saw the funny side. People liked him, but to conventional judges, these were not the signs of a 'good mind' ... [SP]

He is as efficient as he is ethical, a *single-minded type who burrowed into business as soon as he trapped an audience.* [SP] Falco, despite initial suspicion, warms to him: *Of all the men I met on this business, I liked him the most. I never told him that. (I know he realised.) I did tell him, no one but me could have found a case where only the civil servants were straight ...*

When Falco returns to Britain for *A Body in the Bath House*, Gaius is a benign background presence; *The Jupiter Myth* places him centrally, working with Falco to their mutual enjoyment as they tackle gangland crime in Roman London. *He looked a quiet, clerkish, slightly innocent fellow, but I wouldn't take him on at draughts,* says Falco as they inspect a murder victim. *He was dealing with the situation in his usual way: curious, thorough, and unexpectedly assertive.* Gaius is now older, greyer and more haggard; Falco suspects his health is poor. But Gaius and his wife remain the best kind of diplomat: *They were wise; they were fair. They embodied noble Roman qualities.* Though as Falco remarks, *That did not make them popular with colleagues ... They did not seem to notice and never complained. Under a different emperor they might well have dwindled into oblivion. Under Vespasian, they flourished surprisingly.* [JM]

Publius Camillus Meto

Though he dies in the first book, the senator's younger brother has a lasting impact.

A bland unremarkable face and a bland unremarkable head. In my experience, men who sit in corners are the ones to watch ... [SP] At Sosia's funeral Falco notices more detail: *He left a faint trace of myrrh, and he wore a gold intaglio ring with a substantial emerald, slight touches of bachelor vanity which I had missed before ...* [SP] The emerald ring features significantly in *Shadows in Bronze*.

Falco presciently smells danger immediately. Publius had a wild life as a youth in Bithynia, then left Mauretania under a cloud: *political speculation, social scandal, riot, shady business deals, women ...* [SP] We first see him in unpleasant company, with Pertinax. We learn that Sosia resulted from an affair with the married wife of an absent VIP. Publius had to acknowledge the child but dumped her on Decimus and Julia, who brought her up. However, as he presides over Sosia's funeral, Publius seems genuinely in shock. When he angrily blames Falco, the informer spots ambiguity: *It jarred, because Publius Camillus Meto looked like someone whom grief steers into rigid self-control; like a man who would break, but not yet; break, but not in public; not today, not here. He had previously been so persuasive – this loss had shaken him.* [SP] Of course Publius realises the plot is unravelling, due to this annoying man, Falco.

Publius is motivated by resentment; his family lacked money to put him in the Senate, unlike his elder brother, whom he thinks second-rate. Conspiring with Domitian, this hard, manipulative, jealous, striving man will force Falco to take a great step in personal and social development. Fallout from the failed plot will permanently hamper the Camillus family. His young daughter dies. His brother has to commit a terrible, uncharacteristic act. His nephews' promising careers will be blighted. The ghastly disposal of Meto's corpse will haunt Falco, because it is horrific to accomplish and because he dreads Helena and her father learning he was involved. Perhaps one day, they will …

Sosia Camillina

Sosia – sweet, clever, courageous – has a brief presence but a lasting position as the spark that fires the series.

She takes the heroine's role but is savagely destroyed without warning. It was a conscious decision to shake the conventions of gumshoe stories. At sixteen, Sosia is too young for Falco, but she raises important questions about his morality. She develops a crush on him and he falls for her enough to be distraught when she is killed. Maybe we all feel a similar pang. The scene where the vigiles find Sosia's body will always be to me one of the saddest and hardest I have written. But it is crucial for Falco. He grows up that day.

Sosia's life has jolted Falco and her death takes him to Britain. There he meets Helena Justina – who blames him almost as much as Falco blames himself for her young cousin's death. Sosia's murder has given him his part-time career as an imperial agent. He names his second daughter after her.

Like her father, Sosia remains important in the personal stories of other characters, a melancholy motif.

Historical Characters

I have scruples over writing about real people. Suetonius gives us detailed portraits of emperors (his view), but other Romans are barely documented; I am reluctant to impose characteristics they may not have had.

I also hate 'Hello, Chopin, have you met George Sand – oh look, there's supersleuth Napoleon, with criminologist Jane Austen!'

Pliny the Younger? I don't like the cut of his jib. Why should I give him publicity? He's so good at it himself.

So, very few historical figures appear in the Falco series – though there are more than I thought.

The imperial family

Since *The Course of Honour*, I had clear ideas about the Flavians, primarily based on Suetonius' *The Twelve Caesars*.

I like to stress ambiguity. Yes, compared with the previous crazy lot, these are 'good' emperors', but Falco and I ask questions about whether Rome should have emperors at all and the possible abuses of power. The Flavian attitude to informers and Falco's republicanism give me ample scope.

Emperor Vespasian (Titus Flavius Vespasianus Augustus, many times consul, with tribunician power, Father of his Country and Pontifex Maximus)

Once I began the Falco books, I always had a sly retrospective glance at Vespasian's character in *The Course of Honour*. When he first meets Falco – *a cheery old cove came out in his slippers* [SP] – this is a character I know. I had to avoid repetition; that generally solves itself because the Emperor is now seen through Falco's grudging eyes.

With such a mighty reputation – he had now been decreed a triumph over the Jews – Vespasian added eight more consulships to the one he had already earned. He also assumed the office of Censor, and throughout his reign made it his principal business first to shore up the State, which was virtually in a state of prostration and collapse, and then to proceed to its artistic embellishment ...
SUETONIUS

Finally he took a bath and went to dinner, when he would be in such a cheerful mood that members of his household usually chose this time to ask favours of him.
SUETONIUS

He was a big, easygoing, competent character. An organiser, he had the direct glance of a blacksmith, with the country-born arrogance that reminded me of my grandfather. He knew what he believed. He said what he thought. People acted on what he said. They did it nowadays because they had to, but people had been jumping when Vespasian barked since long before he was emperor ... He had held all the civil magistracies and the highest military ranks. Every post in his career through the cursus honorum had been screwed out on merit and in the face of Establishment prejudice. Now he held the final post available. The Establishment was still prejudiced against him, but he need not care. [TTD] That prejudice was to dog Vespasian and even his sons. Falco observes: The Curtius brothers owned a family tree so ancient that Romulus and Remus carved their names in its moss. To them, Vespasian was a nobody. His good generalship meant nothing; nor the forty years of service he had already given Rome. He had no money and no famous ancestors. You cannot let people who own nothing but talent rise into the highest positions. What chance is there then for the upper-crust bunglers and fools? [SB]

Vespasian, who famously disliked the use of informers made by Nero, is nonetheless pragmatic; when he has to deal with plots and provincial problems, he will use a man like Falco, for whom he has a measured respect. For his governing style, I follow Suetonius: My researches show that no innocent party was ever punished during Vespasian's reign except behind his back or while he was absent from Rome, unless by a deliberate defiance of his wishes or by misinforming him about the facts of the case ...

Titus complained of the tax which Vespasian had imposed on the contents of city urinals. Vespasian handed him a coin which had been part of the first day's proceeds. 'Does it smell bad?' he asked. And when Titus answered 'No' he went on: 'Yet it comes from urine.'
SUETONIUS

A communal public lavatory (probably Ostia)

Vespasian never rejoiced in anyone's death and would often weep when convicted criminals were forced to pay the extreme penalty. Of course Suetonius also drums into us Vespasian's money-grubbing. It creates nice tensions with Falco, who has problems obtaining his fee, even where there is one. And there is a topical connection with laundries!

Falco will remain wary. *Finding an emperor with moral values always startled me,* he says. But he needs work and is desperate to improve his social status, a situation Vespasian and Titus exploit. Falco's very curmudgeon-liness means they can trust him more than the normal flatterers. And they can see just how good he is. Theirs will never be an easy relationship, but it works.

Titus Flavius Vespasianus, Titus Caesar

Titus had such winning ways – perhaps inborn, perhaps cultivated subsequently, or conferred on him by fortune – that he became an object of universal love and adoration. Nor was this an easy task, because it happened only after his accession: both as a private citizen and later under his father's rule, Titus had not only been criticised but loathed.
SUETONIUS

We first see Titus immediately after his return from war, excited by his family's new position (a position he very much helped to arrange), determined to consolidate his father's government, testing his own strength as a ruler. *A man my own age, not over tall, with a jutting chin. His body was hard as a brick; his energy made me groan. He waved away the attendants and rushed forwards to greet us himself ... He was bursting with talent. This cheery young general had evidently dealt with Jerusalem, and I quite believed he swept up in his conquest the fabulous Judaean queen ...* [SP] He comes over as brisk and efficient, rigorously testing both Falco and Helena until he can trust them. He has the close-knit Flavians' family loyalties, so despite Domitian's proven plotting, he sticks fast by his brother – outraging Falco after Sosia's murder.

He bore most of the burdens
of government and, in his
father's name, dealt with
official correspondence,
drafted edicts …
SUETONIUS

Titus's brother Domitian took
part in endless conspiracies
against him, stirred up
disaffection in the armed
forces almost openly, and
toyed with the notion of
fleeing to them. Yet Titus had
not the heart to execute
Domitian, dismiss him from
the court, or even treat him
less honourably than before.
SUETONIUS

Titus also assumed command
of the Guards, a post in which
he behaved somewhat high-
handedly and tyrannically. If
anyone aroused his suspicion,
Guards detachments would
be sent into theatre or camp
to demand the man's
punishment as if by the
agreement of everyone
present; and he would then
be executed without delay.
SUETONIUS

Titus was famously in love with Queen Berenice of Judaea; what an exotic madam! During my early books she probably had not brought herself to Rome, so remarriage to produce an heir must be a possibility for Titus. Initially, he has his beady eye on Helena. *He had an attractive personality and was at home wherever he went … an all-round political achiever. On top of that, he was good-looking. I had the girl; Titus Caesar had everything else …* [IHM] Falco feels manic jealousy, darkly distrusting Titus: *Everyone knew Titus had a very pleasant temperament, but he could also have me sent down to Hades by the short route …* [TTD] I don't stress too much how dangerous Titus could be, but it's there: *Titus had a reputation as a nice soft-hearted darling – always a sign of a nasty bastard who could be bloody dangerous.* [OVTM]

In fairness, Titus recognises Falco's worth and their relationship is based on considerable openness:

'Falco, why is it when I talk to you I always end up
    wondering whether I can stand the pace?'
'I'm a sterling debater, Caesar.'
'And modest!'
'And the only kind of fool who'll risk offending you
    … ' [TTD]

People usually worry about Domitian, but even Titus could pose a threat: *One of the worst features of Roman life at the time was the licence long enjoyed by informers and their managers. Titus had these well whipped, clubbed, and then taken to the amphitheatre and paraded in the arena; where some were put up for auction as slaves and the remainder deported to the most forbidding islands.* [SUETONIUS]

Will their good relationship save Falco? See below for my views …

Titus Flavius Domitianus, Domitian Caesar

Domitian is ten years younger than both Titus and Falco. *Solid as a bullock, curly-topped though hammer-toed.* [PG] Statues show him as physically similar to Titus, though to my mind he's even chubbier and soppier. *For Domitian, the courtesy title of Caesar seemed a fragile irony. He had the family curls, the creased Flavian chin, the bull neck,*

square body and stocky build. Somehow he failed to convince.
[SP] Sometimes he comes across well; I allow Falco
hindsight knowledge: *In that moment he enjoyed all the
gifts of the Flavian house: grace, high intelligence, respect for the
task in hand, sturdy wit, good sense. He could have been no
less a statesman than his father or his brother; sometimes he
managed it. Vespasian had shared his own talents with an even
hand; the difference was, only one of his sons handled them
with a truly sure grip.* [SP]

I believe it is crucial that, unlike Titus,
Domitian never shared a military campaign
with his father but was left behind in
Rome. This must have a bearing on his
character, making him introverted and
probably lonely; he was always striving to
impress his father and to equal his more
charismatic brother.

During the Year of the Four Emperors, he had a
narrow escape, having to hide from Vitellian forces at
the Temple of Isis and with a schoolfriend's mother. His
uncle Sabinus, who could have advised him, had been
murdered; once the scary situation was resolved, the
young man of twenty was thrust into power without
supervision; he went wild. *Domitian's idea of becoming a
Caesar was seducing senators' wives.* [SP] But Titus excused
him and Vespasian tolerated these early misjudgements.

Domitian had a reputation as a plotter. Tacitus says:
*It is believed that Domitian sent secret messages to seduce
Cerialis from his allegiance and see if he would hand over the
army and supreme command to himself when they met. He
may have been toying with the idea of fighting his father, or it
may have been a manoeuvre to gain support and advantage
against his brother. No one could tell, for Cerialis steered a safe
course and returned an evasive answer to what he took to be the
idle fancy of a child. Domitian realised that his elders despised
his youthfulness and ceased to discharge even the slight official
duties he had previously undertaken. Assuming an ingenuous
air of abstraction and looking as if butter would not melt in his
mouth, he posed as a connoisseur of literature and poetry …*

This justifies the conspiracy to dethrone Vespasian
which begins my series. So, Domitian is the murderer of
sweet, brave, over-curious Sosia Camillina; surprised, he
stabs her with a pen. He drops his inkwell. Falco finds it
and keeps it as a surety. Domitian knows Falco has it.

Very occasionally – for instance, at Falco's poetry recital in *Ode to a Banker* – their paths cross uncomfortably. In *Poseidon's Gold*, Domitian refuses to upgrade Falco's social rank, and clearly enjoys his revenge. Otherwise I have used their feud lightly, having other ideas to pursue.

Readers seem paranoid about Falco's fate once Domitian is emperor. But Falco still has the inkwell. I can't remember where he's put it, but I've never let him lose it.

Domitian's reign of terror, which caused his eventual assassination, was primarily directed against senators. Besides, Falco is a hero. Heroes escape.

He checked and severely penalised informers who had brought false accusations for the benefit of the imperial treasury. A saying attributed to him runs: 'An emperor who does not punish informers encourages them.'
SUETONIUS

Antonia Caenis

As far as I knew, Caenis did not interfere in politics, although any woman Vespasian had cherished for forty years and whom Titus treated respectfully must have the potential for enormous influence. The freedwoman was a scandal waiting to happen, but the cool glance she gave me said that scandal stood no chance ... [TTD]

Helena introduces Falco to Caenis, hoping for patronage. *If the rumours about how she used her position were true, then more power might be wielded in this isolated villa than in any other private house in Rome.* [TFL] We assume the rumours *were* true; the Census job falls into Falco's lap and subsequently he is raised to the middle rank.

By *Nemesis*, I had discovered that Caenis probably came from Istria. The refurbishment of the amphitheatre in Pula, which we know about from an inscription, forms a useful kink in the plot. Perhaps Anacrites witnesses that very inscription being set up.

This gave her the greatest influence and she amassed untold wealth, so that it was even thought that he made money through Caenis herself as his intermediary. For she received vast sums from many sources, sometimes selling governorships, sometimes procuratorships, generalships and priesthoods, and in some instance even imperial decisions. For although Vespasian killed no one on account of his money, he did spare the lives of many who gave it; and while it was Caenis who received the money, people suspected that Vespasian willingly allowed her to do as she did.
CASSIUS DIO

Queen Berenice of Judaea

Daughter of Herod Agrippa, Berenice was married three times, then rumoured to have an incestuous relationship with her brother. A powerful, wealthy ruler, she was forty when she aided Vespasian in his Jewish Wars, perhaps tickling his fancy; however, it was Titus, ten years her junior, who fell in love with her and she with him. Around AD74–75 she visited Rome with her brother, lived with Titus as a concubine and aroused the hostility of traditionalists, who saw her as a designing Eastern princess like Cleopatra.

I managed to give her a brief plot-line. When Falco and Helena meet Berenice, he says: *No man can possibly answer the question: was Queen Berenice really beautiful? Well, not when any of his womenfolk are listening.* [OVTM] She makes an impression – though, as Helena remarks, shimmering is a neat trick: *Silken robes help. Then it's easy to do if your sandals are difficult to walk in, so you have to sway sinuously so as not to fall over when traversing low steps.* Although Berenice hangs back in the conversation, to the point that Falco actually wonders if she speaks Latin, he then reminds us she can be formidable: *This was the woman who had once protested volubly against the barbarity of a Roman governor in Jerusalem; she was a fearless orator who had appealed for clemency for people barefoot, though in danger of her life.* [OVTM]

Aware that Vespasian won't welcome her as daughter-in-law, Falco evaluates her chances sceptically: *The father had built his imperial claim on high-minded traditional values; a would-be empress with a history of incest and interference in politics could never make a suitable portrait for the next young Caesar's bedroom wall ... Somebody should tell her: Berenice would get the push.* He's right. Berenice was persuaded to return home. She revisited Rome briefly on Titus' accession, was dismissed again, and vanished from history.

Claudia Sacrata

German women obviously like to be at the front of things ... (IHM)

A Ubian woman who lived in Cologne during the turbulent Year of the Four Emperors, according to Tacitus, Claudia Sacrata was rumoured to have a liaison with Petilius Cerialis. Falco's conviction that she is a source of regular R&R for Roman troops may be entirely his imagination, and mine. Or not.

That Claudia Sacrata chose gifts for the prophetess, went with the embassy from Cologne to Veleda, or provided food for the feast when the Chauci and Frisii were locked in a burning hall are my embroideries.

Julius Civilis

This interesting character belonged to the aristocracy of Batavia, an area around the mouth of the Rhine. Batavians were well known for shipping skills and their cavalry could swim in perfect formation in full kit. This was put to good use during the Claudian invasion of Britain. Eight auxiliary cohorts of Batavians were attached to the XIV Legion. Civilis served with the auxiliaries for twenty years and was a Roman citizen.

Once unrest flared in Germany in AD68, Batavian leaders came under suspicion; Civilis narrowly avoided execution twice, by both Nero and Vitellius. Embittered by his imprisonment and the bad treatment meted out to his people, he determined on revolt. Tacitus says he dyed his hair red and refused to have it cut or to shave until the Romans were driven out. Contest beard-growing apparently pre-dated Björn Borg.

In alliance with Veleda, Civilis did enormous damage to the Romans. He may have been aiming for personal power as leader of a huge rival confederation; he certainly made good use of the fighting skills he had learned with the Roman army. His enemies acknowledged him as intelligent and tenacious. In his last reported speech from Tacitus he claims to have been a friend of Vespasian and to have great respect for him – clearly the speech was aimed at repatriating himself.

So perhaps one day he really did meet an envoy who said crisply, *Let's get down to it, Civilis. You took the money. You enjoyed the life. You were grateful to be exempt from taxation and gain the benefits of a regular income and a structured career. You threw it away for a dream that became pointless. You and your family will live at Augusta Treverorum at a fixed address. Xanthus has come to give you a snappy haircut and a shave* ... [IHM]

Petilius Cerialis (Quintus Petilius Cerialis Caesius Rufus)

He has never appeared, but this general took part in major incidents that affect Falco. He may have been a relative of Vespasian, perhaps even married to the Emperor's daughter, **Flavia Domitilla**.

During the Boudiccan Revolt, Cerialis was legate of the IX Hispana legion. He is very briefly glimpsed in *Poseidon's Gold,* when the centurion Laurentius mentions going off into bandit country under this general during service in Judaea.

He supported the Flavian bid for power, at one point disguising himself as a peasant and living in the hills to escape Vitellian forces. After Vespasian's accession, he was sent to Germany, to tackle native revolt and army mutinies. The campaign was successful; we know Roman Germany was pacified. Although Falco discusses acerbically more than one incident where Cerialis looks inept, Tacitus also shows he stabilised the legions and was wise in reconciling Gauls and Germans to Rome. He also sensibly deflected approaches from Domitian to make attempts against Vespasian or Titus.

The feckless – or chronically unlucky – general did lose his flagship at Cologne. It was sent to Veleda, though its history with Falco and friends is of course conjectural. Cerialis was subsequently made Governor of Britain, serving there again in AD71–74, a period when Falco is occupied elsewhere.

Veleda

Her name may be a title meaning 'a seer'. Tacitus says the Germans traditionally regarded many women as prophetic, to the point of divinity, while stressing that Veleda's prestige rested on her success in foreseeing the outcome of defying Rome. I had to describe her with nothing more to go on. I wanted to be believable, but to treat this real person with courtesy. I did it mainly through the impression she makes: *She looked as if she could not only reach decisions, but make other people see that whatever she decreed was their only course … too old to be a young woman, yet too young to be called old. For Rome she was the wrong age altogether. She knew too much to forgive us, and too little to tire of fighting us …* [IHM]

Tacitus describes Veleda's lifestyle among the Bructeri: *Any personal approach to Veleda or speech with her was forbidden. This … was intended to enhance the aura of veneration that surrounded the prophetess. She remained immured in a high tower, one of her relatives being deputed to transmit questions and answers as if he were mediating*

An unmarried woman, who enjoyed wide influence over the tribe of the Bructeri …
TACITUS

between a god and his worshippers … I found a reference to archaeological remains of an early Roman signal tower near the River Lupia: I put two and two together.

In or around AD77, Veleda was captured and brought to Rome by Rutilius Gallicus. *Her local influence was waning and Rutilius Gallicus could have – should have – left her alone … He needed her for his own purposes. Veleda was a symbol. She stood no chance.* [SA]

Her fate is unknown. Speculation that she was made to live at a temple in Ardea is based on the finding of Greek inscription near there, which lampoons her prophetic powers.

Ganna

Described as Veleda's successor, a prophetess called Ganna was received by the Emperor Domitian. It is my invention in *Saturnalia* that she might already have been to Rome and learned home cooking from Ma.

Munius Lupercus

One of the enormous cast of Tacitus' *Histories,* Lupercus was commander at Vetera, then a prisoner sent to Veleda. He was killed during the journey; I decided his fate for *The Iron Hand of Mars*. The method is validated by both archaeology and Tacitus: *Cowards, shirkers and sodomites are pressed down under a hurdle into the slimy mud of a bog.*

The Legionary commander, Munius Lupercus was sent along with other presents to Veleda … But Lupercus was put to death before he reached her.
TACITUS

Rutilius Gallicus (Quintus Julius Cordinus Gaius Rutilius Gallicus)

When researching *Two for the Lions*, I came across a legate who conducted a boundary survey for Vespasian. I could find nothing else about him.

Immediately afterwards, John Henderson brought out *A Roman Life: Rutilius Gallicus on Paper and in Stone*, dissecting the poet Statius' commendatory poem on Domitian's 'Chief of Police' (Urban Prefect, a job equivalent to Mayor of London or New York). *Rutilius Gallicus is unique as a figure from the heyday of the Roman Empire who can be studied in detail through both text and inscription and who isn't part of an emperor's family … Gallicus appears by turns as a formal public servant, a delicate amateur poet-rhetorician, a workaholic chasing an early grave, the darling of his people, the strongman of the tyrant Domitian, the miraculously resurrected patient of Apollo, and a soldier-hero of the Empire* … says Henderson. Sharp intake of breath!

My Rutilius first appears as a solitary expat: *an upright figure, slightly too much flesh, sharp haircut, clean-shaven, bearing himself like a soldier though with too many years out of action to be an army professional. He spoke with an unmistakeable Basilica Julia accent. That greeting alone told me he was freeborn, patrician, tutor-educated, army-trained, imperially patronised and statue-endowed.* [TFL] This is too aristocratic, because he probably began as an equestrian; adoption may have advanced his career. But an inscribed statue base exists, so I guessed right about *that*!

Gallicus oversees the games in Lepcis Magna where Famia goes to the lions and Anacrites fights. Then Falco (now clearly having read Henderson) reassesses him: *When Vespasian became emperor, Rutilius somehow pushed to the front, one of the first consuls of the reign. Nobody had heard of him. Frankly I had taken no notice of the man either – until I met him in Tripolitania. What he did have was ambition. He was stepping up the treads of power as niftily as a roofer with a shoulder-hod of pantiles.* [OVTM]

Next he and Falco host a joint reading event, though they don't gel. We glimpse his wife, **Minicia Paetina.** Falco puts up more markers for the future: *A celebrity in waiting,* [OB] Rutilius wrote epic poetry, his crony Domitian's favourite, but since none survived we only have Falco's verdict: *He was, as I had always suspected, a far from thrilling poet.* [OB]

As governor of Lower Germany, Rutilius led a raid to capture Veleda, bringing her back to Rome for a Triumph, or more correctly an Ovation; we don't know for sure if it happened. Perhaps his glory was clouded by some scandal – as occurs in *Saturnalia*?

Tiberius Claudius Togidubnus

It is possible that King Togidubnus of the Atrebates was one of the tribal princelings sent to Rome to be educated before being installed as a 'client' king (which Tacitus says he was). His forenames indicate he was granted Roman citizenship by Claudius or Nero.

Certain domains were presented to King Cogidumnus, who maintained his unswerving loyalty right down to our own times – an example of the long-established Roman custom of employing even kings to make others slaves.
TACITUS

It seems quite likely that he allowed a Roman military base at Chichester even before the Claudian invasion; the first stage of the Roman Palace (called the 'old house' in my novel) dates from Nero's day. On the invasion the King surely met the young Vespasian, as legate of the Second Augustan legion, capturing hill forts and subduing hostile tribes throughout the south-west. Togidubnus presumably supported Vespasian's bid for the throne and was rewarded with a huge palace makeover seven years later.

Uncertainty about his name devolves from Tacitus who calls him 'Cogidumnus' (in most manuscripts). An inscription at Chichester uses the 'dubnus' ending; unfortunately the first two letters are missing (!) but 'Togi' is preferred by the scholars I prefer. Hence Falco's jokes, trying to pre-empt angry letters.

To look at he was clearly an elderly northerner, his mottled skin now papery and pale. On any formal occasion, he dressed like Roman nobility. I had not deduced whether any rank conferred on him actually entitled him to the broad purple stripe on his toga, but he called himself a 'legate of Augustus' and he wore that stripe with all the confidence of a senatorial bore who could list several centuries of florid ancestors. [JM] I had to invent such details, and also gave him a friendly relationship with Falco in both books where he appears.

Sextus Julius Frontinus

If he was the usual age for a consul he was forty-three; forty-four if he had had this year's birthday. Clean-shaven and close-shorn. A Vespasian appointment so bound to be confident, competent and shrewd. Undeterred by my scrutiny and unfazed by his poor surroundings. He was a man with a solid career behind him, yet the energy to carry him through several more top-notch roles before he went senile. Physically spare, a trim weight, undebauched. Someone to respect – or walking trouble: primed to stir things up. [THF]

It's very difficult to give a physical description of a real person of whom there are no known likenesses! I had to draw conclusions. Frontinus was governor of Britain in the AD70s, in a period of expansion and consolidation: the large reconstruction of Fishbourne Roman Palace and major building in Roman London date from then. In AD95, under Nerva, Frontinus

Julius Frontinus was equal to shouldering the heavy burden and rose as high as a man then could rise. He subdued by force of arms the strong and warlike nation of the Silures, after a hard struggle, not only against the valour of his enemy, but against the difficulties of the terrain.
TACITUS

became Curator of the Aqueducts in Rome; he conducted a detailed survey of the aqueducts and wrote his two-volume work on the subject, from which many details in *Three Hands in the Fountain* derive. It is my conceit that his interest may have been piqued by working with Falco. Frontinus also wrote a book on military strategy.

I have assumed he appreciates Falco's practical sense and efficiency, so he asks for Falco to clear up the troubles at Fishbourne Palace, then quickly hands over the murder of the King's henchman and associated gangster problem in *The Jupiter Myth*. Here, at the start of what was clearly a successful term as British governor, Falco assesses him again and still approves: *Frontinus had all the makings of an old-time Roman in power: soldierly, cultured, intrigued by administrative problems of all kinds, decent, absolutely straight.* After listing in detail the plans Frontinus has, Falco decides: *If all this came off, Britain would be transformed. Frontinus would haul this marginal, barbarian province properly into the Empire.* [JM]

In a few decades' time I could well find myself smiling as the Daily Gazette *saluted an Annio Novus extension, when I would remember standing here above Nero's lake, while an engineer's assistant earnestly propounded his theories …* [THF]

Tiberius Catius Asconius Silius Italicus

He had a heavy build, not grossly fat but fleshy all over as a result of rich living. It had left him dangerously red in the face too. His eyes were sunk in folds of skin as if he constantly lacked sleep, though his clean-shaven chin and neck looked youthful. I put him in his forties but he had the constitution of a man a decade older. His expression was that of someone who had just dropped a massive stone plinth on his foot. [AC]

Classical scholars treat this man with respect, perhaps awed by the fact he produced a historical epic poem, the *Punica*, in no fewer than seventeen books. Its survival makes him better known than his colleague Paccius, though to me they are tarred by the same brush. He was consul in the year Nero died, AD68, and achieved the high honour of being proconsul of Asia – though he had to wait longer than normal for it. This could be due to the taint of his earlier career – 'distinguished orator', according to classicists, yet an informer of the despised Neronian type. When Vespasian assumed the throne, all senators had to swear they had done nothing to harm others; Silius abstained, and was thrown out of the Senate temporarily. After rehabilitation, he seems to have kept his head down, turning to that refuge of politicians and models, writing fiction. At the age of seventy, he committed suicide stoically, while afflicted with a tumour.

Caius Paccius Africanus

Paccius made the mistake of *not* writing a long epic poem, or not one that survived, so scholars don't have to respect him. He too was a Neronian informer. He too was a consul, in AD67, in which year he denounced several enemies of Nero — perhaps being rewarded for this with his consulship. When required to take the oath of not having harmed anyone by his actions, he declined and was expelled by force from the Senate. The results seem to have been no worse than temporary expulsion of a rogue Member from the House of Commons: everyone gasps, but the man sneaks back.

Certainly Paccius survived, and achieved the proconsulship of Africa, the same year as Silius in Asia.

Heron of Alexandria

We paid a guide a bunch of coins to tell us how a window was arranged high up, through which sunlight streamed at break of day, falling so the sunbeam seemed to kiss the god on the lips. It was a device created by the inventor, Heron. [AL]

I've known a few inventive, practical men. I find Heron extremely attractive and several of his inventions are illustrated in this book. He wrote on many scientific subjects and although he is thought to have died around the time of Falco and Helena's visit to Alexandria, I was delighted to introduce him, and to honour him by letting him deduce what really happened in the Great Library the night Theon died. *Could it be ropes and pulleys? Could Theon have worked some pneumatic device from within his private sanctum? Could some incredibly impractical criminal have set up a crack-brained mechanical killing machine? Impossible of course — you would have found the machine afterwards ...* [AL] Part of his answer is practical: an earthquake has caused damage which has not been repaired. It is also based on human understanding: an elderly man became confused and left the door locked unintentionally.

The Public Sector:
Vigiles and Bureaucrats

Lucius Petronius Longus

My good friend Petronius Longus had many fine qualities. He was tough and shrewd, an amiable crony, a valued law and order officer, a respected man in any neighbourhood he graced. [JM]

Every private eye needs a pal in the police. *He was thirty years old. He arrived dressed in various shapeless brown woollen garments, his usual unobtrusive working uniform … Stuck through his belt he carried a thick cudgel for encouraging quiet behaviour on the streets; these he supervised with a light, reasonable hand, backed up by well-aimed bodyweight. A twisted headband rumpled the straight hair on his broad head. He had a placid mentality he certainly needed when picking through the grime and greed at the low end of Roman society. He looked solid and tough, and good at his job − all of which he was. He was also a deeply sentimental family man − a thoroughly decent type.* [PG]

Petronius is a certain type of man: a cautious investor, suspicious of banks. He takes care of his possessions like a typical ex-soldier; he is a good packer of luggage; he never throws anything away; he has a medicine chest; his spare sword is handy; he carries a substantial note-tablet for making notes about suspects. He is calm and unperturbed. He cares about food less than Falco; he doesn't go home for lunch, though he routinely has dinner with his children, and slips off from work if he has a household job pending; he is a keen and competent carpenter. Petro has a legendary love of wine, much like my editor, though Petro also likes a bargain: *Once he found a crisp white at a few coppers an amphora (with a pétillance he described to me lovingly, as connoisseurs do) Petronius Longus acquired as much as he could: while I left him on his own he had bought a culleus. Seriously. A huge barrel as tall as his wife. At least twenty amphorae. Enough to put a thousand flasks on the table if he kept an inn. More, if he watered the drink.* [SB]

As a vigiles officer, Petronius is thoroughly sound. We see his stubbornness when he pursues the apparently untouchable gangster Balbinus; again in his long-term obsession with Balbinus' heir Florius. And he's a good commander. *He had strong bonds with his man. He always led from the front. He pulled his weight in routine enquiries and on surveillance he mucked in as one of them … His quiet manner tended to disguise how powerfully built he was. Slow of step and wry of speech, he could lean on wrong-doers before they even saw him coming, but once Petro applied weight, resistance caved in fast. He ran the watch without seeming to exert himself although in private he worried deeply about standards. He achieved the highest. His was a lean, competent squad which gave the public what they paid for and kept the villains on the hop.* [TTD] Like Falco, he is several times badly beaten up – usually finding women to nurse him back to health.

He may be deceptive. Falco says: *He has a mild-mannered reputation – behind which lurks the most devious, evil-minded investigation officer anywhere in Rome!* [TTD] Petronius certainly lives up to this in *Nemesis*. The boy Zeno is typically deceived: *What the boy saw was a big man waiting silently with a friendly expression, someone who might throw a beanbag about in an alley with the local children.* But he's also *an officer whose slam-bang interrogation methods were a legend. Petronius could persuade incorrigible criminals to bleat out damning evidence against their favourite brothers. He could make them do it even if the brothers were innocent, though mostly he did prefer confessions of real guilt.* [STH]

His friendship with Falco is embedded in their army service. I doubt they were as laddish as they make out but Petronius may have been worse than Falco. Good colleagues so long as each remains in his own sphere, when they work as formal partners they find unexpected problems: *Petronius was going to sort out our business. (He was going to sort out me.) He would impose order. He would attract new work; he would plan our caseload; he would show me just how to generate wealth through blistering efficiency … He spent a lot of time composing charts, while I plodded around the city delivering court summonses. I brought in the meagre denarii, then Petro wrote them up in elaborate account systems.* [THF] Sometimes, Falco and Petronius quarrel bitterly, almost like a husband and wife using one another to release unbearable tension.

'You'll have to stop chasing the women. A few well-positioned cuts might have made you look romantic – but that's just ugly.'
'I'll stop chasing when I find the right one,' said Petronius. [OB]

In his love life, according to Falco, *He had always been attracted to dainty girls with flat chests and scornful voices who ordered him about.* [SB] During his first marriage, *no one spotted that he liked to flirt with risk.* [BBH] Yes, Petronius Longus cheats on his wife, to our knowledge with Aemilia Fausta in *Shadows in Bronze* (who bears his child) and, disastrously, with Balbina Milvia, the gangster's daughter, which precipitates his marriage breakdown. I take the blame here. As Falco settled down respectably I chose to balance that with Petro making a muck of things. Writing about honest, faithful characters is less fun than writing about reprobates. (Incidentally, Ben Crowe, the actor who plays Petronius on radio, was distraught over the Fausta incident, refusing to believe his decent character would really behave like that. Sorry, Ben!)

When Petro acknowledges feelings for Maia, Falco hates watching their relationship stumbling to life: *I had cursed when I found one of my sisters wanting to berth alongside my dearest crony. That can damage a male friendship. But it was far more uncomfortable when Petro was dumped ... I would never forgive my sister.* [BBH] Things do not go smoothly. Helena tells Petro: *You drink too much, you flirt too much, you do dangerous work. You are a risk to a woman who wants a good life – but Maia Favonia is aching to take that risk. You must be the most exciting man who ever courted her. Maia wants you – but she doesn't want to be deceived by you. Her children love you – but she doesn't want them to be let down.* [JM]

It is, I feel, a subtlety of characterisation that despite his own behaviour, Petro believes in old-fashioned Roman rectitude for everyone else. He has no truck with the liberal freedoms Falco and Helena exercise, such as sharing confidences about work and travelling together. *Will Maia bring him round?*

We rarely hear about his early background, but he has a much older brother (**Petronius Rectus**, who appears in *Nemesis*), also cousins with whom he and Rectus jointly own the ox, **Nero, aka Spot**. After featuring in *Shadows in Bronze*, Nero reappears in *Nemesis,* where he is stolen, features in a 'missing' poster, and is found in the possession of a serial killer. Petro's devoted **Auntie Sedina** owns a flower-shop in Rome.

Arria Silvia

We first meet Petro's wife on holiday (never a good situation) in *Shadows in Bronze*. Falco says she and her father eyed up Petronius as a potential husband *like two old women in a market selecting a fresh sprat for their festival treat* – though he admits Petro was keen on the copper-beater's cash. Initially, the marriage is successful. Petronius loves his three children and demonstrates romantic feelings for his wife. *A slightly built, pretty woman; she had small hands and a neat nose, with soft skin and fine eyebrows like a child's. But there was nothing soft about Silvia's character, one aspect of which was a searing opinion of me ...* [IHM]

In *Time to Depart,* Falco says Silvia brings him out in a rash. Their antagonism is mutual, although in early books, when Falco and Helena are starting out together and it still looks as if Silvia's marriage to Petronius is sound, the two couples enjoy a friendly relationship.

Despite her being abrasive, it's clear that during most of their marriage Petro and Silvia rub along well. *She was weeping, reduced to a disappointed young woman who felt exhausted beyond her strength. Petro was letting her snuffle on his great shoulder while he went on dreaming to himself ...* [SB] She genuinely cares for him; we see that when he is knocked unconscious and again when he is devastated by the doctor's murder in *Time to Depart.* Under impossible pressure Silvia leaves Petro, taking the children to Ostia when she gets a boyfriend, a potted-salad seller. Petronius then gets himself stationed at Ostia (though partly for my convenience). Silvia seeks a reconciliation – sadly too late. Petronius has moved on. The implacable author has other plans for him. In *The Accusers* Silvia is depressed and even speaks of suicide, though no more is heard of that.

Petronilla, **Silvana and Tadia** are the three Petronius daughters. Silvana and Tadia die of chickenpox in *The Jupiter Myth,* causing their father anguish and guilt for leaving them.

Tadia Longina's need for a comfort stop in *Shadows in Bronze* saves Falco from being roughed up or worse by Pertinax's thugs.

After the break-up of her parents' marriage, there is a touching scene where Petro and Petronilla are seen at the Games together: *They were both eating pancakes. Petronilla had managed hers quite daintily for she had inherited her mother's daintiness. Her father had a sticky chin and honey sauce down his tunic front. Petronilla noticed this. She soon cleaned him up with her handkerchief. Petronius submitted like a hero. When his daughter sat back he slung an arm around her while she snuggled up against him. He was staring at the arena with a set expression; I was no longer sure he was watching the race.* [THF] After her sisters die, life is even harder for Petronilla; she lives with her mother but does regularly see her father.

In the IV Cohort of Vigiles

Marcus Rubella

In *Time to Depart,* the new appointee Rubella is *big physically; quiet, not tired by life. His grey hair was close-cropped in the military manner, giving him a tough appearance. His strength was enough to move an ox aside merely by leaning on it. The knowledge soothed him. Rubella took the world at his own pace. He was utterly composed.* About fifty, this slightly sinister character left the legions as a retired ex-chief centurion, and is gruesomely ambitious to join the Praetorian Guard. He is suspicious of Falco, whom he views as an uncontrollable amateur. He lacks a sense of humour and earns a lot of insults: *He could be one of those dark types who like to pretend they never lift a digit, while all the time they have a swift comprehension of events, a warm grasp of human relationships, and an incisive grip on their duties in public life. He could be loyal, trustworthy and intelligent. On the other hand he could be just as he appeared: a lazy, carefree, overpromoted swine …* [TTD]

When he first arrives, the cohort are obsessed by trying to categorise their new commander: *whether he is an ineffectual layabout who needs a diagram in triplicate before he can wipe his backside clean – or whether he's so poisonous he's actually corrupt.* [TTD] Then at the brothel fight, it is Rubella who deals with the bent centurion from the Sixth Cohort: *He was locked in a hold with Tibullinus, a hold of painful illegality … he broke a bone somewhere in the centurion with a horrendous crack, then put in a punch like a pile-hammer. He jerked his chin up derisively …* [TTD]

Lieutenant Byrnes was the man in charge of the 87th Detective Squad. He had a small compact body and a head like a rivet. His eyes were blue and tiny, but those eyes had seen a hell of a lot, and they didn't miss very much that went on around the lieutenant. The lieutenant knew his precinct was a trouble spot and that was the way he liked it.
McBAIN

He always kept his inkpot full and his sand tray topped up. [THF]

As we learn more about him, I love portraying Rubella as the archetypal 'boss': paranoid, obsessed with his own status, and deviously manipulating. *He liked to think of himself as a dangerous spider twitching the strands of a large and perfectly formed web.* [THF] For Petronius he will always be *an ambitious, unscrupulous, discipline-mad, tyrannical hard man who could never wipe his bum with a latrine sponge without consulting the rules to see if a ranker was supposed to do it for him.* [OVTM]

However, he is brutally good at his job: *For him 'interviews' were never an intellectual exercise. Marcus Rubella was a master of pain management, the excruciating mixture of torture and delay.* [STH] My favourite Rubella scene is at the Fourth Cohort's drinks party: *in order to show how conscientiously he threw himself into occasions of cohort festivity, Marcus Rubella (a staid man, conscious of his dignity) was wearing a silly hat, winged sandals and a very short gold tunic. I noticed with a shudder that he had not shaved his legs.* [SA]

Martinus

Originally Petro's deputy, Martinus shamelessly tries to usurp Petro's position. He's forty, unmarried, and has *straight brown hair, cut neatly across the forehead, heavily shaded jowls and a dark mole on one cheek.* [TTD]

Capable, but pedantic and painfully slow, he has a scene in *Time to Depart* where he secretly watches a brothel with Falco. He turns out to be devoted to draughts. Likening the game to investigation, Martinus says, '*You need mental agility, strength of will, powers of bluff, concentration ...* ' '*And little glass balls,*' replies Falco balefully. However, Falco watches Martinus on surveillance in the Forum and realises the man misses nothing. Falco decides he must be 'straight', because he is too lazy to be bent.

Eventually he applies for promotion in the Sixth Cohort, which suits everyone.

Fusculus

Right-hand man to Petronius, Fusculus is *a round, happy fellow, about thirty-five years and a hundred and eighty pounds. Balding on top, the rest of his hair ran around his skull in horizontal ridges. It had remained dark and he had almost black eyes. Though rotund, he looked extremely fit.* [TTD] From his first appearance he is the man who studies lovingly the Forum scams and scammers' patois. This starts with him listing 'scratchers' who steal gilding from statues, tanners who emit noxious smells, street fights and escaped wolves, then it progresses to detailed examples of criminal slang (all invented by me; see the Afterword to *Saturnalia* for comment).

Sergius

Sergius enjoys his work. *Sergius was the Fourth's punishment officer – tall, perfectly built, permanently flexed for action, and stupendously handsome. Flicking his whip gently, he was sitting on the bench outside, killing ants. His aim was murderous. Muscles rippled aggressively through gaps in his brown tunic. A wide belt was buckled tightly on a flat stomach, emphasising his narrow waist and well-formed chest. Sergius looked after himself. He could look after trouble too. No neighbourhood troublemaker whom Sergius looked after bothered to repeat his crime. At least his long tanned face, dagger-straight nose and flashing teeth made an aesthetic memory for villains as they fainted under the caress of his whip. To be beaten up by Sergius was to partake in a high-class art form.* [THF]

Scythax

Scythax was a brusque Oriental freedman who seemed to suspect malingering. He expected people to cry ouch as soon as he entered a room; he viewed 'headaches', 'bad backs' and 'old knee trouble' with little patience. He had heard it all before. To get sympathy from Scythax, you had to produce a bright red rash or a hernia, something visible or proddable ... His hair lay in a perfectly straight line on his eyebrows as if he had trimmed it himself using a cupping vessel on his head as a straight edge. [TTD] Falco later comments: *Since the vigiles acted as a fire brigade, his unwillingness to soothe burns did hamper him, but he had worked with the Fourth Cohort as long as anyone could remember and the vigiles dislike change.* [AC]

Although the Romans lacked forensic science as we know it and autopsies were illegal, Scythax often provides medical insights about how a victim has died. He does his best over the severed hands found in aqueducts, though has little to go on and clearly dislikes being asked. *He was a hard man with the living. Apparently we had found his weakness with our sad sections of the dead.* [THF] Before we actually see a post-mortem in *Alexandria*, Falco comes to believe that Scythax is performing autopsies illegally on bodies that are dumped for him. [SA]

His brother, **Alexander**, also a doctor, is murdered in *Time to Depart* as a reprisal for helping Petronius prosecute Balbinus.

Passus

Passus joins the Fourth in *Ode to a Banker;* later Falco says he was head-hunted by Petronius. *He was a short, shock-haired neat type with a belt he was proud of and stubby hands. He had a quiet manner and was no raw recruit. His air was competent but not pushy. He was carrying a set of waxed tablets, with a bone stylus bending his right ear forward, for taking notes.* [STH]

Like many an off-duty policeman, he reads novels.

Palace Bureaucrats and Spies

Of course it is not due to my first career that I see bureaucracy as a byzantine tangle, peopled by slyly grappling mandarins!

Falco takes a sceptical position: *It was perfectly possible to substantiate a million-sesterces fraud, yet still to encounter some slimy high-powered bureaucrat who would decide there were policy reasons, or ancient precedents, or issues affecting his own pension, that made him advise his great imperial master to shelve the exposé.* [TFL] Finding himself a patball in the power struggle between Laeta and Anacrites, he groans: *This was the kind of situation where the general good could be overturned in the pursuit of some disastrous administrators' feud. And it was a situation where Rome could, yet again, end up in the grip of sinister forces who ruled by torture and infamy.* [DLC]

There is the tricky question of bribes, the Roman equivalent of supposedly 'normal' sweeteners, whether it is big banks paying massive bonuses 'to keep our executives' or arms manufacturers handing illegal sums to sheikhs 'because it is expected in their culture'. Bribery must be how Narcissus became a multimillion-aire under Claudius, and it was said that Caenis amassed a fortune. I suggest Laeta may be deliberately creating an olive oil cartel, aiming to be bribed himself and to serve his master with profits. It was a real charge against Vespasian that he cornered the market in special commodities, which he then sold off at high prices.

Intelligence is gathered and used by the most benign rulers. *Vespasian maintained a pretence that he hated spies and informers – yet the imperial intelligence service still flourished. Titus Caesar had made himself commander of the Praetorian Guard, who ran the spies network (on the rationale that they were using it to protect the safety of the Emperor). From what I heard, rather than disbanding it, Titus was planning to restructure and expand the team.* [BBH]

It is believed Titus did so, but naturally we don't have the top-secret records.

'Oh let's pretend Vespasian does not know what his Chief Spy fixes – or his filthy methods. No. Be realistic. Vespasian does not want to know.'

'Inform Vespasian if you want to, Marcus – but he won't thank you!' [BBH]

Tiberius Claudius Laeta

Laeta, to whom I have given the position of chief secretary, creeps up on us in *Time to Depart,* though his full importance emerges in the following book, where his rivalry with Anacrites starts to show; it is *Saturnalia* before Falco tells us *he had some undefined oversight of both home security and foreign intelligence.* As he lurks in the old Palace of Tiberius on the Palatine where he has an enormous suite, working obsessively, Falco suspects that his position at the top can be lonely. Laeta likes it that way.

He could be any age between forty and sixty. He had all his hair (dry-looking brown stuff cut in a short, straight, unexciting style). His body was trim; his eyes were sharp; his manner was alert. He wore an ample tunic with narrow gold braid, beneath a plain white toga to meet Palace formality. On one hand he wore the wide gold ring of the middle class; it showed some emperor had thought well of him. [DLC]

As he looms into Falco's orbit, Laeta is hoping to dominate the bureaucracy and even manipulate the Emperor. Falco considers his background: *an imperial ex-slave, born and trained among the cultivated, educated, unscrupulous orientals who had long administered Rome's empire. Nowadays they formed a discreet cadre, well behind the* scenes, but I did not suppose their methods had changed from when they were more visible … [DLC]

His aims are long-term and self-serving. Above all, he revels in his feud with Anacrites: *Cracking heads wasn't necessary. Laeta's not vicious. He's not crude. He's quite clever enough to outwit Anacrites, and depraved enough as a bureaucrat to enjoy finessing him. Laeta wants a classic power struggle. He wants Anacrites alive so he knows he has lost the game. Where's the art otherwise?* [DLC]

His relationship with Falco is cautious on both sides: *He was a silken-tongued twister I had never trusted. He saw me as a grimy thug who possessed intelligence and other handy talents. We dealt with one another, when we had to, politely.* [SA] Laeta sees, and is too astute to ignore, that Vespasian and Titus think well of Falco; Falco suspects Laeta has found out that there is a secret reason for his own feud with Domitian.

Laeta's position in *Nemesis* is as ambiguous as we would expect.

Tiberius Claudius Anacrites

Initially, I had no plans for the Chief Spy. In *Shadows in Bronze,* he was just background, useful for making Falco feel out of place among the 'official' palace team. *He called himself a secretary … He had a tense compact frame and a bland face, with unusual grey eyes and eyebrows so faint they were nearly invisible.* [SB] Even here he is jumpy – tight-lipped, an insecure type – and as he checks documents, Falco notices presciently that he uses *the fine detail of an auditor who expects another auditor to be round later checking him.*

By *Venus in Copper,* I had seen Anacrites' potential. Every hero needs a rival to hamper and annoy him.

There are explanations for his behaviour: *His was a classic case of career blight. He must have studied his craft under Nero, those crazy years of suspicion and terror when prospects for intelligence agents had never looked more golden. Then as he reached his prime, he found himself stuck with the new Emperor Vespasian, a man so irredeemably provincial that he did not really believe in palace spies. So instead of enjoying himself at the centre of some crawling network of undercover termites, Anacrites now had to devote every day to proving that his place on the payroll was justified …* [VC] Having been a civil servant in Margaret Thatcher's Britain, I wrote those words with insight and passion!

The intelligence service was part of the Praetorian Guard; Anacrites does call on the Guards' thumping brutality on occasions, and after he is badly wounded, he receives protection in their camp. His subordinates are a motley crew. Apart from Perella, he uses the derisible staff **'Footsie and the dwarf'**; **Valentinus** is of higher calibre, though unfortunately killed. Then Anacrites takes on the **'Melitan brothers'**, who will develop far beyond their original jokey sighting.

Anacrites has built up a nest egg (Laeta complains about his seaside house at Baiae). Falco reckons he takes bribes; once he gains higher status after the Census, these bribes will be larger. He thinks himself a financial wizard (though comes a cropper when advising Ma); originally he lives at the Palace, yet he ends up in a desirable old republican house by the Palatine. This kind of discreet, expensive, securely protected private house can be seen in central Rome; I have speculated often on who can possibly live there. Probably faded aristocracy, not intelligence agents – though who is to know?

Physically Anacrites is *tight-lipped and tense, pale eyed, obsessively neat.* [PG] He is a dandy, well manicured, consciously choosing tunics with a racy cut in odd shades that make him unobtrusive, but adorned with dashing braids. He wears his hair slicked back in a style Falco hates. Those eyes, it slowly emerges, are two-tone. This was decided at a conference, where a very unhelpful waiter served breakfast to Ginny, Michelle and me. His sinister eyes were different colours – and we thought he came from Croatia …

His damaging head wound has a profound effect: *He remembered nothing about the evening he was battered. This troubled him. For a man whose career involved knowing more about other people than they chose to tell even their mistresses and doctors, losing part of his memory was a terrible shock. He tried not to show it, but I knew he must lie awake at night, sweating over the missing days of his life.* [OVTM] It affects his ability to function: *since his head wound had made him erratic, he could take a decision to spend large sums of our so far unearned money without turning a hair. Of course tomorrow the same erratic behaviour would make him change his mind …* [TFL]

His best agent – a man I reckoned I would have liked. I could walk away from the palace intrigue, but the dead Valentinus would continue to haunt me. [DLC]

As a well-placed slave at the Palace whose work involved discovering facts that people wanted to hide, he must often have come across unsought bankers' orders propped against his favourite stylus box. They might be anonymous – but he would know exactly who was asking him not to lean on them. [OB]

A good spy, lacking character himself, he could blend into the background like fine mist blurring the contours of a Celtic glen. [TFL]

'This is a filthy job.' For once Anacrites and I spoke the same language.

I agreed with him. *'Sometimes I have nightmares that just by being involved in scenes like this some of the filth might rub off on me.'*

'You could leave it to the vigiles.'

I gave Anacrites a rueful grin. *'I could have left it to you!'*

Holding up the torches, he returned the wry look. *'That wouldn't be you, Falco. You do have to interfere.'*

For once the comment was dispassionate. Then I felt horrified. *If we shared many more foul tasks and philosophical interludes, we might end up on friendly terms.* [THF]

Anacrites is not adept socially. It is never clear whether he has a love life. In *Saturnalia*, Falco and Petro discover he has a secret cabinet of pornographic Roman material. In *Nemesis* we have his formal dinner party; he is definitely an awkward bachelor and has to hire party-planners.

He can be professional. In *Nemesis*, Laeta says he was always seen as intelligent, and even physical; indeed, as a gladiator in *Two for the Lions*, he survives, though lacks stamina and has to resort to a sly move called 'Trainer's Cheat'. He is a good public speaker (which can make him very dangerous) with a light, cultured voice. When they work on the Census, Falco observes him at close quarters: *He conducted an unforced style of interview, making copious notes in a large loose hand. His manner was calm, as if merely familiarising himself with the local scenery. It was not what I had expected. Still, to become Chief Spy he must have been successful once.* [TFL]

There are unsettling moments when he and Falco are equals, such as their frightening descent into the Cloaca Maxima in *Three Hands in the Fountain* and their necessarily hasty search of the dead gladiator's room in *Two for the Lions*. Then, Falco admits they respect one another. *How Anacrites would manage in a real tussle, without a bank of torture irons and a set of pervertedly inventive assistants, was less clear. I suppose somehow I trusted him. Maybe he even had some faith in me.* [TFL] It emphasises that Anacrites *could* have chosen Falco's virtuous path. Being treacherous is deliberate.

Work is critical to understanding Anacrites. *He liked to see himself as an expert at dealing with tricky characters in dangerous locations, but the truth was he led too soft a life and had lost the knack.* [LAP] This explains his fear of Falco as an imperial favourite; it explains, though it does not excuse, Anacrites' long series of attempts to eliminate Falco. The spy's mixture of envy and mimicry will take him from landing Falco in prison over the lead ingots, through trying to have Falco killed in Nabataea, yet obsessively worming his way close to Falco's family. Anacrites' head wound makes their relationship more fraught: his life is saved by Falco and Ma. Anacrites is torn between resentment and his obligation to Falco and pitifully wanting to be one of the family. In *Two for the Lions* their tetchy partnership increases his envy and his yearning to enjoy freedoms he sees Falco enjoying.

His attentions to Maia fail. When, to our relief, she dumps him, his reaction is vindictive and shocking. By the time I wrote this episode, Anacrites had finessed himself into having a reader fan club, who begged me to give him a 'happy ending'; the violence wreaked on Maia's home in *A Body in the Bath House* deliberately restated his danger. His overtures are sinister. When thwarted he is vicious. In *Nemesis,* we will learn that the wrecking incident could have had even worse consequences.

Falco reluctantly tries to live with the situation, though he never forgets. In *Nemesis* we will discover the secrets in Anacrites' background and genes.

> 'Falco,' said Anacrites plaintively, 'I thought that was what you would have done yourself.'
> Dear gods, the madman wanted to be me. [TFL]

Momus

Momus never really changes from his off-putting debut in *Shadows in Bronze: a typical slave overseer: shorn head to deter lice, wine gut, greasy belt, grubby chin, croaky voice from the diseases of his trade, and tough as an old nail stuck in wood. He was clearing out the personnel ... He was crooked, filthy, slapdash and devious – a pleasantly clear-cut type.* Eventually he works at the Palace: *Anacrites always thought Momus had been put on the same corridor so he could report on him to his superiors, or to watch him for Claudius Laeta. Momus encouraged this fear by giving himself increasingly dark titles, such as Inspector of Audit Inspectors. (This also upset Internal Audit).* [SA]

Falco associates with him occasionally; in *Nemesis* he seeks Momus' advice about the hold criminals have over Anacrites. Momus helps Falco and Petronius deal with an unwanted suspect, but he is as uncooperative as Laeta over the real problem.

Perella

With Perella I take delight in overturning Falco's pre-conceptions. She is *a short, stout, surly blonde* [DLC], a dancer, but one of mature age: *as a companion in a wine bar she might be cracking good fun. She was of an age where you could rely on her having a fair old amount of experience –*

in almost anything. In fact she is a merciless state assassin. *Perella looked like a housewife with a headache on the bad day of the month. She was the deadliest intelligence agent I had ever met.* [OB] She is most dangerous in *A Body in the Bath House,* where she continues her role as Anacrites' field agent, bloodily eliminating a fraudulent architect, though her real mission is to persecute and perhaps attack Maia for the spy.

Here we see Perella's method most closely. Falco says Perella will *station herself near her quarry, working as a dancer in some sour dive. There she would listen, watch, make herself known in the district until nobody thought twice about her presence. All the time she was planning her move … When Perella found her victims, she took them out, fast and silently. A knife across the throat from behind was her favourite method. Without question, she had others.* [BBH]

Her dance, a grand scene, is heart-stopping. It sums her up: she looks insignificant, but she is very, very good. *Perella danced at first with such restraint of motion it seemed nearly derisive. Then each fine angle of her outstretched arms and each slight turn of the neck became a perfect gesture. When she burst forth abruptly into frantic drumming of her feet, whirling and darting in the confined spaces available, gasps turned to stricken silence.* [BBH]

As a woman, Perella has to fight for her position; even Falco steals the credit for a job she had wanted in *A Dying Light in Corduba.* While she finds it convenient, Perella works for Anacrites, though there must be an element of doubt about her loyalty, and in *Nemesis* she admits she wants his job. Aware of Anacrites disgracing himself at Lepcis Magna, she claims she won't interfere in Falco's hoped-for revenge on the spy.

The Melitan brothers

They sidle into the series gradually, first seen watching Falco's house: *A couple of shady characters in bum-starver cloaks were lurking on the Embankment outside …* [AC] He calls them *short hairy idiots* and *beetle-browed,* then jeers at Anacrites: *I see you're still employing top quality!* [SA]

They start as minor characters. Then, as you do in a series, I pick them up and make them significant. They are *not* from Malta.

Other Regular Characters

I don't have space to talk about every character. These are people who appear in more than one book:

Julius Frontinus

In *The Silver Pigs,* Falco meets this hard-bitten Praetorian, a friend of his late brother Festus. The purpose of the scene is threefold: to show that Falco has wandered into a new and frightening milieu; to gain new facts in the plot; and to show him as a detective in that archetypal situation, being forced to get very, very drunk with a witness who won't talk otherwise.

Poor Frontinus then gets stuck with the task of helping Falco dispose of the revolting ten-day-old corpse in *Shadows in Bronze.*

If I had been more familiar with historical figures then, I would have given him another name. You learn.

Apollonius

We meet Apollonius as an elderly beggar failing to obtain alms on a barrel outside Flora's Caupona. He has been an unsuccessful teacher at the infant school Falco and Maia were sent to: *He had always been a failure. The worst kind: someone you could not help but feel sorry for, even while he was messing you about. He was a terrible teacher. He might have been a snappy mathematician, but he could not explain anything …* [PG]

At first pedantic, Apollonius settles in with a veneer of culture; he is prone to disappearing out the back to read, so nobody can get served. He gives Falco advice; in *Poseidon's Gold,* he is an early advocate of Falco aiming high, even though Helena Justina is a senator's daughter.

As he gains confidence he acquires a nice cynical wit. He copes well with having Junia in charge, though Falco says in *Scandal Takes a Holiday* that Apollonius fiddles the figures and cheats her of profits. He has little appearances right through to *Nemesis.*

Placing a cup two inches from my elbow and following it with a neat little dish of exactly twenty nuts. [PG]

Lenia

Falco's friend, ally and bugbear at the Eagle Laundry,
Fountain Court, Lenia is nosy, frequently tipsy, with no
discernment in men. Briefly – very briefly – she
becomes wife to the landlord Smaractus, as a ploy to
grab his money. Their marriage takes several books to
occur, a fortnight to disintegrate after a flaming first
night, and several more books to conclude in divorce
(has it even happened?).

*I found her in the corner she used as an accounting room,
sitting in her greasy slippers while she sipped mint tea. Until
this pitiful ninny decided to invest in real estate (and real
misery) by planning to marry our landlord Smaractus, she had
been one of my shabby friends; once I could persuade her to
ditch the brute she would be again. Lenia was a sagging drab
about five times stronger than she looked, with startling snag-
gles of henna-red hair which constantly worked free of a limp
scarf around her head ... she had sickly eyes and a voice like
forty dried peas rattling in a pannikin.* [SB] She does not
improve. *Her face was white, her deportment unstable. She
surveyed me with eyes that needed an oculist ...* [PG] Or later:
*She was a wild-eyed, snaggle-haired fury who carried too
much weight but was otherwise pretty muscular. Her hands
and feet were swollen and red from being in warm water all
day. She had a voice that could have carried half way to the
Palatine, with all the sweetness of a one-note trumpet giving
the orders to a military parade ...* [THF]

From time to time we catch a frightful glimpse of
Lenia's sassy staff. They tease Falco whenever they
see him and are based on traditional spirited factory
girls who live hard lives and stand up for themselves.
*They were sweethearts as singletons but together they turned
into a hooting, foul-mouthed obscene little clutch. If you saw
them coming, you wouldn't just cross to the other pavement,
you'd dive into a different street. Even if it meant getting
mugged and your money pinched.* [THF]

Smaractus

Just a blotch of local slime ... [SP] *the most stinking, greedy,
heartless and degenerate Aventine landlord.* [TFL]

Until Falco moves to live above the basket weaver's,
he constantly dodges his landlord, whom we therefore
don't meet in person until *Time to Depart* on the eve of

his wedding to Lenia – during which festivities we also learn he has a doughty mother. He is wary of Falco: *I was lean and hard and I hated his guts.* [TTD]

His half-starved enforcers come from a seedy gymnasium he runs for the lowest type of gladiator – *all black eyes and dirty bandages.* [SP] *He took them around for protection; I mean to protect the rest of the populace from what these idiots might get up to if Smaractus left them unattended … Smaractus himself was perfectly capable of forcing his debtors to turn out their purse if he caught them in.* [TFL] Smaractus nonetheless dreams of greater things for his fighters, especially in *Two for the Lions,* where he fondly hopes to cash in when the Flavian amphitheatre opens.

His name, which you can spit well, causes great difficulty to the BBC radio drama actors, who cite this as unfair treatment.

Rodan and Asiacus

The two gladiators from the landlord's gym whom we met. *They were ill-fed, unhealthy specimens, kept on short rations by Smaractus' meanness. He had owned them for years. They were slaves, of course, pallid bruisers in leather skirts and with their arms wrapped in dirty bandages to make them look tough. They fought even more dirtily than the Roman crowd liked.* [TFL]

Rodan was the one with the broken nose. A tenant had hit him in the face with a mallet when Rodan tried to forestall a moonlit flit. Asiacus was the rude one with the pustular skin complaint. [TFL]

Cassius

The baker at Fountain Court; his produce is excellent and he is sympathetic to Falco. His wood store causes the fire that disrupts the wedding night of Lenia and Smaractus.

Ennianus

Another Fountain Court regular: he rents a shop to sell baskets, though he lives out on the Campagna; Falco and Helena rent a room above his shop in *Time to Depart,* rent-free in return for watching his lock-up.

Appius

The barber's shop serves as a refuge when Falco thinks his apartment may be visited by undesirables. *Appius was fat, florid, and had the worst head of hair between here and Rhegium. Thin, greasy strands were strung over a flaking scalp. He hardly ever shaved himself either.* [THF]

The **barber's boy** can be useful, though he is somewhat vague.

Glaucus

Glaucus, my trainer, was as sharp as a kitten's claw. A short, wide-shouldered Cilician freedman ... he knew his regulars better than they knew themselves. Probably none of us were at all close to him. After twenty years of listening to other people revealing their secrets while he worked on their muscle tone, he knew how to avoid that trap. But he could tease out embarrassing information as smoothly as a thrush emptying a snail shell. [THF] Clearly an excellent trainer, he does not spare his clients. *For a steep fee, Glaucus would give you a lesson that was almost as uncomfortable as being ridden down by murderous tribesmen galloping on wild horses.* [AC] He teaches Anacrites Trainer's Cheat, the move that saves him in the Lepcis arena.

Unfortunately! [MDF]

In *See Delphi and Die* Falco is entrusted with his beloved son, the obsessed athlete **Young Glaucus**, for their trip to Greece. Glaucus falls for Albia, but she brushes him off.

Marponius

A judge in the murder court, he is an irritant to Petronius Longus, interfering in investigations and agitating to be chosen for trials; he also runs up against Falco several times. In *Poseidon's Gold* he arrests both Falco (on suspicion of killing Censorinus) and Helena (as an accessory); they have to be rescued and bailed by their fathers. He loves being a judge, is fascinated by crime, and boasts to Helena Justina that he is 'a man of ideas'.

Ambitious, nasty, narrow-minded and famous for spouting bigoted drivel, [AC] he has *a flat-topped head and a lather of light, curly hair, receding each side of his rather square brow.*

His backside was too large, so he tended to strut like a pigeon with too much tail ... [PG] He is a 'New Man', who has made his money selling copies of encyclopaedias.

A childless widower, Marponius lives austerely in a detached town villa just off the Vicus Longus, where Falco and Petronius speculate rudely about his rather solitary life. Though the rabbit pie gives him indigestion, he is an habitué of somewhere called Xero's pie shop: *His special haunt when he wanted to look like a man of the people (and to overhear, incognito, the public's views on how he ran his case).* [AC] He is a man with a mission – to clean up Rome. But he comes good for Falco because of their shared background: *We both grew up in the shadow of the Temple of Ceres, we both played in the gutters under the Aqua Marcia, we had the same mud on our boots and we recognised one another for lowborn tykes with equal disadvantages and the same points to prove. If the senatorials tried to be too clever, Marponius would side with me.* [AC]

Thalia

She was a big girl. By which I mean ... nothing. She was big, all over; she was young enough to be described as a girl without too much irreverence; and I was able to see that her assets were entirely in proportion to the height of her. Her attire was what the well-dressed artiste was wearing that month: a few stars, a couple of ostrich feathers, a skimpy drape of transparent stuff – and a necklace. [VC]

I soon saw the potential of this sparkling character. Originally intended only as a colourful witness, she reappeared in *Last Act in Palmyra* as a client, who becomes a friend, after saving Helena's life when she is bitten by a scorpion. In *Two for the Lions,* she dispenses salves and inside knowledge of the arena business. *I thought I liked her,* says Falco. *It seemed the best attitude to take.* By now she has progressed from being a down-at-heel exotic dancer, though she continues to perform; inheriting the circus business from Fronto, who was eaten by a panther, she has become an experienced manager – a role she will reprise in *Alexandria.*

Thalia's relaxed sexual lifestyle has tricky results. A liaison struck up during *Alexandria* – it is uncertain *which* liaison – ends in her becoming pregnant. This is a surprise to everyone, and in *Nemesis* I hint at a lifetime of problems to come. She manages to lumber Falco with it.

Jason, Thalia's python

The necklace might pass for coral, until you observed that its jewelled folds sometimes shuddered with a sluggish allure ... Every time she moved, that creature perked up and started inspecting if I was properly shaved and whether I had nits behind the ears ... [VC]

Of modest size but gigantic curiosity, Jason's favourite trick is to panic Falco. He is like a dog that knows you are afraid of it, or a cat fixing on me when I don't want it on my lap. *Jason liked to curl up right in the exit to a tent where he could look up people's tunic skirts. He wasn't even pretending to be asleep. He was staring right at me, daring me to approach ...* [TFL]

Thalia has a much larger python called **Zeno**, and briefly she owns a cobra too.

Davos

Encountered as a leading actor in *Last Act in Palmyra*, Davos knows Thalia and we leave them apparently about to go into partnership, both business and private. We have not seen him since, however!

'Love of my life,' Thalia assured me. 'I can't get enough of his thundering virility or the way he picks his teeth ... ' [AL]

Davos had a square face with quiet, regretful eyes. Short, no-nonsense black hair topped his head. He was built like a cairn of Celtic rocks, basic, long-lasting, dependable, broadly based; not much would topple him. His view of life was dry. He looked as if he had seen the whole spectacle – and wouldn't waste his money on a second entrance fee ... [LAP]

The only certain thing about Thalia's pregnancy is that Davos cannot be the father.

Byrria

In *Last Act in Palmyra*, Byrria is a young, very beautiful actress, aware of her own talent and trying to make a career. *She had a triangular face with green eyes like an Egyptian cat set wide above high cheekbones and a thin, perfect nose. Her mouth had a strange lop-sided quirk that gave her an ironic, world-weary air. Her figure was as watchable as her face, small and curvaceous, and hinting of unrevealed possibilities. To finish the business she had a dramatic knack of looping up her warm brown hair with a couple of bronze hairpins, so it not only looked unusual but stayed in place, showing off a tantalising neck. Her voice seemed too low for such a neat person; it had a huskiness that was completely distracting when combined with her experienced manner.* [LAP]

She falls hopelessly in love with **Musa**, the handsome Nabataean priest. She is passed off as the daughter of grande dame, Phrygia – after which Byrria is guaranteed the best parts. We may want to imagine that back in Rome, Byrria may be the unnamed beautiful actress with whom Justinus has an infatuation.

She is a character I have placed where she *could* be useful again if I wanted (as could Musa). *Perhaps one day in the future, when Byrria had exhausted her dreams, they would meet again and it might not be too late …* [LAP]

Cornix

This Cornix was an obscene bully of a foreman, a real specialist in administering tortures to slaves. A slab-shouldered sadist with a face marbled like a side of beef by his depraved life. He had picked on me mercilessly from the day I arrived, but owned just enough working ooze in his chickpea brain to be wary in case one day I went back to some previous life and talked … [SP]

First encountered as one of the miseries at the Mendips lead mine, Cornix is deeply corrupt; he breaks several of Falco's ribs with a pit prop then nearly kills him through deliberate neglect. Eight books later, at the Castulo mine in Baetica, Cornix reappears: *Of all the pig-ignorant debauched men in the Empire, he was the last man I would ever wish to see …* [DLC] But I am not merciless to my boy. Positions are reversed. Another gallery prop is swung, and I am with Falco when he says: *Suddenly I felt a lot better about a lot of things.*

Lentullus

Lentullus arrives in *The Iron Hand of Mars,* the dimmest recruit ever, a role he still occupies when we meet him again years later: *the daftest, silliest, clumsiest and untidiest. He had no idea. He had no luck either. If there was a large hole with a great notice beside it saying* Don't fall in here; this

'Have you learned to march
yet?'
'No he bloody hasn't!' [SA]

means you, Lentullus! *Lentullus would home in and tumble head first down the hole.* [SA]

Given to stumbling on horrors, in Germany he is nonetheless brave, swinging on the tail of the mighty aurochs. Back in Rome, he loyally defends Justinus, gaining a near-fatal leg wound which forces him to leave the army. Justinus takes him in, Lentullus strikes up a friendship with Albia, and he may have a future role.

Cornella Flaccida

Wife to the gangster Balbinus, Flaccida was first described as a hard moll: *a short, thin woman, a blonde of sorts, about forty-five. From twenty strides away she would have looked fabulous. At six feet she showed signs of a troubled past. She wore a gown in material so fine its threads were tearing under the weight of its jewelled fastenings. Her face and hair were a triumph of cosmetic attention. But her eyes were restless and suspicious. Her mouth set in a hard straight line. Her hands were too big for her arms. Size mattered here. On both wrists she wore bangles that were trying too hard to tell people how much they cost, and on her fingers two full rows of high-budget rings. Her voice had a smoky rasp that came from a mis-spent life in ill-lit places. She would lie even if there was no reason to do so. Lying was her way of life.* [TTD]

This is a dangerous woman, capable of the worst legal shenanigans and terrible physical cruelty. Soon she is aiming to take over where her husband left off; initially she out-manoeuvres Florius: *scheming to beat him to the profits, a hard-faced bitch whose idea of a quiet hobby was arranging the deaths of men who crossed her.* [THF] We glimpse her, arrayed in finery paid for with cash her late husband secreted away, living with her daughter. *There was a reason why other people stayed honest. Who wants to be parboiled, roasted, skewered through every orifice, and served up trussed in a three-cheese glaze with their internal organs lightly sautéed as a separate piquant relish?* [THF] She furiously tries to prevent Petro's affair with Milvia, no doubt aware of its dangers, but also perhaps trying to stop his influence with Milvia.

She must have thought she
would never be missed, and if
missed never traced ... Once
the narrowness of her escape
hit home, she subsided into
deep shock. [THF]

But Flaccida becomes the victim of a terrible crime herself; she is physically abused and mentally crushed so badly that it will end her brief criminal ascendancy.

Balbina Milvia

She was about twenty, dark, sharp-faced, very pretty. She was dressed in an extremely expensive gown, none too practical for eating pears in a sloppy honey sauce. I doubted whether young Milvia had ever worried about a laundry bill. She saw us without any chaperone, so I could not check whether the maids who wielded the curling tongs in this mansion had to endure being thrashed if they misplaced a ringlet. Milvia had a bright intelligent expression that suggested she could manage staff by guile. Or bribe them, anyway. [TTD]

Neglected by her husband, Florius, Milvia claims to be unaware of the criminal background that supplied her education and luxurious home lifestyle; this innocent bud is fair game for Petronius Longus, who shamelessly has an affair with her. If Petronius forms this liaison in order to spy on the gangsters, he never really articulates that. *I found myself wondering whatever possessed Petro to involve himself with miniature puppets like this: all big trusting eyes and piping little voices, and probably just as deceitful under the heartfelt innocence as the bold, bad girls I once fell for myself ... I wondered whether to tell Milvia about all the others, but it would only give her an opening to assume she was the one who was different. As they all did.* [THF] As Petro's marriage unravels because of her, any innocence Milvia once had disappears. *The truth was, the glitter covered dirt. Milvia could no longer pretend not to know that her finery was financed by theft, extortion, and organised gang violence. She gave me a bad, metallic taste in the mouth.* [THF]

Milvia settles back down with Florius, just as he begins to take over her father's crime empire. I left her positioned where she could reappear if I wanted.

Florius (Gaius Florius Oppicus)

Florius starts as an incidental wimpish character – though gangland families traditionally have a tight bond and I became more interested in him as I wrote. Characters who change are always good value.

First he is *a shapeless lump, too heavy for his own good.* His dress and personal hygiene are neglected; left to his own devices, and with his arranged-for-legal-skulduggery marriage to Milvia faltering, he is an obsessive gambler. *I had seen him scribbling away with his stylus so rapidly that in minutes his squiggly figures filled a whole waxed board.* [TTD] Witnessed surveying his dead father-in-law's properties – a natural equestrian action, thinks Falco – it's in fact a short leap to Florius taking over the crime empire. Falco realises that destroying Balbinus Pius has not destroyed his evil. *I had a dark sensation as Florius loped off with his scrolls and stylus. Maybe I had just witnessed the beginning of another depressing cycle in the endless rise and fall of villains in the underworld ...* [TTD]

I first intended to leave it at that. As I conceived *The Jupiter Myth* (eight years later), I saw how to set up Petronius with an ongoing crime-fighting feud. Florius now poses a much greater threat: *All agree he is vindictive, cruel and out to prevent any attempts by the authorities to interfere.* [JM] Toughened up and running protection rackets and brothels, he is physically unrecognisable: *lean, tanned, and shaven-headed. He wore natty dark brown leather trousers and navvy's boots; he had bare arms tightly tied up with rope bracelets to make the muscles stand out. He looked like any tough from the Subura, and that's a scary look.* [JM] Of course he is a coward. *He may have shaved his head, but he still had all the personality of a dirty rag. He was so scared he was dribbling.* But he fights dirty and, although he normally lets others do his killing, almost to his own surprise, he kills Chloris. He has already debauched and raped Albia. Then his torture of Petronius in the supposed kidnap of Maia is evilly conceived and near-fatal.

Will Petronius Longus ever catch him? You have to have faith that the answer is yes. There must be a book there.

Gloccus and Cotta

Coming on the scene in *One Virgin Too Many*, these monsters of bathroom supply cause gasps of recognition wherever they are mentioned. I am proud to have devised the bastards – aided as I was by enraging encounters with modern tradesmen.

They were late starting; their previous contract overran. They have to keep returning to Rome for more materials – disappearing for the rest of the day. They need money in advance but if you pay them upfront as a courtesy they take advantage and vanish again. I gave them a clear list of what I wanted but every item they supply is different from what I chose. They drink; they gamble, and fight over the results. If I come here to work on other parts of the house, they interrupt me constantly, either asking for refreshments or announcing that I have a problem with the design. Every time I take them to task, they just admit they have let me down in an intolerable fashion, apologise cringingly, promise to apply themselves diligently from now on – then vanish from sight again. [OVTM]

I never had a bathroom contractor who left a dead body under the floor. But it was inevitable Gloccus and Cotta should fire up the plot in *A Body in the Bath House*. There we meet them. Gloccus, in a scruffy old tunic but good boots (stolen from the murder victim) could be anyone who has worked on your house. *He needed a shave and a haircut. He was one of those men who looks as if he never settled, but wears an outsized wedding ring. He was well-built, at least around the midriff; he could be prosperous. He had a direct, friendly air.* [BBH] As Falco prepares to arrest him, Gloccus bolts for freedom and is killed. *I can still hear Gloccus in his dying moments. I mention it purely to give comfort to those of you who have found raw sewage backing up a waste pipe in your new caldarium, three days after your contractors vanished off the site.* [BBH] I wrote the scene for the same reasons.

Next Cotta, disguised as a dentist in an old forge: *The tooth-puller was a skinny stoat, with nervous eyes and thin tufts of hair. He had perfected a manner that must make all his patients terrified ...* Just in time, Falco realises his personal danger, captures the man and tells him he must go to the silver mines to die a slow death.

> *'Falco, what have I ever done to you?'*
> *'Something really criminal. You built my bath house, Cotta' ...* [BBH]

Minas of Karystos

As soon as Aelianus steps off the boat at Piraeus, he is snatched to become a pupil of this gregarious professor: *He earns his money. He takes me to the very best dinner parties, sometimes several in an evening. He introduces fabulous women and exotic boys. He shows me drinking games, dancing girls, flautists, and lyre players – and then we talk. We talk at length, and about all moral issues – though in the morning I remember not a word.* [SDD] There were contemporary complaints about the hard partying of Athenian academics, so don't blame me!

Minas made a curious figure. He was small, elderly and keen, like a grandfather taking his grandsons to a stadium. He wore a long tunic in a gaudy hue, with a six-inch embroidered border in which precious metal glinted. Beneath a neatly placed wreath of flowers, grey hair hung in wet straggles. [SDD] He manages to organise a party where the killer will be revealed: *'It is a long while since I conducted a murder trial.'* *He was planning to enjoy it.* [SDD] When he comes to Rome, intent on social advancement, he behaves like a drunk until the senator is being subjected to a house search. Minas rallies (in order to advertise himself to neighbours): *He rushed from a late breakfast to pronounce loudly on the rights of a citizen to live without interference. Unbeknown to us previously, he was a populist democrat, fiery on the subject. Even with omelette in his curly beard, he was good.* [NM]

We never see his wife, but his daughter **Hosidia Meline** appears in *Nemesis* when Minas arrives in Rome. Her presence causes Albia much grief.

The Vestal Constantia

Constantia was a game girl. So friendly, in fact, that in the confines of my home, I preferred not to mention her. [AC]

Constantia approached the ancient watering hole with the stately gait that her sisterhood cultivates. Carrying a water vessel on the head certainly draws attention to a full womanly figure … She looked to be in her early twenties. She must have completed the first ten years of learning her duties and was now equipped to carry them out in a reverential – though slightly distracting – style. [OVTM] From the moment she slips on moss and lets out an expletive, we know this young lady is a tease and a terror, not above groping an innocent man who just happens to be hiding with her in a dark secluded place. Personally I am shocked and distressed to have to write about such scandalous behaviour.

She made an impression on Falco; he mentions her with slightly nervous recollection in *The Accusers*.

Aedemon

Aedemon, an Egyptian from Alexandria, *weighed about three hundred and sixty pounds. Like many overweight men, he gave no sign of recognising that he was enormous. He was an empiricist. He believed all disease started in the bowels. The only cure was purging and fasting. He had a square, dark-skinned face with lightly crinkled hair, but almost European features. He seemed honest, and perhaps he was, yet he gave the impression he was alien and devious.* [SA]

He returns to Alexandria to join the academic board of the Museion, giving Falco useful advice about the victim and suspects when the Librarian is killed.

Nothokleptes

Dr Jenny March assured me the nickname means *thieving bastard* in Greek.

Falco's banker, who would probably describe himself as put-upon and patient, haunts the series, but only really appears in *Ode to a Banker: He was seedy and suspicious, just about convincing as a Roman citizen, yet by birth probably Alexandrian. A heavy man, with jowls that were designed for pegging a napkin under his chin. He spent a lot of time at his barber's where you could find him at ease as if the shaving chair were an extension of his business premises.*

Falco hires a bank box from Nothokleptes which contains important documents like his legionary discharge but often not much else. *We had held many conversations about whether it was even worth my while to pay the hire-fee. On these difficult occasions, Nothokleptes had impressed me with both his commonsense and his ferociously unyielding attitude. Like many men who wield power over unfortunates, he looked like a soft slob who would never find the energy to come down on them. How wrong that was … He enjoyed handling money the way tailors fondle cloth.* [OB]

In *Nemesis,* Nothokleptes claims he always knew Falco would come good, though for nineteen books it must be merely a fond hope.

Place

Place is extremely important both to Falco as a Roman and to me as a writer. Our maps have to be crude at this size, but at readers' request I have included a Gazeteer by province/country.

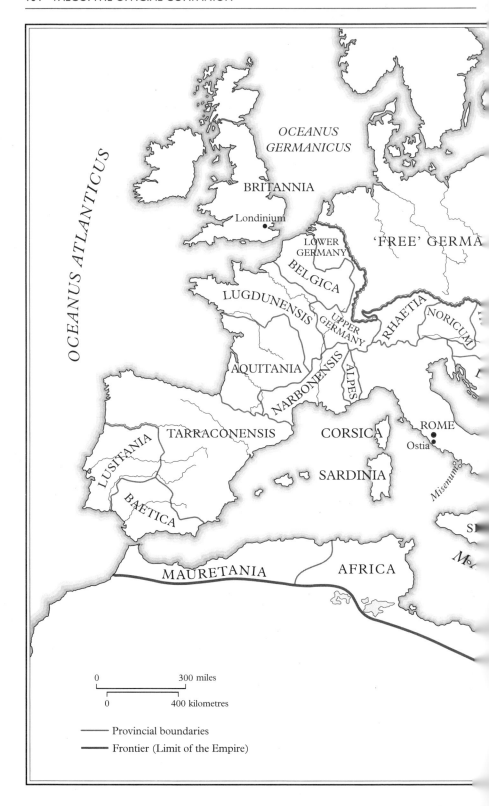

The Roman Empire

N
SPQR

PONTUS EUXINUS

OESIA

THRACIA

ACEDONIA

PIRUS

ACHAIA

ASIA

PONTUS et BETHYNIA

GALATIA

LYCIA

CILICIA

CAPPADOCIA

ARMENIA

PARTHIA

SYRIA

Athena

RHODUS

CYPRUS

CRETA

JUDAEA

TERNUM

Alexandria

ARABIA

CYRENAÏCA

AEGYPTUS

SINUS ARABICUS

Gazetteer with Modern English Place Names

Achaia (Greece)

'What's the attraction in Athens?' 'You mean apart from art, history, language and philosophy?' [SDD]

Alphaios	River Alpheus
Athenae	Athens
Chaironia	Chaeronea
Copais	(lake now drained) Kopaida plain
Corinthos	Corinth
Delphi	Delphi
Dodona	Dodone
Elis	Elis (Ilia)
Epidauros	Epidavros
Helike	Mount Helicon
Hercyna	River Herkyna
Itea	Itea
Karystos	Karystos
Kenchreai	Kenchreai (eastern Corinth)
Lebadeia	Levadhia
Lechaion	Lechaion (western Corinth)
Letrinoi	Pyrgos
Megara	Megara
Olympia	Olympia
Patrae	Patras
Pheia	Feia
Piraeus	Piraeus
Rhodus	Rhodes
Tegea	Alea

Aegyptus (Egypt)

Alexandria	Alexandria
Crocodilopolis (Arsinoe)	Medinet El-Fayum
Giza (Babylon)	Cairo
Heliopolis	Heliopolis
Lake Mareotis	Lake Mariout
Naucratis	Naucratis (Kom Gi'eif)
Nicopolis	Nicopolis

Africa Proconsularis

Carthago	Carthage
Cydame	Ghadames
Lepcis Magna	Lepcis Magna
Marcomades	Sirte
Oea	Tripoli
Sabratha	Zouagha

Arabia Felix

Yemen

Arabia Nabataea

Bostra	Bosra
Canatha	Qanawat
Petra	Petra

Batavia

The Island	The Rhine Delta area (Netherlands)
Noviomagus Batavodurum	Nijmegen

Belgica

Augusta Treverorum	Trier

Britannia

Britain, where whichever way you turned, somehow the filthy weather always met you in the face. (SB)

Abona	Sea Mills, Avon
Aestuarium Sabrinae	Bristol Channel
Aquae Sulis	Bath
Camulodunum	Colchester
Dubris	Dover
Durnovaria	Dorchester
Eboracum	York
Fretum Gallicum	Straits of Dover
Glevum	Gloucester
Isca Dumnoniorum	Exeter
Lindum	Lincoln
Londinium	London
Mona	Anglesey
Oceanus Britannicus	English Channel
Rutupiae	Richborough

Sabrina	River Severn
Tamesis	River Thames
Vebiodunum (deduced from Veb …)	Charterhouse (in the Mendips)
Vectis Insula	Isle of Wight
Verulamium	St Albans
Viroconium	Wroxeter

Chersonesis Taurica (the Crimea)

It was a terrible place to be sent. If he wasn't eaten by brown bears, he would die of cold or boredom, and however much money he managed to take with him, there were no luxuries to spend it on … [TTD]

Commagene

'Stuff Commagene' (a small, previously autonomous kingdom) … [LAP]

Crete and Cyrenaïca

Antipyrgos	Tobruk
Apollonia	Marsa Susah
Berenice (Euesperides)	Benghazi
Cyrene	Shahhat
Ptolomais	Tolmeitha
Tocra	Teuchira

Dalmatia (former Yugoslavia)

Istria	Istria
Narona	Viol, Croatia
Pola	Pula
Pucinum	Sovinjak
Salonae	Split

Gallia (France)

That's as in 'Caesar divided Gaul into three parts', which every schoolboy is compelled to know … The Gauls have a crazy standard of values. They are wine-mad and spend like lunatics in the quest for liquor … [IHM]

Arelate	Arles
Cavillonum	Châlon-sur-Saône
Durocortorum	Reims

Gesoriacum	Boulogne
Lugdunum	Lyons
Massilia	Marseilles
Mosa	River Meuse
Narbo	Narbonne
Rhodanus	River Rhône
Valentia	Valence
Vienna	Vienne

Germania Libera (east of the Rhine)

Endless tracts of territory where 'free' meant not only free from Roman commercial influence, but with a complete lack of Roman law and order too ... [IHM]

Castellum Mattiacorum	Mainz-Castel
Flevo Lacus	The Zuiderzee
Lupia Flumen	River Lippe

Germania Superior and Inferior
(west of the Rhine)

Geographically, what Rome calls Germany is the eastern flank of Gaul. Sixty years ago, Augustus had decided not to advance across the natural boundary of the great River Rhenus, a decision forced out of him by the Quinctilius Varus disaster ... Even so long after the massacre, I myself felt extreme reluctance to spend time where it had occurred ... [IHM]

Argentoratum	Strasbourg
Asciburgium	Asburg
Bonna	Bonne
Borbetomagus	Worms
Castrum ad Confluentes	Koblenz
Colonia Claudia Ara Agrippinensium	Cologne
Gelduba	Gellep
Moenus	River Main
Moguntiatum	Mainz
Mosella	River Moselle
Novaesium	Neuss
Noviomagus	Neumagen
Rhenus	River Rhine
Rigodulum	Riol
Vetera	Xanten

Hispania (Spain)

I had never been to Barcino. I had no idea what
Barcino was storing up for me ... [DLC]

Astigi	Ecja
Baetis	River Guadalquivir
Barcino	Barcelona
Cartago Nova	Cartagena
Castulo	Caslona
Corduba	Cordoba
Empuriae	Empuries
Fretum Gaditanum	Straits of Gibraltar
Gades	Cadiz
Hispalis	Seville
Iluro	Mataro
Italica	Santiponce
Malaca	Malaga
Montes Mariana	Sierra Morena
Sisapo	La Bienvenida
Tarraco	Tarragona
Turris Caepionis	Chipiona
Valentia	Valencia

Italia

Antium	Anzio
Arretinum	Arezzo
Augusta Taurinorum	Turin
Baiae	Baia
Bedriacum	Tornata (though often called Cremona)
Bruttium	Calabria
Buxentum	Policastro di Santa Marina
Cape Colonna	Capo Colonna
Capreae	Isle of Capri
Capua	Santa Maria di Capua Antica
Circeii	San Felice Circeo
Cosentia	Cosenza
Croton	Crotone
Formiae	Formia
Fregellae	Ceprano
Fundi	Fondi
Herculaneum	Hercolano
Lactarii Montes	Lattari Mountains

Lanuvium	Lanuvio
Latium	Lazio
Lepini Montes	Volscian Mountains
Magna Graecia	'Greater Greece' (Southern Italy)
Melita	Malta
Misenum	Capo di Miseno
Neaethus	River Nieto
Neapolis	Napoli/Naples
Nola	Nola
Norba	Norma
Nuceria	Nocera
Oplontis	Torre Annunciata
Ostia/Portus	Ostia Antica/Fiumicino
Paestum	Paestum
Pompeii	Pompeii
Praeneste	Palestrina
Puteoli	Pozzuoli
Ravenna	Ravenna
Rhegium	Reggio
Roma	**Rome**
Salernum	Salerno
Satricum	Le Ferriere
Scylacium, Gulf of	Squillace
Sila Plain	La Sila
Stabiae	Stabia
Surrentum	Sorrento
Sybaris	Corigliano
Tarentum	Tarento
Tarracina	Terracina
Tibur	Tivoli
Tusculum	Tusculo (Frascati)
Veii	Veii
Velia	Velia/Elea
Volsiniensis Lacus	Lake Bolsena
Vulturnus	River Volturnus

Pontus and Bythinia (Turkey)

Pessinus	Ballihisar

Syria

Abana	River Barada
Antiocha	Antioch

Beroia	Aleppo
Bethel	Beitin
Emesa	Homs
Epiphania	Hama
Mount Hermon	Mount Hermon (Jabal al Sheikh)
Orontes	River Orontes
Palmyra/Tadmor	Palmyra
Sidon	Sidon/Saida
Tiberias Lacus	Lake Tiberias/Sea of Galilee
Tyre	Tyre

The Decapolis

... a Greek federation in central Syria ... whichever order you flog around these ten gracious metropolitan sites, she's bound to be in the last town you visit ...
[LAP]

Abila (Seleucia) *(not officially in the league)*	Hartha
Canatha	Qanawat
Capitolias	Beit Ras
Damascus	Damascus
Dium, Dion	? Aydoun
Gadara, 'The Athens of the East' *(for Athens, see Greece)*	Umm Qais
Gerasa	Jerash
Hippos	Sussita
Pella	Tabaqat Fahl
Philadelphia	Amman
Scythopolis (Nysa)	Beth Shean
Tiberias	Tiberias

Map of Rome, City and Vigiles Jurisdictions

People like to point out that the line around this map appears to be the Aurelian Walls, which were built later than the First Century. Please take the word of a bureaucrat: when Augustus defined the fourteen regions, their outer boundaries were indicated by a line on the map. Rome always had an outside edge, which administrators could ink in, between the gates, just as we do here.

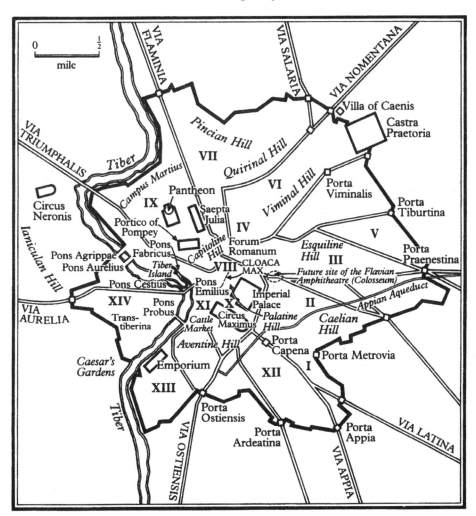

Jurisdictions of the Vigiles Cohorts in Rome
Coh I Regions VII & VIII (via Lata, Forum Romanum)
Coh II Regions III & V (Isis and Serapis, Esquiline)
Coh III Regions IV & VI (Temple of Peace, Alta Semita)
Coh IV Regions XII & XIII (Piscina Publica, Aventine)
Coh V Regions I & II (Porta Capena, Caelimontium)
Coh VI Regions X & XI (Palatine, Circus Maximus)
Coh VII Regions IX & XIV (Circus Flaminius, Transtiberina)

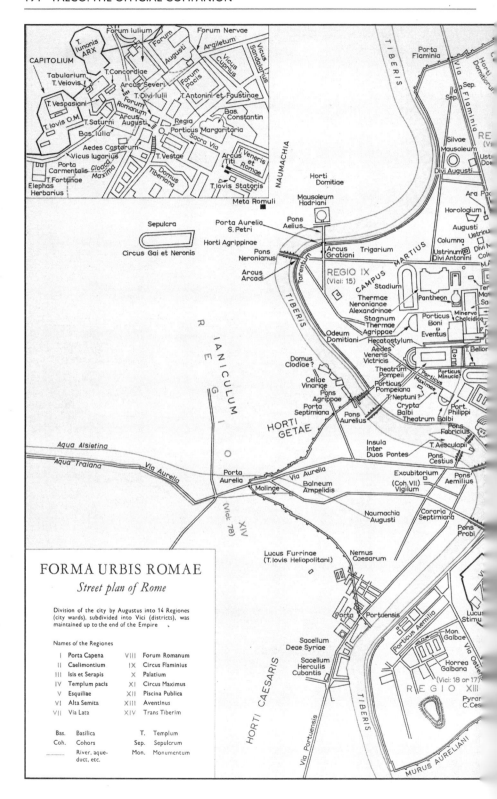

FORMA URBIS ROMAE
Street plan of Rome

Division of the city by Augustus into 14 Regiones (city wards), subdivided into Vici (districts), was maintained up to the end of the Empire

Names of the Regiones

I	Porta Capena	VIII	Forum Romanum
II	Caelimontium	IX	Circus Flaminius
III	Isis et Serapis	X	Palatium
IV	Templum pacis	XI	Circus Maximus
V	Esquiliae	XII	Piscina Publica
VI	Alta Semita	XIII	Aventinus
VII	Via Lata	XIV	Trans Tiberim

Bas.	Basilica	T.	Templum
Coh.	Cohors	Sep.	Sepulcrum
———	River, aqueduct, etc.	Mon.	Monumentum

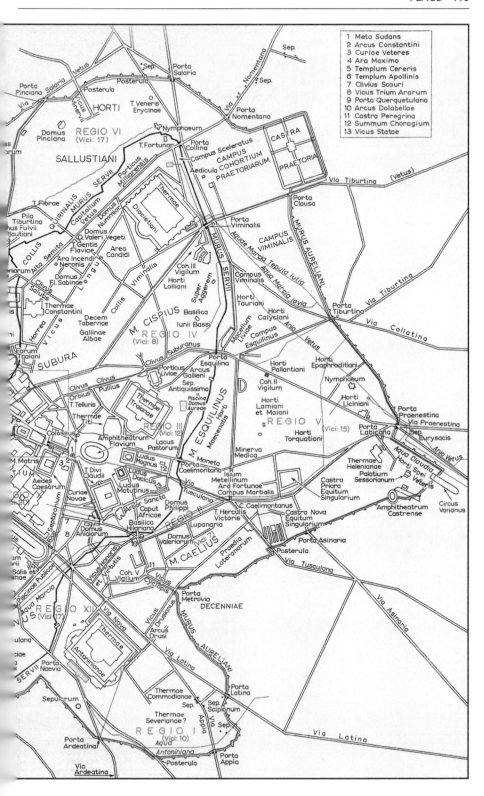

1 Meta Sudans
2 Arcus Constantini
3 Curiae Veteres
4 Ara Maxima
5 Templum Cereris
6 Templum Apollinis
7 Clivius Scauri
8 Vicus Trium Ararum
9 Porta Querquetulana
10 Arcus Dolabellae
11 Castra Peregrina
12 Summum Choragium
13 Vicus Statae

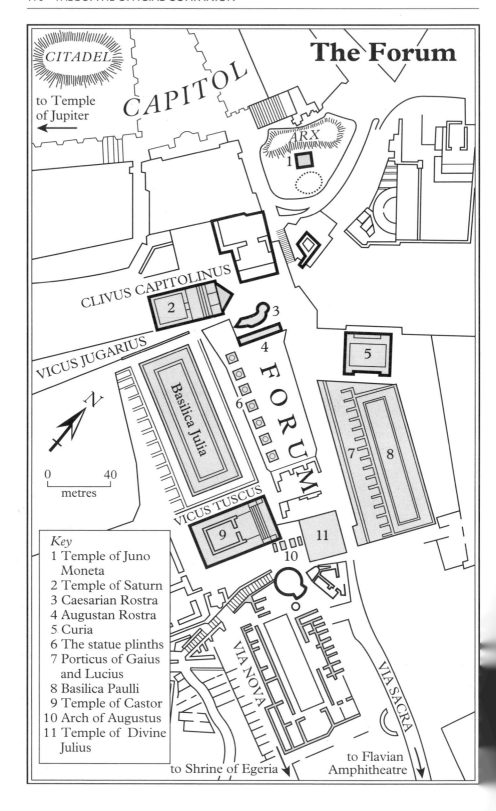

CITADEL

The Forum

to Temple
of Jupiter ←

CAPITOL

ARX

1

CLIVUS CAPITOLINUS

2

3

4

5

VICUS JUGARIUS

Basilica Julia

N

6

F O R U M

7   8

0   40
metres

VICUS TUSCUS

9

11

10

Key
1 Temple of Juno
  Moneta
2 Temple of Saturn
3 Caesarian Rostra
4 Augustan Rostra
5 Curia
6 The statue plinths
7 Porticus of Gaius
  and Lucius
8 Basilica Paulli
9 Temple of Castor
10 Arch of Augustus
11 Temple of Divine
   Julius

VIA NOVA

VIA SACRA

to Shrine of Egeria ↓

to Flavian
Amphitheatre ↓

Falco's Rome

Imperial Rome was continually forced to juxtapose her splendid monuments to an incoherent confusion of dwelling houses at once pretentious and uncomfortable, fragile and inordinately large, separated by a network of gloomy, narrow alleys. When we try to reconstruct ancient Rome in our imagination, we are ever and again disconcerted by the contrast of modern spaciousness with primitive medieval simplicity, an anticipation of orderliness that is almost American with the confusion of an oriental labyrinth.
CARCOPINO

It is very important to me to give a sense of a city in flux. There was a conscious decision to mend the destruction of the civil wars, when buildings that were central to the Roman psyche had been lost from a once-famous skyline. New monuments began to rise

Aerial view over Rome, from the south east [Rome Reborn]

too. It makes a good background for crime novels. As the city changes, people see an opportunity to shake up their lives, to strive for something better, by fair means or foul ...

Roma Resurgens

Vespasian's campaign to restore the city and empire was called Roma Resurgens. *Rome itself was to be rebuilt, its most famous monuments meticulously restored while carefully chosen additions to the national heritage would be positioned at suitable spots: a Temple of Peace, nicely balancing a Temple of Mars; the Flavian arena; an arch here; a forum there; with a tasteful number of fountains, statues, public libraries and baths.* [PG]

Creating Falco's Rome starts with the physical: *the temples and fountains, the astonishing height of the gimcrack apartments, the arrogance of the sophisticated slaves who barged along the highroad, the drips on my head where my road dived under the gloom of an aqueduct ...* [SB] I have learned which buildings were contemporary, though sometimes I slip up; people are most helpful in alerting me. I add colour either through the people present or, so often, through smells – for which, apparently, I am famous: *stale garments and fresh tempers, a sweet tang of myrrh among the sour reek of brothels, a fresh hint of oregano above the old and indelible reek of the fish market.* [SB]

Falco's love of Rome

Falco is completely devoted to his home city. Nowhere is this so apparent as when he leaves it and grows homesick. He romanticises: *I was sick of stones in my shoes and the raw smell of camels' breath. I wanted glorious monuments and dubious fish that tasted of Tiber grit, and to eat it gazing over the river from my own grubby nook on the Aventine while waiting for an old friend to knock on the door. I wanted to breathe garlic at an aedile. I wanted to stamp on a banker. I wanted to hear that solid roar that slams across*

Chariot race scene

the racecourse at the Circus Maximus. I wanted spectacular scandals and gigantic criminality. I wanted to be amazed by size and sordidness. I wanted to go home. [LAP] Stuck in Britain, in *A Body in the Bath House* and *The Jupiter Myth* he shows his homesickness several times, especially when comparing the civic deficiencies of Londinium with Rome.

Here, in a bit of a jumble, because I see no way to be more organised, are places we have seen with him.

The Aventine Hill

The Aventine was partly in the Thirteenth region, where Falco lives, and partly the Twelfth, where Helena's family are.

Once it had lain outside the pomerium, *the official city boundary that had been ploughed out by Romulus. That original exclusion had allowed the positioning here of shrines that possessed for our forefathers a remote, out-of-town mystique; in the quieter squares of the modern Aventine they still maintained their historical air of privacy ... We who lived here now could still see the river and the distant hills, or in open spaces feel close to the sky and the moon.* [OB]

The Aventine today is a very quiet, gracious suburban area. The big church of Santa Sabina dominates on the northern side, alongside which are the Gardens of the Orange Trees, where I like to go to look at the view across the river or sit in the sun. In Roman times, plebeians were allowed to buy freeholds on the Aventine, which is why I gave it that teeming character. You can still climb up from beside the Circus Maximus on the Clivus Publicius.

There were many great temples, including those of Ceres, Diana, Venus, Isis, the Sun and Moon, Mercury, the seasonal god Vertumnus, and Liberty, which was where freed slaves traditionally congregated to celebrate their liberty (wearing the Phrygian caps that much later were associated with the French Revolution). Minerva, goddess of reason and the arts, had a temple here, home of the Writers' and Actors' Guild. The Bona Dea, whose mystical, orgiastic cult was reserved for women and notorious among men, had a grotto on the Aventine.

Fountain Court

(which had never possessed a fountain and wasn't a court) ...
[SB]

This is an invented location. I cannot place it on a map. You will not find it on the modern Aventine.

Streetscene
[Rome Reborn]

Stay in Rome or any other big, sunny city. Go to the alley at the back of your hotel. Stand quietly in the narrow space between tall, multi-occupied buildings; listen to people you cannot see, as they go about their lives nearby. Look at the washing lines, discarded crates and gutter-litter. Sniff, if you dare. Here; you've found it.

Of all the groaning tenements in all the sordid city alley-ways, the most degrading must be Fountain Court. It was five minutes off the great road from Ostia, one of the most vital highways in the Empire, but this ulcerous spot in the armpit of the Aventine could have been a different world. Up above, on the double crests of the Hill, were the great temples of Diana and Venus, but we lived too close to see their lofty architecture from our deep, dark warren of aimless, nameless lanes. It was cheap (for Rome). Some of us would have paid the landlord more just to have him hire a pair of competent bailiffs to evict us into the fresher air of a better street ... [VC]

It is narrow, dank and dirty, full of dubious smells, morose people and decrepit small businesses: we know the laundry, a funeral parlour, barber's, basket weaver's, baker's, a rope-maker, ink-making and poultry-keeping. People lead sorry lives: *Even in the dead of night there was usually some husband receiving brain damage from* an iron pot, a pigeon being tortured by delinquent youths, or an old woman screaming that she had been robbed of her life savings ... [PG] And they are imbued with curiosity: *You couldn't squeeze a pimple in Fountain Court without three people telling you to leave yourself alone.* [TTD] It might be good to think there is local loyalty, but Falco says everyone who lives there is trying to leave.

He and Petro revisit for a mournful scene: *This was a lonely place, a sordid place, a noisy, half-derelict heart-breaking location ... But in this backstreet byway a man who lay low could be ignored by the world.* [ST] In *Nemesis*, the apartment which has been so many kinds of refuge comes into its own again.

Falco's apartment

You won't find this, either – just be grateful!

A striking discovery of my early research was that, with land at a premium and a poverty-stricken multitude, Rome was not all white marble temples and mansions, but full of crowded apartment buildings. *Two apartments per storey, two or three rooms per apartment, two and a half families per dwelling and as many as five or six people to a room. Sometimes there were fewer occupants, but they ran a business, like the mirror-polisher and the tailor. Sometimes one room contained an old lady, who had been the original tenant, now almost forgotten among the rumbustious invaders to whom Smaractus had sublet parts of her home 'to help her with the rent'.* [TTD]

One of these tenements, crumbling and exposed like a bombed building in my childhood, hangs tentatively on the Capitol today. Archaeology has produced many, with identically arranged flats and cramped common areas, generally with commercial premises at ground level, like Lenia's Laundry. After the Great Fire, Nero decreed that six was the maximum number of storeys allowed.

From the beginning, we are under no illusions; Falco has *two rooms on the sixth floor of a dank tenement where only the dirt and dead bedbugs were cementing together the walls.* [SP] I allude to both ancient and modern literature, beginning with Juvenal's *If the alarm goes at ground level, the last to fry will be the attic tenant, way up among the nesting pigeons, with nothing but tiles between him and the weather.* Raymond Chandler's Philip Marlowe is a lessee in Los Angeles: *I had an office in the Cahuenga Building, sixth floor, two small rooms at the back. One I left open for a patient client to sit in if I had a patient client … I looked in the reception room. It was empty of everything except the smell of dust. Three hard chairs and a swivel chair, flat desk with a glass top, five green filing cases, three of them full of nothing, a calendar, and a framed license on the wall, a washbowl in a stained wooden cupboard, a hatrack, a carpet that was just something on the floor, and two open windows with net curtains that puckered in and out like the lips of a toothless old man sleeping: not beautiful, not gay, but better than a tent on the beach.*

Fumbling to provide a Roman equivalent, I gave a nod to this famous passage, using archaeology: *There was an outer room in which a dog might just turn round, if he was a thin dog with his tail between his legs. A wonky table, a slanty bench, a shelf of pots, a bank of bricks I used as a cooking stove, a gridiron, winejars (empty), a rubbish bucket (full). One way out to the balcony for when you got tired of stamping on the cockroaches indoors, plus a second opening behind a curtain in bright welcoming stripes; this led to the bedroom.* [SP] Under the floorboards is Falco's wine stash. That small balcony outside becomes the scene of many poignant moments in the series. He pees off it illegally. A gecko lives on the ceiling, tolerated, unlike the cockroaches. A tile on the outside landing advertises Falco.

Even when he and Helena obtain better conditions, Falco retains his apartment. It is his office while he lives opposite. It provides Petronius with a temporary home, shelters Justinus and will be a refuge for Albia. Every time Falco returns, it provides moving nostalgia for him and us.

The Eagle Laundry, Fountain Court

Many Roman dwellings incorporated commercial premises … *the cut-price, clothes-stealing wash-shop which occupied the ground floor of our building.* [IHM] We see Lenia's laundry in many of the books, often briefly. It provided that particularly fascinating detail: human urine was used by fullers – to fix dyes – and by laundries; Vespasian imposed a lucrative tax on it (see Historical Characters).

Flora's Caupona

Flora's made the average seedy snack shop look chic and hygienic. It squatted on the corner where a dingy lane down from the Aventine met a dirty track up from the wharves. It had the usual arrangement with two counters, set at right angles for people in the two streets to lean on reflectively while they waited to be poisoned. The counters were made from a rough patchwork of white and grey stone ... each had three circular holes to take cauldrons of food. [PG] *Sinister stews in anaemic hues, thickened with what seemed to be a mix of lentils and pavement dust. As the lukewarm pots fermented, from time to time half a gherkin or a lump of turnip would pop up through the slime, then softly sink to its death.* [SA]

You can see remains of street bars at archaeological sites. Flora's has the staple furnishings: tables and benches, a barrel outside, a rack of amphorae, a shelf of beakers and a price list of wines written on one wall. At the back is a kitchen, where the waiter lives; sometimes lodgers hire tiny rooms upstairs. A horrible cat called **Stringy** lurks, *with a fat brindled tail and an unpleasant leer;* when first seen he is sturdy but later becomes older and emaciated. I love describing the food, a chance to dwell

A caupona waitress, expecting a large tip

on ghastliness – and to remember a favourite snack bar when I was a civil servant; the paint-stripper Brie sandwich with grey mayonnaise was unforgettable.

Flora's is a watering hole for Falco's brother Festus, for Petronius Longus on his way home from a shift, sometimes for Falco himself. We first encounter it in *Poseidon's Gold,* where Falco indignantly learns the owner is his father's girlfriend. After Epimandos dies, the thankless task of waiter passes to Falco's run-down ex-teacher, Apollonius. After Flora's death, Falco's unsuitable sister Junia runs the place. We can assume it will stay in the family.

The Valerian

Opposite Flora's is a much better run, well-scrubbed but much less popular caupona. *The Valerian had a quiet atmosphere and quite good wine ...* [PG] But *Nobody went there.* * *People were afraid the cleanliness would give them hives. Besides, when nobody goes to a place there is no atmosphere.* [OB]

* Author's note: wrong, Apollonius wisely eats there!

The River Embankment

Below the Aventine, the south bank of the Tiber was reinforced with an embankment, much as today, though without thundering motor traffic. You can still see the outlet of the **Cloaca Maxima**, the Great Drain built in Etruscan times to carry away water from the marsh area of the Forum. This features in *The Silver Pigs* and again in *Three Hands in the Fountain.* Once he lives in Pa's old house, Falco often walks along the Marble Embankment. On unavoidable occasions, he meets his brother-in-law Lollius, the water-boatman, there.

Pa's house, which eventually becomes Falco and Helena's settled home, is a narrow town house, prone to flooding. I have imagined layout and decor – for instance the salon with battered antique furniture where Falco and Helena impress the travel agent in *See Delphi and Die.* Its roof terrace is a favourite hideaway, also useful for observing Anacrites' men's antics. Then as now, Romans decorated their houses with plants. *It had troughs filled with plants, bulbs, even small trees. Shaped trellises were curtained with roses and ivy. At the parapet more roses were trained along chains like garlands. There between*

Rome had been founded upstream on high ground at the earliest bridgeable point on the Tiber – but that presupposed ours was a useful river. Romulus was a shepherd. How would he know? Compared with the grandiose waterways in most major provincial capitals, old Father Tiber was a widdle of rat's piss. [STH]

The Cloaca Maxima and its brother under the Circus kept the centre of Rome habitable and its institutions working. The Great Drain sucked down standing and surface water, the overflow from fountains and aqueducts, sewage and rainwater. [THF]

tubs of box trees, stood two lion-ended seats, providing a vista across the water to Caesar's Gardens, the Transtiberina, the whale-backed ridge of the Janiculan ... [PG]

Falco, who once used to brood on the Embankment, takes a particularly lonely decision here on his own rooftop, at the start of *Nemesis*.

The Emporium

Into her three ports of Ostia, Portus, and the emporium beneath the Aventine poured the tiles and bricks, the wines and fruits of Italy; the corn of Egypt and Africa; the oil of Spain; the venison, the timbers and the wool of Gaul; the cured meats of Baetica; the dates of the oases; the marbles of Tuscany, of Greece and of Numidia; the porphyries of the Arabian desert; the lead, silver and copper of the Iberian peninsula; the ivory of the Syrtes and the Mauretanias, the gold of Dalmatia and of Dacia; the tin of the Cassiterides, now the Scilly Isles, and the amber of the Baltic; the papyri of the valley of the Nile; the glass of Phoenicia and of Syria; the stuffs of the Orient; the incense of Arabia; the spices, the corals and the gems of India; the silks of the Far East.
CARCOPINO

The Emporium, which incorporated an earlier store called the Aemilian Portico, was a long, secure building on the Embankment. Here barges from Ostia brought every kind of import. Scenes from several novels in the series take place at the Emporium, which lies close to Pa's house. *You can smell it from the water. A blind man would know he had arrived. Here anything buildable, wearable or edible that is produced in any province of the Empire comes to be unloaded at the teeming wharves. The slick stevedores, who are renowned for their filthy tempers and flash off-duty clothing, then crash the goods onto handcarts, dump them in baskets, or wheel about with great sacks on their shoulders, ferrying them inside the greatest indoor market in the world. Cynical sales are conducted, and before the importer has realised he has been rooked by the most devious middlemen in Europe, everything whirls out again to destinations in workshops, warehouses, country estates or private homes. The moneychangers wear happy smiles all day ...* [TTD].

Balbinus Pius organises a raid, after which Petronius gets into trouble for closing the place. Falco makes enquiries in the German trading community in *Saturnalia*.

The Forum Boarium

The meat market, close to the river and near the starting gate end of the Circus Maximus, with its rough traders and smell of dried animal blood, makes a frequently apt scene. Ideas for the smell and atmosphere come from a street of butchers' stalls near the Piazza Vittorio Emmanuele, where at one time Richard and I used to stay. *There must have been a landing place and a market here since long before Romulus grew up and identified the Seven Hills as an ideal development site.* [TTD] The corpse in a gangster killing is found there in *Time to Depart;* another scene occurs in *Saturnalia*, where the Praetorian Guards get short shrift from the butchers' wives.

Two exquisite Roman temples have survived nearby, their dedications uncertain but now identified as most likely a Temple of harbour god Portunus (the rectangular one) and the round Temple of Hercules Victor.

The Circus Maximus

The four-horse chariot of the Blues,
When Catianus plies the whip,
Drops back – to win the bribe and lose
The race. Consummate jockeyship!
MARTIAL

Today, as in Roman times, the huge long hollow of the Circus lies between the Aventine and Palatine Hills, an inescapable barrier to walkers.

Prostitutes haunted the colonnades; they were called 'night moths'. *Filling the outer vaults was the usual scene of deplorable commerce, a strange contrast to the delicacy of the paintings and gilt decoration which adorned the stucco and the stonework under the arcades. In the cookshops and liquor stalls*

View from Lower Aventine, across the Circus Maximus, with Capitol and Palatine behind. [Rome Reborn]

the hot pies were lukewarm and greasy, and the cool drinks came in very small containers at twice the price you would pay outside. The loose women were plying for hire noisily, vying with the bookies' touts for spectators who were still trickling out ... I entered by one of the gates on the Aventine side. I had the president's box to my far left above the starting gates, the glittering imperial balcony immediately opposite me against the Palatine Hill, then the apsidal end with the triumphal exit away to my right. The dazzle off the first two tiers of marble seats was sizzling hot by then, and even in the lull at lunchtime I was met by a wall of sound ... [SB]

The Capena Gate

One of the oldest gates, inside the city by Falco's time, where two aqueducts, the Appian and Marcian (which were notoriously leaky), crossed. This is where the senator lives, Helena's family home. *The Camilli owned a pair of houses near the Capena Gate. They had all the amenities of the nearby busy area around the Via Appia, but were ensconced in a private insula off a back street where only the upper classes were welcome. I could never have lived there. The neighbours were all too nosy about everyone else's business. And someone was always having an aedile or a praetor to dinner, so people had to keep the pavements clean lest their highly superior enclave be officially criticised.* [THF]

This was close to the sacred spring where the Vestals filled their water jugs; so in *One Virgin Too Many* it is where Constantia slips on the moss and says a rude word.

The Forum Romanum

It was the usual scene in the Forum. We had the Record Office and Capitol Hill hard above us on the left; to the right the Courts, and the Temple of Castor further down the Sacred Way. Opposite, beyond the white marble rostrum, stood the Senate House. All the porticos were crammed with butchers and bankers, all the open spaces filled with sweaty crowds, mainly men. The piazza rang with the curses of strings of slaves crisscrossing like a badly organised military display. The air simmered with the reek of garlic and hair pomade. [SP]

The main Forum was absolutely crowded with temples and other buildings, so that many emperors built new fora alongside to act as overflows. At the **Temple of Venus Genetrix** in the **Forum of Caesar**, Falco has a bad experience being picked up, then later dumped semi-conscious, by the crook Priscillus in *Venus in Copper.*

Almost every book set in Rome has scenes in the Forum Romanum.

View of the northern end of the Forum [Rome Reborn]

The Tabularium

This partly survives below the Campidoglio; we think it was the record office. On its wall, in *The Iron Hand of Mars,* Falco chalks up his advertisement, after washing off a candidate's election puffs from the Manicure Girls at the Agrippan Baths.

Didius Falco
For All Discreet
Enquiries + Legal
Or Domestic
Good Refs + Cheap
Rates
At Eagle Laundry
Fountain Court

The Temple of Saturn

The series begins with Falco on the steps of this important temple, where the Treasury was housed in the base-
ment. As he and Sosia rush inside to escape her
pursuers, he mentions the dignified beauty of the Ionic
portico; eight columns and part of the portico remain.
The cult statue is supposed to have been wooden, and
filled with oil, a fact I had fun with ... This is the scene
of the *lectisternium,* or outdoor public banquet for the
god, in *Saturnalia.*

Forum; the remains of the
Temples of Saturn and of
Castor and Pollux

The Temple of Castor and Pollux

Often shortened to omit Pollux; three columns still
stand in lonely grandeur. Falco's favourite bath house
and Glaucus' Gym are around the back of this very old
temple, which commemorated a myth that after assist-
ing the Romans at a battle, the Dioscuri had watered
their horses in the Forum. The **Basin of Juturna** was

the sacred spring where this happened; it is glimpsed briefly in *Three Hands in the Fountain*, as is the **Arch of Augustus**, one of the sites where speeches could be made, a kind of Hyde Park Corner. Falco seems unimpressed by the principle of free rhetoric: *there various hotheads waved their arms as if they were trying to lose a few pounds while they declaimed against the government in a manner that could land them in jail being beaten up by unwashed guards – another offence against their liberty to roar about. Some of them wanted to be philosophers – all long hair, bare feet and hairy blankets – which in Rome was a sure way to be regarded as dangerous. But I also noticed cautious souls who had taken care to come out girded with water gourds and satchels of lunch.* [THF] In the same passage he also mentions the ancient **Shrine of Venus Cloacina**. You can spend a lot of time wandering around the Forum today, trying to pinpoint these features. Sometimes they are labelled (often the labelling is disputed by scholars …)

Glaucus' Gym

Establishments like this were meant to be sociable, like sports clubs today; Falco's choice has a strict entrance policy, and sounds like an enlightened gentleman's club. *The one I used was run by an intelligent Cilician called Glaucus. It had the unusual distinction of being respectable. Glaucus kept a casual exercise ground where likeable citizens brought their bodies up to scratch with their minds (which were on the whole quite good), then enjoyed pleasant conversation in his bath house afterwards. There were clean towels, a small library in the colonnade, and an excellent pastry shop beside the portico steps.* [SP]

It has the usual manicure girls, a sneery barber, and a huge, pain-inducing masseur from Tarsus. We learn more: the gym *usually stayed open until after dinner time. It was well lit, with pottery lamps lining all the corridors, yet at this time of night the place assumed a certain eeriness. There were attendants lurking somewhere who would scrape you with a strigil if you wanted to shout out to them, yet most people who came at dusk managed alone. Many clients were middle-aged grafters with proper jobs of work. Designers of aqueduct systems and harbour engineers who sometimes worked late at emergencies on site. An academic type who had lost all sense of time in the library at the Portico of Octavia and*

A sleek fellow who took off two days' growth with an expression as if he were cleaning a drain. [TFL]

then came here stiff and bleary-eyed. Men in trade, arriving from Ostia after an afternoon tide. And one or two offbeat, freelance freaks like me, whose weapons training Glaucus personally supervised and who worked at odd hours for reasons which his other customers never asked about ... [SB]

Glaucus allows Falco to introduce Camillus Verus, so in *The Accusers* they are able to meet there to plot. In *Three Hands in the Fountain,* the crook Florius discovers enough about Falco's haunts to send thugs after him; Glaucus and his clientele set to eagerly with flying fists, to save him.

The Rostra

Between the Basilica Aemilia and the Basilica Julia stood the raised platform from which public orations were made. It was adorned with the prows of ships captured in battle, from which it took its name (*rostrum* means beak or prow).

The Basilica Julia

One of the finest buildings in the Forum, it had been rebuilt by Julius Caesar. The steps remain, complete with scratched gaming boards, though last time I went, access was disallowed. *The long rectangular hall, roofed in wood over a fifty foot span, has a double row of colonnades on each long side, paved with more glittering slabs, so a ponderous chill strikes the bones in winter and an important hush lies everywhere, except when barristers are arguing among themselves in the side aisles. The colonnades have upper galleries, where people can observe proceedings, eat nuts, then throw down pistachio shells into the toga folds of the legal teams.* [AC]

Home to the Centumviral Court, it was closed from September to mid-October for summer recess.

The Golden Milestone, *Milliaria Aurea*

... the Golden Milestone, from which all the roads in the Empire take their distance. [SP]

Sosia asks Falco to meet her there in *The Silver Pigs*; when he fails to turn up, she goes to her death alone. Ironically, the Golden Milestone stood close to the Temple of Saturn, where Falco rescued Sosia in the first scene of the book. In *The Iron Hand of Mars*, Falco tells Xanthus to meet him there before they set out for Germany: *on a journey this long, I always start from Zero ...*

Built by Augustus around 20BC, the Golden Milestone may have inspired the phrase *All roads lead to Rome*. Of unknown form and decoration, it was either the same as, or adjacent to, the *Umbelicus Urbis Romae* (the Navel of the City). A stone in the Forum today claims to be the base of the Golden Milestone but is probably nothing to do with it; the Umbelicus, once clad in marble, exists only as a pile of bricks.

The Basilica Aemilius (Basilica Paulli)

A long, very narrow building with a wooden roof, which was fronted by a two-storey colonnade called the Porticus of Gaius and Lucius. Dating from the age of Augustus, it was beautifully decorated in many-coloured marbles and had the frieze showing scenes from Roman history and the larger-than-life statue of a barbarian that Falco describes when he visits his banker in *Ode to a Banker*. It was a retail outlet and haunt of bankers; lawyers too: *Here we sat, among the fine Doric columns of black and red marble in the Porticus of Gaius and Lucius, named for the grandsons of Augustus, lost golden boys whose early deaths symbolised dashed hopes. We occupied a peaceful corner outside the shops, close to one of the staircases that took people up from this gracious porch-like frontage to the richly ornate upper gallery of the Basilica Paulli. This was sophisticated living ...* [AC]

Only the floor, still beautiful, survives.

Behind the Porticus was the **Janus Medius**, a meeting point to discuss financial business.

All could have found a more congenial place to discuss the news ... By gathering in this dead-end passage they were consciously setting themselves aside in a private clique. [OB]

The Temple of Vesta and House of the Vestals

In *One Virgin Too Many* we glimpse an elderly Vestal going in procession: *She glanced about with the truculence of a loopy old lady who has men who should know better being respectful to her all day.* Is she the friend of Helena's mother and grandmother? Don't ask me; I only write this stuff.

View past the Temple of Vesta towards the Capitol [Rome Reborn]

Praetors, consuls and dictators would sacrifice before this flame upon taking up office, but a mere Procurator of the Sacred Poultry would have to find a damned good reason before approaching the sanctum. [OVTM]

It used to be possible to walk around the Vestals' House and its garden, though more recently it has been cordoned off. The first time we really see the temple, Marina's friend is being sick on the Corinthian columns and Marina herself shouts *'Bitches!'* Rebuilt after Nero's Great Fire, the temple has been partially reconstructed in modern times too so you can appreciate what its delicate columns and famous latticework were like. Standing on a high podium, it *was supposed to resemble an ancient hut built of wood and straw though the mock-antique construction appeared pretty crisp.* [THF] Mopped out in a daily ritual, this was a place of extreme sanctity, housing a perpetual fire and the mysterious Palladium.

The Temple of Venus and Rome

Mentioned by mistake. (Don't write in!) All right, all right; Hadrian built it.

The Temple of the Divine Julius

Also called the Temple of the Comet, because a comet was supposed to represent Caesar's soul among the gods.

The Regia

The ancient palace of King Numa Pompilius was taken over by the College of Pontiffs, then reconstructed in majestic style by a wealthy consul. It contained the Temple of Mars where military dedications were made. Rutilius Gallicus gives Falco a commission in the oddly shaped triangular courtyard that you can still make out today; its purpose is that old archaeological standby 'not fully understood'. *Coolly paved in white and grey marble slabs. Around it were various old rooms used for meetings, and scribes' nooks occupied by guardians of the archives and annals which were stored here ... In the centre of the courtyard was a large underground cistern, possibly an old grain silo from centuries ago when people actually lived in Numa's Palace.* [OVTM]

The Domus Aurea – Nero's Golden House

After the Great Fire of AD64, which he may or may not have conspired to start, Nero took over large parts of the centre of Rome to build his famous property. *Its lofty structures leapt between the crags, a feast of fabulous architecture. The interior décor was unbelievable, its richness and imagination surpassing anything artists had previously created. If the architecture was amazing, despite representing such blatant megalomania, even more dramatic was this entire landscape surrounding the halls and colonnades: a natural countryside within the city walls. Here there were parks and woodlands where wild and tame animals had roamed, all dominated by the famous Great Lake. It had been the tyrant's private world, but Vespasian, in a calculated propaganda coup, had thrown it open to everyone as a vast public park – Smart work, Flavians!* [PG]

Domitian was later to build imperial apartments on the Palatine, grand remnants of which you can see today. But Vespasian and Titus lived at the Domus Aurea when they were in Rome. In *Time to Depart* Falco goes to the west wing and in a secluded interior garden has his first meeting with Caenis.

One of the most famous rooms is the dining room with a revolving ceiling, which hosts my conference about organised crime: *The room was full of light. There was an open aspect to the south, with a heart-stopping view that we would not be gazing at. There was a theatrical cascade (turned off). There were curtained side rooms in which scenes of revolting debauchery had once occurred (now empty). Above our heads had been the legendary revolving ivory ceiling that had showered gifts down upon lucky diners (dismantled; no presents for us).* [TTD]

I was privileged to see the Golden House and this room before the monument was open to the public. Subsequently it was opened to small groups. Damage to the frescos caused by light and people's breath became immediately apparent. The hill above, where Trajan's Baths were built, lets in water. Public access became uncertain again, though there has been further investigation of the rooms.

The Colosseum

Coin of Titus showing the Colosseum

The Colosseum, with the Arch of Titus and the Colossus [Rome Reborn]

The Great Lake next to the Domus Aurea was drained by Vespasian for the Flavian Amphitheatre, the Colosseum (named after an enormous statue of Nero in a radiate crown). Throughout my series, the iconic building is slowly rising on its substructures.

It had three rows of arches, with columns in the three decorative orders; clad in marble, it featured triumphal quadrigae and other statues – many provided by Didius Geminus, according to *Nemesis*. An efficient system allowed rapid emergence of the audience. There were complex underground areas for the wild beasts and gladiators. Sailors hauled canopies across from the roof to give shade.

The Palatine

The Palatine today is a wonderful place to visit, though the ruins are hard to decipher and much of what you see dates from later than Falco – including Domitian's Palace. So don't be fooled into thinking Falco saw this. But you can have an atmospheric wander under the pine trees, with the perpetual traffic noise muffled. There is a small museum (with loos) and from time to time (depending on the vagaries of Roman museum opening) you can see the House of Livia, where Caenis lived. There were other buildings on the Capitol, such as the Temples of Apollo, Victory and Cybele, the House of Augustus, and presumably the house where the Flamen Dialis lived.

In Falco's time the main building was the old palace of Tiberius, adapted by Caligula, where he has many meetings with bureaucrats. Nero's Golden House extended right across the Forum to here. At the north end of the Forum, then as now, there was a route up into the main buildings, via a street called the Clivus Victoriae and entry through the Cryptoporticus, a formal covered passageway.

Supposedly unassuming … that miniature palace with every pampering amenity where our first emperor liked to pretend he was just a common man. [TFL]

Prisons

The Romans used prisons as holding cells rather than for punishment. Falco has experience of the two state prisons. *I was in the Lautumiae Prison, along with various petty felons who could not afford a barrister, and all the Forum pickpockets who wanted a rest from their wives. The Lautumiae was a rambling affair, built to house squadrons of prisoners from provinces which were restless … Things could be worse; it could have been the Mamertine: the short-stay political holding cell with its twelve-foot-deep dungeon, whose only exit for a man without influence was straight down into Hades … In the Mamertine nothing breaks the monotony until the public strangler comes in to measure your neck.* [VC]

Being caught in the House of the Vestals, for which the penalty is death, in *One Virgin Too Many* does bring him to the Mamertine, or Tullianum, which you can visit at the foot of the Capitol today, where the Gemonian Stairs used to be.

That bare, stinking hole near the Tabularium, from which the public strangler extracts his victims when they pay the final, fatal price for being enemies of Rome … a crude prison. Strong stone walls enclose irregular cells that used to form part of a quarry. Water runs through it. It was pitch dark. It was chilly. It was solitary and depressing. [OVTM]

Nero's Circus

Situated at the foot of the Vatican Hill, adjacent to the Janiculan on the north bank of the Tiber, this arena could apparently be flooded and was a favourite venue for *naumachiae,* mock sea battles. Its red granite obelisk had been brought from Egypt (Heliopolis) by Caligula in a ship that was then sunk to form the mole across the harbour at Ostia. You can see the obelisk, now topped by a Christian saint, in St Peter's Square at the Vatican.

Falco first meets Thalia there, in her tent. It is while watching attempts to train a tightrope-walking elephant (supposedly a popular trick) at the start of *Last Act in Palmyra* that Falco accepts Thalia's commission to go to the East.

The Auditorium of Maecenas

Called the Mecenate, this is sometimes open to the public – or not: no bad thing in this case, because the frescos have deteriorated visibly.

The floor and walls, and the frames and ledges of numerous niches in the walls, were all marble-clad ... The décor was entrancing. All the rectangular wall niches were painted with glorious garden scenes – knee-high cross-hatched trellises, each with a recess in which stood an urn, a fountain, or a specimen tree. There were delicate plantings, perfectly painted, amidst which birds flew or sipped from fountain bowls. The artist had an astonishing touch. His palette was based on blues, turquoise and subtle greens. He could make frescos that looked as real as the live horticulture we could see through the wide doors which had been flung open opposite the apse to reveal views over a lush terrace to the Alban Hills. [OB]

The Capitoline Hill

This important landmark has been completely altered since Roman times. Michelangelo and Victor Emmanuel left their marks in very different ways. Try not to shrink too much from the vainglory of the Campidoglio, which is sometimes called the 'Wedding Cake' – though I have never been to a wedding which had a triumphal quadriga galloping on its fruitcake ...

Imagine instead what Falco would have seen: twin peaks, the Arx and the Capitol; the Saddle between them was where Romulus traditionally granted refuge to riff-raff in order to people his new city – for the Rome of the Caesars was founded by criminals, rejects and fugitives, thereby setting up a good class of inhabitants for a series like mine.

Temple of Jupiter Optimus Maximus
(Jupiter Best and Greatest)

The largest temple ever, it had a golden roof that gleamed for miles. When Vespasian came to power, this fundamental temple had been destroyed by fire, so during the series it is a building site. Inaugurating its restoration, the Emperor carried away the first sack of rubble himself; he made special efforts to have copies created of all the ancient inscriptions that had been lost in the fire.

Temple of Juno Moneta (Juno the Admonisher)

Another great and very visible temple, which gave its name to the modern word 'Mint'.

The Auguraculum

This was a consecrated platform which formed a practical, permanent augury site. An augur was supposed to mark out with a special curly stick the area of sky he intended to watch, then the area of ground from which he would operate and within which he pitched his observation tent. He sat inside from midnight to dawn, gazing out southwards or eastwards through the open doorway until he spied lightning or a significant flock of birds. [OVTM]

The sacred geese and augurs' chickens

Ever since a monstrous army of Celts once raided Italy, a permanent gaggle of geese had been given privileged status on the Arx, in honour of their feathered forebears who had raised the alarm and saved the Capitol. I had imagined the big white birds led a pampered life. This lot looked a bit wormy, to tell the truth. [TFL] Falco is perturbed that the Arx is an unsuitable location for geese – too rocky and with incorrect vegetation, and when he is forced to officiate at the annual ceremony he hates it.

They accomplished the climb so quietly that the Romans on guard never heard a sound, and even the dogs – who are normally aroused by the least noise in the night – noticed nothing. It was the geese that saved them – Juno's sacred geese, which in spite of the dearth of provisions had not been killed. The cackling of the birds and the clapping of their wings awoke Marcus Manlius.
LIVY

The Campus Martius

Many public buildings have been inflicted on the Campus by men who thought they should be famous – all those pompously named theatres, baths, porticoes and crypts, with the occasional temple or circus to keep tourists agape ... [PG]

Falco is beaten up here by Priscus and his thugs in *Venus in Copper*. Some of the buildings he visits in the series are:

The Porticus of Pompey

This is where Geminus often holds auctions. Porticoes were something like Lincoln's Inn or the Palais de Justice in Paris. They had colonnades enclosing gardens, statuary and libraries. Pompey's Porticus had the Library of Octavia where Caenis helps with the catalogue in *The Course of Honour.*

Heavy architecture on four sides formed a secluded interior where men could hang about pretending to admire works of art while they hoped something more lively would turn up – an invitation to dinner, a quarrel, an expensive boy with a body like a Greek god, or at least a cheap female prostitute. [PG]

The Pantheon

A masterpiece, and one of the first buildings ever to use that newfangled stuff, concrete. Behind the main building were baths where Agrippa bequeathed to the people permanent free access.

People scold me that the Pantheon was built by Hadrian. Thank goodness Hadrian's inscription actually *says* it was created by Marcus Agrippa (in the reign of Augustus). Hadrian raised the height of the dome and restored it. That doesn't mean Falco can't go there. And he does, particularly in *Time to Depart* when he meets Florius.

You can still see the Pantheon, though it is regularly made inaccessible by use as a Roman Catholic church. As if there were not plenty in Rome!

The Saepta Julia

Beside the Pantheon Baths: its exact purpose is debated. It was a large enclosed building in two parts; at one end the Dolabrum may have been used for elections. It is said that the main part was flooded like an arena for mock sea fights, though Falco comments on the inconvenience, if so. Built on two levels, it had shops for gold-smiths and jewellers, so it is where I placed Geminus as an antique dealer and auctioneer. The Saepta was famously a haunt of informers. Both Titus and Domitian tried to clear them out (see Frequently Asked Questions).

Geminus has a suite on the top floor and a ware-house for storing goods more conveniently at ground level. From his upper office, where he tends to lurk with a packed lunch and wine, he can stroll out on to the bal-cony and look down into the enclosure. His bank box is bricked into a wall of the office.

Falco and Anacrites work at the Saepta temporarily in *Two for the Lions*, in an insalubrious office Anacrites hires. Falco comes back there in *Nemesis*.

I could see why he loved this place. There was never a dull moment, as fat jewellers and paranoid goldsmiths swaggered around trying to bamboozle would-be customers, while pickpockets tailed the customers and guards wondered absently whether to tackle the pickpockets. There were constant cries from food-sellers who wandered the building with gigantic trays or weighed down by garlands of drink flagons. Wafts of grilled meat and suet patties vied with the reek of garlic and the stench of pomade. Every now and then some man of note – or a nobody who thought he was one – pressed through the throng with a train of arrogant slaves in livery, trailing sweaty secretaries and put-upon fan-danglers. [NM]

The Janiculan Hill

> *My friend's few happy acres vie*
> *With the Hesperides; they lie*
> *On the Janiculum's long spine,*
> *A flat crest with a mild clime …*
> *On starry nights when there's no cloud,*
> *The graceful gable of his proud*
> *Villa lifts gently towards heaven.*
> *From one side you can see the seven*
> *Sovereign hills*
> *A bird's-eye view*
> *Of all Rome.*
> MARTIAL

I can't really remember if that poem inspired the crook Priscus having a villa on the Janiculan, which makes Falco covet this location. Helena buys him his villa, but they find it too inconvenient for working in Rome. After a house swap with Pa, the bath house Helena began is found to contain the body that initiates *A Body in the Bath House*.

Scenes in *Nemesis* are poignantly set at the villa.

The Servian Walls (the Embankment)

Once past the squeaking booths of the puppeteers, the men with trained marmosets and the self-employed loom workers plying for hire, the ancient Servian ramparts form a breezy promenade ... [SP] *We went up the Embankment – the great ancient rampart built by the republicans to enclose the original city. Rome had long outgrown these battlements, which remained now as a memorial to our forefathers and a place to climb to view the modern city ...* [PG]

Horace mentions this recreational feature that had been improved when Maecenas took over the Esquiline paupers' graveyard to create his Gardens:

> *Now the Esquiline Hill is a healthy place*
> *To live in; you can stroll along the wall in the*
> *   sunshine where recently*
> *You had a grim view of white bones strewn on the*
> *   ground ...*

Falco and Helena have a significant walk there on first returning to Rome in *The Silver Pigs*, a moment when they begin to relate to one another properly. In *Poseidon's Gold* they return nostalgically and plight their troth after Helena points out that, according to the Roman legal definition, they are man and wife.

The Praetorian Camp

In the north-east of the city, just outside the walls; this presumably noisy district is where Caenis had her house (a memorial stone was discovered, put up by her steward Aglaeus). Her house is now under the Ministry of Transport and a hectic modern spot, but the Camp can still be envisaged from its enormous outline.

Close by is a wine bar used by soldiers where Falco gets inordinately drunk with Festus' friend, the Praetorian Guard Frontinus, in *The Silver Pigs*. Falco also visits the Camp while chasing the serial killer in *Three Hands in the Fountain*.

The camp itself is a monstrous spread in the shadow of the Servian Walls, mirrored by an even more gigantic parade ground that takes up most of the space between the Viminal and Colline gates; the troops inside are bastards to a man. [THF]

The Pincian Hill

In the north of the city, this area still has gardens (the Borghese, with its dinky museum) and large residences, some diplomatic. The British School at Rome, a restrained Lutyens building, is in the Piazzale Winston Churchill off the Via Gramschi above the Villa Giulia Etruscan Museum.

Falco comments that this is an area of shuttered mansions belonging to the rich and he several times has trying experiences here: visiting the Hortensius freedmen in *Venus in Copper,* or trying to see the ex-Praetor Pomponius Urtica: *Nice district. Patrician open spaces with panoramic views that were interrupted only by tall, elderly pine trees where doves cooed. Beautiful sunsets over the Tiber. Miles from the racket of the Forum. Clean air, peaceful atmosphere, stunning property, gracious neighbours: wonderful for the smart élite who inhabited that fine district – and miserably inconvenient for the rest of us if we came visiting.* [TFL]

The Transtiberina

Nowadays called Trastevere, it is full of tourist restaurants in season, though a bit of a blank at other times.

The fullest description, too long to quote, occurs in *Shadows in Bronze* when Falco trails 'Barnabas' over there. This region had been outside the official boundary of Rome until Augustus rearranged the regions; I see it very much as an immigrants' quarter, as derived from similar haunts in modern cities, particularly Paris – districts that are colourful, exotic, secretive, a little sinister to outsiders. Such places are regarded as trouble spots by the authorities, with the implication that some occupants may be there illegally. For that reason, they stare after strangers. People are poor, and have to struggle to make ends meet either through outright begging or selling cheap trinkets that no one really wants. Unregulated children often help in this.

Falco recognises dangers: *Only an informer with the kind of brain disorder that needs his doctor to send him on a six months' cruise with a huge bottle of purgatives and a fierce course of exercise goes into the Transtiberina at night.* [SB] The hard round cake he eats, wanting to throw it down a drain but thinking it would cause a blockage, commemorates a very particular North African item Richard and I once bought from a booth in St-Michel in Paris. We hated waste but never managed to eat it.

Ostia/Portus

Outside Rome, but so close it could be reached in a day and linked to it by road, river, trade and tourist route,

the port of Ostia and its newer harbour basin at Portus
are an essential start to most overseas travel for Falco
and Helena. The first significant scene is in *Time to
Depart,* where Petronius sees off the crook Balbinus (he
thinks). We glimpse the famous lighthouse with its sea-
god statue, and when the thieves Gaius and Phlosis try
to snatch Falco's cargo of glass, we are introduced to
some of the scams that will be explored much more
fully in *Scandal Takes a Holiday.*

Ostia was discovered when the airport (Fiumicino)
was built; Portus lies on private land but has recently
been explored by archaeologists from the British
School. You can still easily get to Ostia Antica by road or
rail; it is a very enjoyable site, one of my favourites.

Lindsey's Favourite Roman Places

People write and ask me where to go. I can't mention
everywhere I've been in the past twenty years, but here
are ideas for anyone starting from scratch:

In Italy the two main areas are, obviously, Rome and
the Bay of Naples. Sicily has stunning remains but
when I went, many years ago, I found the atmosphere
so threatening it's enshrined in Falco's visit to Croton
in *Shadows in Bronze.* But one day, Piazza Armerina ...

Rome

'Falco's Rome', above, gives a few ideas.

My little tour would start with the Forum, including the Colosseum; don't omit the Palatine. I'm looking forward to visiting the new '3D immersive
infotainment centre' where Rewind Rome presents
the models I've been able to use in the *Companion.* Add
the Pantheon, the Mecenate (the Auditorium of
Maecenas) if it's open, the Ara Pacis (Augustus' Altar of
Peace) and a couple of museums, say the Vatican (go
early) and the National Museum of Rome (Palazzo
Massimo) by the Baths of Diocletian. Should the
Domus Aurea (Golden House) be open, beg for a timed
ticket. Then try just walking about, soaking up atmosphere. You'll need to do this, won't you, as you plan
your next delicious Italian meal?

A must is Ostia Antica. It can be reached easily and cheaply by train. I always cover my legs because the grass gives me a rash.

Of course Rome has wonderful museums and monuments from other periods (which I do grudgingly pop into …) There are lovely trips out, to Tivoli in particular where you can see Hadrian's Villa as well as the Villa d'Este.

The Bay of Naples

Every time I visit this area, I think Vesuvius may blow again soon and we'll lose it all – so better enjoy it!

For many years, after I had handed in my manuscript each autumn, Richard and I took a short November holiday in Naples. We never cared for Sorrento or Capri. We preferred Herculaneum to Pompeii, while our favourite site was the villa at Oplontis (Torre Annunciata). If you have time, go south to Paestum. I have fond memories of having Herculaneum almost to ourselves on balmy autumn days. Once, before the site dogs were cleared out, a keen doggie who knew a soft Englishwoman when he saw one acted as our guide, running eagerly from ancient house to house, as if wanting to show us all the best mosaics. Once we came across another couple – who were reading a Falco book; they looked bemused, and possibly nervous, when my beloved bounded up and announced who I was.

'A place that intends to last!' One of my sharper remarks. All right; I do know what happened at Pompeii – but this was eight years before Vesuvius exploded. Any student of natural science who did notice that their local mountain was shaped like a volcano deduced it was extinct. Meanwhile the Pompeian playboys believed in art, Isis, Campanian gladiators, and ready cash to purchase gorgeous women; few of the flashy bastards were great readers of natural science. [SB]

In Naples the National Museum is unmissable – though check opening times and, as always in Italy, be prepared for unexpectedly closed galleries. We had favourite spots that were not Roman at all: the Castel d'Ovo (which we only managed to visit on our very last trip); the Galleria Umberto IV (which had and maybe still has a private detective's office adjacent); the Café Gambrinus and the Royal Palace, a delightful late discovery.

Naples was one of 'our' places. I'll go back, of course. But it can never be the same.

Roman Britain

See Hadrian's Wall (Vindolanda and the other forts, Arbeia and the reconstructed baths at Newcastle). See

Fishbourne; Bath; St Albans; a villa (my local is
Lullingstone); Dolaucothi gold mine if you are tough.
Trimontium (Melrose) has special Roman facilities for
visitors. Soak yourself in Roman artefacts at the British
Museum and Museum of London.

Use the *Ordnance Survey Map of Roman Britain* to
pick out other places or just browse.

Some other ideas

Diehards will love Syria and Libya but unless you speak
and read Arabic, I'd recommend joining an organised
tour with a specialist guide. I really like to have remains
explained properly. I'm keeping Tunisia in reserve ...

I love museum visits. From Paris, travel out by train
to Saint-Germain-en-Laye, a gracious town in itself
with a superb archaeological museum in a palace (*and
amazing lunch across the square!* adds Michelle). Cologne
and Mainz have special Roman collections. Recently at
Zaragoza I was impressed by the explication of the
Roman river port and only barely resisted formally
committing myself to setting a Falco story there.

This is just the tip of a fabulous iceberg. I haven't
tried everywhere myself yet. Explore; that should be
part of the fun.

Romans and the Country

> *In Rome you long for the country; once there, you*
>   *praise to the skies*
> *The city you've just left.*
> HORACE

Romulus and Remus were shepherds. In the Republic,
the ideal life for Romans was working on a farm, being
called away only in times of emergency when a good
man would do his duty, even though his heart was in
the land. The financial qualifications for rank were to be
invested in Italian land. In the country you could
throw off your toga; you were not pestered with
responsibilities.

For this reason, I gave Falco a country connection.
His mother came from a market garden on the

Campagna (the area around Rome – not to be confused with Campania, a district further south which included Naples). In troubled times, Falco has spent time at the market garden and when it suits a novel's plot he revisits. He himself buys a run-down rural retreat close to, or perhaps the site of, Hadrian's future villa at Tivoli.

I am a city girl and though I garden, I view the country as a place where I visit good friends, then scarper. Not for me a writer's cottage with roses round the door at the end of an inaccessible lane, surrounded by cows, cowpats and dodgy country characters. I want to live in a street, close to shops. This may explain the joy I take in writing about the Campagna market garden, making Falco equip it with a crazy excrescence of agricultural myth. *They are always going off for a foreign love affair, or to recover from a fit of remorse because their cart ran over a grass-cutter. Then just when someone is delivering twins on the kitchen table and the radish crop has failed, they arrive home unexpectedly, all eager to rape the goatherd's teenage daughter and full of mad ideas for horticultural change ... Unless Uncle Fabius discovers he has an illegitimate son by a woman with a weak heart who is threatening a lawsuit, he counts the day lost ...* [PG]

Poets are always praising the simple life (while yearning for Rome!). As early as *The Silver Pigs,* we find Falco, at the procurator's villa, musing: *I was enjoying*

This is what I prayed for.
A piece of land – not so very big,
With a garden and, near the house, a spring that never fails
With a bit of wood to round it off.
HORACE

myself in this hospitable house. By day I read, wrote letters, or limped around the farm. The staff were friendly and being pampered felt quite acceptable. Every evening I talked cheerfully with my host. Even in Britain this was the ideal Roman life ...

So maybe, as Helena Justina jokes, a villa in a remote rural location will be Falco's eventual retirement.

Travel and Transport

The Roman roads ran absolutely straight in all directions and all led to Rome
SELLAR AND YEATMAN

As he and Pa make their way down the Via Appia to Capua, Falco remembers Horace: *a farrago of crooked landlords, potholes, house fires, gritty bread and infected eyes; of being packed into a ferry to cross the Pontine Marshes ... of staying awake half the night all keyed up for a girl who never bothered to turn up ...* [PG]

Falco and Helena travel a lot; they like it and so do I. It enables me to visit new places – some, like Syria and Libya, where I might never have gone otherwise. The Romans did travel for leisure and education, which seems so modern.

I suppose it is unlikely that individual Romans visited quite *so many* provinces as Falco and Helena, though they could. Senators were supposed to stay in Italy unless they had permission (this was to stop them going abroad to plot rebellion) but for anyone else there were good roads, fairly good shipping connections, a common currency, common languages (both Latin and Greek) and the right to go for trade or tourism wherever they wanted.

Maps existed, showing distances between towns and posting stations, with inns identified: *our inn, which Helena had rightly identified on her pictograph map as a four-tower effort.* [SDD]

The Imperial Post

Because Roman travel was slow, for logistical reasons I have Falco using the imperial transport system when I need to move him around quickly. Only the Emperor

... The Appian is easier when you take it slowly.
Here I declared war on my stomach because of the water which was quite appalling, and waited impatiently as the other travellers enjoyed their dinner ...
The blasted mosquitoes and the marsh frogs made sleep impossible ...
From there we bowled along in wagons for twenty four miles putting up at a little town which can't be identified in verse though it can very easily by its features; they sell the most common of all commodities – water, though their bread is quite unbeatable, and a traveller, if he's wise, usually carries some with him on his journey ...
... a long stretch of road damaged by heavy rain. On the next day the weather was better but the road worse ...
HORACE

could issue passes; we see Pliny the Younger sycophantically asking Trajan for permission to let his wife use one after a family bereavement.

Falco spells out how it worked: *Use of the imperial courier service is a dismal privilege. The special messengers on horseback travel fifty miles a day. We classed ourselves as a less urgent despatch and took an official carriage: four wheels on stout axles, high seats, change of mules every dozen miles, and after the double distance food and lodging – all charged to the locals thanks to our pass.* [SP] In *A Dying Light in Corduba*, he takes advantage of an official pass to gallop desperately in search of Helena who is about to give birth to Julia, then in *Three Hands in the Fountain* he gets away with an outdated Baetican pass, during his headlong flight after the serial killer.

Up to now, Sir, I have made it a rule not to issue anyone a permit to use the Imperial Post unless he is travelling on your service, but I have just been obliged to make an exception. My wife had news of her grandfather's death and was anxious to visit her aunt …
PLINY THE YOUNGER

Transport

I don't talk about car designs in real life. Transport was requested – but I'm not going to do it!

Falco of course hankers for a boy-racer chariot. It's a dream, Marcus.

Time

A First Century Roman Timeline

Note: I generally use the BC/AD system for dates, rather than BCE/CE, because it will look more familiar to the majority of my readers.

Novels	Private events	AD	Emperor	Public events
		9	**Augustus** (from 27BC)	Varus Disaster in Germany Vespasian born
The Course of Honour begins		14	**Tiberius**	
		37	**Gaius (Caligula)**	Death of Antonia
	M. Didius Falco born L. Petronius Longus born	41	**Claudius**	
		42		
	Maia Favonia born	43		Roman invasion of Britain
		44		Triumph
		45		
		46		
		47		
	M. Didius Favonius leaves home Helena Justina born	48		
	A. Camillus Aelianus born	49		
		50		
	Q. Camillus Justinus born	51		
		52		
		53		
		54	**Nero**	
		55		Death of Britannicus
		56		
		57		
		58		
	Falco and Petronius join army	59		

Novels	Private events	AD	Emperor	Public events
		60		Boudiccan Revolt in Britain
	Falco and Petronius army scouts	61		
		62		
		63		
		64		Great Fire in Rome Building of Domus Aureus
		65		
	Falco and Petronius return to Rome	66		The Jewish Revolt
		67		Nero in Greece
		68		The German Revolt
	M. Didius Festus dies	69	**Galba Otho Vitellius Vespasian**	
The Course of Honour ends		70		Capture of Jerusalem
The Silver Pigs		71		Triumph for Vespasian and Titus
Shadows in Bronze				Q. Petilius Cerialis governor of Britain
Venus in Copper	Helena & Falco live together			
The Iron Hand of Mars				
Poseidon's Gold		72		
Last Act in Palmyra				
Time to Depart	Lenia and Smaractus marry			
A Dying Light in Corduba	Julia Junilla Laeitana born	73		
Three Hands in the Fountain				S. Julius Frontinus consul
Two for the Lions	Famia dies	74		Census
				Q. Rutilius Gallicus legate in Africa
				? Antonia Caenis dies
				? Berenice in Rome
One Virgin Too Many	Justinus and Claudia marry			
	Flora dies			
Ode to a Banker				

Novels	Private events	AD	Emperor	Public events
A Body in the Bath House		75		S. Julius Frontinus governor of Britain
The Jupiter Myth	Sosia Favonia born			
	Petronius children die			
The Accusers	Maia and Petronius live together			
Scandal Takes a Holiday		76		
See Delphi and Die				Q. Rutilius Gallicus governor of Germany
Saturnalia				
Alexandria		77		
Nemesis	M. Didius Justinianus born and dies			
	M. Didius Favonius dies			
	M. Didius Alexander Postumus born			
	Aelianus married			
		78		
		79	**Titus**	Eruption of Mount Vesuvius
		80		Fire in Rome; inauguration of Flavian Amphitheatre
		81	**Domitian**	
		94		'Reign of terror' begins
		96	**Trajan**	

Significant Events

The Battle of Actium

The crucial sea battle where Octavian, the future Emperor Augustus, defeated Antony and Cleopatra in 31 BC. Although long before Falco's time, this period had a profound effect on the Roman psyche. He makes regular reference to it, especially in *Alexandria*. Cleopatra remained the archetypal femme fatale, an exotic threat to the Roman world in the Roman mind; she was a comparison for Boudicca and Veleda (and later Xenobia). Actium led to the end of the Republic and the rise of the Julio-Claudian imperial dynasty –

that vivid mix of scandal and sound political administration. Vespasian owed his career to association with Claudius in particular. A wish to emulate Augustus' acquisition of Egypt may have lured first Gaius (Caligula) then Claudius to plan an invasion of Britain.

The Varus Disaster in Germany

In AD9, P. Quinctilius Varus was consolidating the Roman presence east of the Rhine. He was lured into a trap by a German leader the Romans called Arminius, a catastrophic military defeat, with the loss of three legions. The distraught Augustus famously beat his head against a wall, crying, *Varus, Varus, give me back my legions!* His stepson Germanicus visited Germany with a handful of survivors, buried some bodies and recaptured the legions' eagle standards, which were deposited in the Temple of Mars in Rome.

The battle location was unknown for centuries until an off-duty British army officer found evidence near Kalkriese; this led to a firm identification of the site, new understanding of how the massacre occurred, documentaries and a museum.

The Boudiccan Revolt in Britain

In AD60, the widowed Queen of the Iceni, a wealthy tribe in East Anglia, was targeted by brutal imperialist greed. Her two teenaged daughters were raped by Roman soldiers in front of her. Taking advantage of the Roman governor's absence on campaign, Boudicca raised a rebellion, which nearly succeeded in driving the Romans out. They were defeated in battle, a tactical triumph for Suetonius Paulinus, who lured the tribes into a trap, perhaps at Letocetum – Wall in the Midlands, close to where I grew up. Archaeology has long revealed the terrible devastation that happened at Colchester, London and St Albans.

The Icenian Revolt was brought about by the combination of indifferent politicians, overbearing armed forces and ill-judged financial control. This had alienated the populace, with results that were sheer murder. [DLC]

The time when Paulinus, the British governor, decided to invade Mona – Druids' Island – to clear out that rats' net of troublemakers once and for all. Paulinus left us at Isca, guarding his back, but was accompanied by our commandant in his advisory corps. We were stuck therefore with an incompetent Camp Prefect named Poenius Postumus, who called Queen

Boudicca's Revolt 'just a local tiff'. When the governor's frantic orders arrived, informing this halfwit that the Iceni had swept a bloody swathe all through the south, instead of haring off to join the beleaguered field army, either from terror or further misjudgement Postumus refused to march out ... After the rebels were annihilated and the truth came out, our pea-brained Camp Prefect fell on his sword. We made sure of that. But first he had forced us to abandon twenty thousand comrades in open country with no supplies and nowhere to retreat, facing two hundred thousand screaming Celts. Eighty thousand civilians had been massacred while we polished our studs in barracks. We might have lost all four British legions. We might have lost the governor. We might have lost the province ... If a Roman province had fallen, in a native rebellion, led by a mere woman, the whole Empire might have blown away. It could have been the end of Rome. [SP]

Falco has terrible memories of this event. It helps give him the bitterness a fictional detective should have. His legion's disgrace is a leitmotif. Things are desperately tricky in *The Iron Hand of Mars*, when Falco must investigate the XIV Gemina – one of the three legions who were let down by his. And it haunts him again when he revisits London.

The event left Falco and Petro scarred for life. They found excuses to leave the army and came back to Rome to pursue other careers. The experience is part of the great bond between them.

The Year of the Four Emperors

It was longer than a year, but basically AD69.

Nero, the last of the Julio-Claudian emperors, had ruled for fourteen years, with increasingly eccentric behaviour. His outrageous behaviour as a Games participant in Greece colours *See Delphi and Die*, while the ensuing nightmare of civil war is still recent when the Falco series begins. Rome, including Falco, accepted Vespasian to end the destruction, waste and bloodshed. Competing for the throne were:

Galba

Seen as old and failing, who made his bid using legions from Spain. He was brutally killed in the Forum. *First Galba, a doddering old autocrat ...* [SP]

Otho

Otho, who according to Tacitus *had nothing to hope for from settled conditions; his whole policy was based on exploiting chaos:* portrayed by contemporaries as a bewigged dilettante who was only redeemed by the dignified manner in which he committed suicide. *Next Otto, who had been Nero's ponce, so judged himself Nero's legitimate heir ...* [SP]

Vitellius

After him, Vitellius, a bullying glutton, who drank himself into and out of the job with a certain ironclad style, then had a recipe for mushy peas named after him ... [SP]

Vespasian

If one except his meanness in money matters he was a worthy successor to the commanders of old [TACITUS] He benefited by having two adult sons who could guarantee the succession and stability.

At the end of the struggle, as Falco says, *Three Sabine provincials no one had ever heard of until last year had, with good luck and some merit, made themselves dynastic princes in Rome.* [SP]

The eruption of Vesuvius

24 August, AD79. What happened to Pompeii and Herculaneum has to overshadow any novel set in First Century Italy. It was a climactic event for Romans (which Falco clearly knows about with hindsight), and its time capsule of remains has provided – and continues to reveal – much of what we know about Roman life.

Whether or not I ever write about the eruption, we have the joke of Falco claiming *Pompeii was a town that intended to last.* [SB]

My own twenty-year relationship with Naples and its archaeological sites resonates through the series.

The Daily Routine and the Hours of the Day

The Daily Routine

Crimes are deplorable. To set this in social perspective and heighten our sense of outrage it is important to show the cycles of *normal* life against which occur murders and other murky things Falco investigates; in other words, to show the life that a reasonable person would think was desirable. Roman writers describe a daily routine for the man about town:

> *Often in the evenings, I stroll around the Circus and*
> *Forum*
> *Those haunts of trickery; I loiter beside the fortune*
> *tellers; then*
> *I make my way home to a plate of minestrone with*
> *leeks and peas.*
> *Then I go off to bed with no worries about having*
> *to be up early in the morning …*
> *I stay in bed till ten, then walk; or else after reading*
> *Or writing something for my private pleasure I have*
> *a massage …*
> HORACE

(Falco reads Horace too, being a similar laid-back entity.)

Compare the poem with: *I stayed in bed long enough to prove that I wasn't a client who needed to leap out and grovel for favours at some rich patron's house. Then I showed myself to the eager populace in the Forum, though most were looking the other way. I dodged my banker, a girl I preferred not to recognise, and several of my brothers-in-law. Then I sauntered into the men's baths at the back of the Temple of Castor for a complete physical overhaul …* [PG]

This is Mediterranean life, where things that would be only incidental in other societies are the driving force. This life has its casual side; people are passionate about that.

The Hours of the Day

Strangely to us, the Romans divided days and nights into twelve hours each, according to light and dark; so in winter an 'hour' might be as little as forty-five minutes and in summer seventy-five. People rose at dawn, or earlier (ugh!), and even for labourers the working day ended around the sixth hour, when most bath houses opened. Dinner would be around the eighth or ninth hour, perhaps carrying on into the night. Brothels were supposed to remain closed until the ninth hour – though did they? Some trades, as always, had to take advantage of any chance to make money, so barbers were famous for staying open until late and the Saepta Julia might have shops open until the eleventh hour, when it must have been growing too dark to see much.

The system bears some relation to modern life around the Mediterranean, where many businesses close at midday, allowing a period of rest or mischief in the afternoons.

The first two hours of the morning tax
Poor clients, during the third advocates wax
Eloquent and hoarse; until the fifth hour ends
The city to her various trades attends;
At six o'clock the weary workers stop
For the siesta; all Rome shuts up shop
At seven; the hour from eight to nine supplies
The oiled wrestlers with their exercise;
The ninth invites us to recline full length
Denting the cushions. At last comes the tenth …
Then my jest books can appear …
MARTIAL

Status, Family and Empire

Social Status

On his first visit to Camillus Verus, perhaps his first ever close encounter with a senator, Falco assesses himself: *A free citizen, his importance signalled by the length of his train of slaves — in my case, none.* [SP] This introduces the financial qualifications for rank, the custom of paying morning visits to patrons (Falco isn't a client, but he will be), the acceptance of slavery and the importance of show. All will colour the series. Falco does not take kindly to the superior ranks: *how clannish these people can be: little pockets of reliable friends sewn into every province from Palestine to the Pillars of Hercules ...* [SP]

Besides physical reconstruction of the city, Vespasian set out to purge corruption and scandal from Roman life. This tends to make Vespasian touchy about Helena Justina allying herself with a plebeian. However, it offers Falco the lure of promotion; Titus suggests he might aim for the middle class. But in *Poseidon's Gold*, even though Falco has borrowed enough cash, Domitian refuses to promote him; his status as an informer damns him.

He reformed the Senatorial and Equestrian Orders, weakened by frequent murders and longstanding neglect; replacing undesirable members with the most eligible Italian and provincial candidates available.
SUETONIUS

Rome was an unforgiving society. An illustrious pedigree was vital and a family could be permanently damaged by a wrong move. It happens to the Camilli, as Falco foresees: *In a Roman scandal none of the family escapes. Unborn generations, judged by the honour of their ancestors, were already condemned by this act against the state ...* [SP]

The Emperor

Augustus devised the famous phrase *primus inter pares,* first among equals, to excuse his position as emperor, or permanent dictator. He pretended he still lived as a private citizen, ostentatiously keeping an ordinary house — though rather specially located on the Palatine. Falco, an unrepentant republican, rejects the principle: *Every free man should have a voice in the government of the city where he has to live. The senate should not hand control of the empire for life to one mortal, who may turn out insane or corrupt or immoral – and probably will.* [SP]

Augustus and subsequent emperors were declared 'divine' after they died. This was what caused difficulties for Christians. It was also the source of Vespasian's wry joke when dying, *Dear me, I think I must be turning into a god!*

Senators

There was a financial qualification for the Senate: at least one million sesterces invested in Italian land. Most senators in fact owned *much* more than that. However, the Emperor had a right of veto. Strictly, 'patricians' were members of only a handful of ancient, snobbish families. The Camilli belong to one such, but I suspect mine are from an inferior branch.

There were responsibilities, sometimes expensive. Falco tells King Togidubnus: *Lavish spending is the duty of a wealthy Roman. It demonstrates status, which glorifies the Empire, and it cheers up the plebs to think they belong to a civilised society.* [BBH]

There were rules. Senators could not marry slaves or freedwomen; this prevented Vespasian marrying Caenis. Senators could not leave Italy without permission. It was forbidden either to be or to marry an actor, gladiator or prostitute – though it happened. *I'm a senator's offspring,* Helena scoffs. *Disgracing myself is my heritage. Every family my mother gossips with has a disgruntled son no-one talks about who has run off to scandalise his grandfather by acting in public.* [LAP]

Falco is contemptuous: *nobody needs exorbitant talents like judgement, or even a sense of honour, to vote in an assembly three times every month* ... [TTD] He reserves particular satire for senators' wives and daughters (except the one he wants). *Senators' wives, in my scheme, fall into three types: the ones who sleep with senators, but not the senators who married them; the ones who sleep with gladiators; and a few who stay at home.* [SP] Then, *Mothers regarded it as a duty to educate their daughters to be rebellious. Daughters revelled in it, throwing themselves at gladiators, joining queer sects, or becoming notorious intellectuals. By comparison, the vices open to boys seemed tame* ... [LAP]

Falco loathes people in authority who are not up to it. He is haunted by *my* prejudices: fast-track admin trainees: PhDs who lack intellectual rigour; modern politicians, who go from university to being a 'political researcher' then jump into a Parliamentary seat without ever having held down a job or even run a household.

Equestrians

The middle-rank qualification was 400,000 sesterces – less than for the Senate, but still a lot of cash. It is the rank from which Vespasian rose, and many others.

This was where opportunists could make their mark, and perhaps make money. Procurators, in executive positions, ran branches of government. Camillus Meto, himself equestrian, sums it up derisively: *Life with a high moral tone, and so little else! Trapped among third-grade tax collectors, freed imperial secretaries, the Admiral of the British Channel Fleet! Hard work on a mean salary or struggling in trade. No ceremony abroad, no style or power at home.* [SP] Falco, ironically, takes a different view: *I thought of what it meant – not simply the land and the rank, but the kind of life they enabled me to lead. Like Flavius Hilaris, ploughing a useful furrow in his own way – so passionately – and enjoying quiet, comfortable houses with a wife he dearly loved, the life of my choice among people I liked, where I knew I could do well.* [SP]

Falco's first (so far his only) government position is as Procurator of the Sacred Geese of Juno. *'You deserve it,'* grinned the Emperor. *The job was rubbish; we both knew that. For me the future looked dreary. I had risen above generations of rascally Didii – to what? To being a rascal who had lost his place in life.* [OVTM] It has dangers too; being accused of neglecting his duties in *The Accusers* nearly wipes him out financially and socially.

Falco is hard on himself when he reaches his equestrian rank: *a sinecure, a placeman, a careerist, and a half-hearted one at that.* [OB] However, I feel he deserves it – and the rank certainly deserves him.

Plebeians

These are the poor. Their privileges are few, but they can vote and appear in court; they have tribunes to

So farewell Rome. I leave you
To sanitary engineers and
 municipal architects, men
Who by swearing black is
· white land all the juicy
 contracts
Just like that – a new temple,
 swamp drainage, harbour-
 works,
River-clearance, undertaking,
 the lot – then pocket the
 cash
And fraudulently file their
 petition for bankruptcy.
JUVENAL

It's the rich wot gets the
pleasure and the poor wot
gets the blame!
MUSIC HALL SONG

speak for them. In theory a plebeian with funds and influence can enter the Senate at the age of forty and even become consul at forty-two (Falco could do this – only he will reach forty just as Domitian's reign begins …) Most work too hard and die too young.

It was worse than slavery to be free but very poor: *Being a menial among people who have no regular income is worse than captivity on a rich landowner's farm. No-one here cared whether Congrio ate or starved. He was nobody's asset, so nobody's loss if he suffered.* [LAP]

Freedmen

A freed slave who had been set up with a little money, and who had initiative, could be extremely successful. Placidus, the procurator for port taxes, says, *I bought my freedom, worked in commerce, earned enough to be granted equestrian rank, and offered myself for useful posts … Some of us really try to do a decent job, but we're thwarted at every turn.* [DLC] The aristocracy, who could not engage in trade legally, were allowed to use their slaves as commercial intermediaries, so many freed slaves understood business and gained useful contacts. There was a tendency for everyone else to look down on them as uncultured and showy, but like yuppies today, why should they care? The Hortensii in *Venus in Copper* are a picaresque example: people even Falco views with a Roman shudder.

Imperial freedmen were powerful in government. In the Julio-Claudian period, the most famous – and richest – was Narcissus. The strong Flavian emperors will have had their mandarins, but they worked in the background.

Any slur about having been a slave seems only to have lasted one generation. One of Trimalchio's cronies in the *Satyricon* says: *I'm a man among men, and I walk with my head up. I don't owe anybody a penny – there's never been a court order out for me. No one's said 'Pay up!' to me in the street. I've bought a bit of land, and some tiny pieces of plate. I've twenty bellies to feed, as well as a dog. I bought my old woman's freedom so nobody could wipe his dirty hands on her hair. Four thousand I paid for myself. I was elected to the Augustan college and it cost me nothing. I hope when I die I won't have to blush in my coffin* [PETRONIUS].

These coarse, clever, thrusting ex-slaves, most often of foreign extraction, suffered from none of the crippling conventions and moral beliefs that every upper-class Roman inherited as part of his emotional baggage. What enabled them to amass gigantic fortunes, and to force their way into positions of political power, was by no means only their native ability. They were cashing in on their masters' ignorance of, and contempt for, a world ruled by commerce and industry.
PETER GREEN

Slaves

Slaves had no legal identity. They were property. Causing harm to someone else's slave was actionable as an injury to their owner. Slaves could possess money only in limited circumstances, and could not marry. They were never to be armed. They could be sold, whatever heartache was caused, with no redress. In good homes they were treated as one of the family, though in bad they were violently abused. Satirists frequently show women screaming at their maids, pulling their hair and beating them, for imagined slights. A slave, male or female, could be used sexually by their own master or others on the master's say-so; it was common and expected. Pertinax is half-brother to Barnabas, fathered on a slave. *When sleeping with a slave, why should he care? A birth only meant one more entry in the plus column of his accounts.* [SB] The two men remain close; Barnabas is one person for whom Pertinax shows genuine affection.

The position of rural slave labour was often grim; for farm work, olive oil production and so forth, large numbers were barracked in poor accommodation, badly fed, forced to work long hours. Worst of all was the lot of slaves in metal mines. It was expected that they would die; being sent to the mines was a criminal punishment – usually intended as a death sentence. Falco may sometimes seem a clown, but subjecting himself to this voluntarily in *The Silver Pigs* is an act of extreme courage.

The liberal Falco is close enough to poverty to feel awkward. He and Helena need domestic help, but his first visit to a slave market is unproductive.

No matter how brazenly he was defying me, I knew better than to beat up another citizen's slave [TFL]

I'm glad to hear that you live on friendly terms with your slaves. It is just what one expects of an enlightened, cultivated person like yourself. 'They're slaves,' people say. No. They're human beings. 'They're slaves.' But they share the same roof as ourselves. 'They're slaves.' No, they're friends, humble friends. 'They're slaves.' Strictly speaking they're our fellow slaves, if you once reflect that fortune has as much power over us as over them.
SENECA

> '*I want a clean woman with experience of headstrong children who would fit in with a young, upwardly moving family.*'
>
> '*You've got expensive taste! We do a basic model with no trimmings. Lots of potential but you have to train the bint yourself. You can win them over with kind treatment, you know. Ends up they would die for you.*'
>
> '*What – and land me with the funeral costs?*'
> [BBH]

Slavery exists in the modern world, particularly in the sex 'industry'. In opulent countries people work illegally in sweatshops or labour gangs, below the authorities' sightlines. We can share Falco's uneasiness about live-in domestic workers: *Some ill-trained, immature, uninterested foreigner for whom our baby represented a spoiled, rude Roman brat with spoiled, rude Roman parents, all of whom Fortune had spared from slavery and suffering for no obvious reason – unlike the conjectural nurse who would think herself, but for Fortune, as good as us. As, but for Fortune, she might well have been.* [OVTM] Any modern yuppie would recognise this.

Runaways

To run away, to lure away a slave, or to harbour a runaway was theft, depriving the owner of his property. The vigiles would apprehend suspicious characters and start a search for their owners. Petronius jokes, *not to fear: all anyone had to do to be in the clear was to produce his valid certificate of Roman citizenship.* [STH] Where masters were not found, runaways became public slaves, working in latrines, hypocausts or even the mines.

Women

It is commonplace to say that a Roman woman had no legal identity. A man had to speak for her, and in the absence of a father and husband, like a juvenile she had an appointed 'guardian'; I feel giving Roman women guardians may just have given them more wimps to push around. At least, unlike Greek women, Roman women went out to dinner with their husbands or were joint hosts at home. However, the man was the head of the household, received the corn dole, answered the Census call, registered the children, appeared in court, served on juries, and according to Carcopino even did all the shopping … Let me point out, gently, that a tradition of Roman marriage was that a new wife was formally handed the keys to her husband's store-cupboards.

Rights given to a mother of three children (four in Italy, five elsewhere) did allow her to manage without a guardian and to make her own will.

'Our history is written by men and perhaps they underestimate the part played by women in real life. The Empress Livia, it is well known, was a rock to Augustus throughout the decades of his reign; he even allowed her to use his seal on state papers. And in most family businesses the husband and wife play an equal part. Even ours, Falco!' [OB]

I was Maia's older brother and Helena's chosen partner. According to the ancient laws of Rome, my word should be law: fat chance. These were women of character and I was just the poor duffer who had to do his best for them. [THF]

In practice, it is clear that among the lower orders, women were their husbands' life and business partners. On tombstones or in paintings they sit side by side, equal in size, which is indicative in ancient pictorial art. Any society where women are visible, which respects mothers and daughters, or where marriage – hence divorce and dowry management – is by mutual consent, will have loud, self-confident women who bully husbands and sons, spend at will, and do not suffer fools gladly. Roman women were the ancestors of modern Italian women. They, too, could be said to live in a paternalist society, but from an old village granny to a celluloid celebrity, you don't cross them.

Where there was a shop, Roman women minded it. If it is true the husband spent a lot of time out shopping, then for the wife to take charge of the business in his absence would be a necessity!

Girls who worked, as many must have done at the poor end of society, would have had their own style – for instance, women like the *pistachio-chewing, mulsum-swigging, parasol-wielding, late-staying, man-baiting members of the Braidmakers' Old Girls.* [THF]

The *cursus honorum*

Critically, most people were trying to improve their social standing. For a senator the traditional career, or course of honours, involved varied posts, with a deliberate mix of both civil and military service. If only this applied to politicians today!

At twenty-five came entry to the Senate. A man who was elected immediately he became eligible was said to be *suo anno*, 'in his year'.

Tribune of a legion

This and/or law-court experience was the starting point for politicals. For instance, we see Camillus Justinus growing in confidence during his tribunate in Germany, then returning with hopes of advancement in Rome.

'the collecting, disbursing, safeguarding, managing and controlling of public funds' [DLC]

Quaestor

Responsibilities were mainly financial: at the Treasury in Rome, as a paymaster to a general, or as financial secretary to an overseas governor. A quaestorship was called a magistracy and when properly carried out involved serious responsibilities.

I equate these 'high-flyers' to admin trainees or yuppies with business management degrees. That is why so many in the Falco series are described cruelly: *Bound to know nothing. Bound to have messed up. Bound to get uppity if I ever told him so.* [SDD] Of course there are exceptions, such as Cornelius in *A Dying Light in Corduba*. Mostly they are a menace. Quinctius Quadratus in the same book is so amoral and dangerous even the governor sends him on 'hunting leave'. But we warm to Aquillius in *See Delphi and Die*.

Aedile
Not obligatory, but this post could showcase an ambitious man. The functions, all in Rome, involved responsibility for roads, public buildings such as temples and aqueducts, supervising markets, the corn dole and festivals.

Legate of a legion
Commanding a legion involved both military and diplomatic skills, not to mention man-management.

Praetor
By imperial times this was a legal position, at minimum age thirty-nine. There were eight; their responsibilities included an annual round-up of legal statutes and cere-monial duties organising the Games (which was per-sonally expensive). The VIP magistrate in *Time to Depart* is presumably one of the praetors, though on legal advice he is never identified.

Consul
The minimum age was forty-two. There were two a year, which was then named after them. In imperial times they frequently stood down to give others a chance.

Governor of a province
Ex-praetors, and especially ex-consuls, would 'draw' a foreign province to govern, Africa and Asia being the

best. It was possible to acquire great wealth through a governorship; famous legal complaints were brought by provinces that had been badly treated. *The men Vespasian chose to establish order in the Empire were of a dry, down-to-earth type. They got on with the job, fairly and quickly …* [TFL]

There were other senior positions, often to do with administration in Rome. For instance, Falco mentions the three senators of consular rank who form the Board of Commission for the aqueducts: *These worthy old codgers clearly held seniority over the Curator. Luring just one of them into taking an interest in our story could have acted as a fulcrum under the Curator's arse. Unfortunately for us, the three consular commissioners simultaneously held other interesting public posts, such as governorships of foreign provinces. The practice was feasible because the Commission only met formally to inspect the aqueducts for three months of the year.* [THF]

Influence

There were other kinds of influence. The complex and ancient institutions of Rome, many based on myth and superstition, arouse Falco's wrath. When the Arval Brethren are covering up a murder he gives it full rein: *All the colleges of priests are élite cliques, where power is traditionally wielded by non-elected, jobs-for-life patricians, all dressing up in silly clothes for reasons no better than witchcraft and carrying out dubious, secretive manipulation of the state.* [OVTM] He has already lambasted augurs: *One reason I despised the College of Augurs was that they could manipulate state business by choosing when the auspices should turn out favourable. Lofty personages who held opinions that I hated could affect or delay important issues. I don't suggest bribery took place. Just everyday perversions of democracy.* [OVTM]

He is equally scathing about the Vestals' 'lottery' and, in other books, oracles.

Patronage

For non-senators there was no formal route to advancement. Those without paying trades (which I'm afraid tended to mean writers) had to rely on the goodwill of wealthy men.

Maecenas came to regard me as one of his friends
Or at least he was willing to go so far as to take me
  with him
When making a journey in his carriage and to risk
  casual remarks
Like 'What time do you make it?' 'Is the Thracian
  Chick a match for the Arab?'
'These frosty mornings are quite nippy; you've got to
  be careful.'
HORACE

This great 'friendship' produces – food. Each meal,
However infrequent, your patron reckons against you
To square his accounts.
JUVENAL

What use are our poor efforts, where does it all get us,
Dressing up while it's dark still, hurrying along
To pay our morning respects to a couple of wealthy
Maiden aunts?
JUVENAL

This cringing life is not for Falco. However, he butts up against people who do have that kind of dependence, particularly the downtrodden authors in *Ode to a Banker*.

Political association

For the working classes, anything like a trade union had to be organised with caution. People gathering in groups could be plotting. So, in *A Dying Light in Corduba*, the credentials of the Society of Olive Oil Producers of Baetica, a dining club with trade connections, are carefully massaged. The only permitted reason to associate is to further a funeral club for members: to form any wider kind of power base is suspicious. The Ostia builders were definitely dodgy. Pliny, in Bithynia, even feared a town establishing its own fire brigade, because it would be like a private army.

When life is tough, people with similar backgrounds or interests do tend to bond together. However, an informer, working alone and without an association, must be a social outsider.

The Family

The family was the official social unit. The Emperor Augustus had encouraged marriage and procreation by legislation. Bachelors were penalised; widows must remarry within six months; people should have three children to be patriotic ... Incitements were cunning: the right to benefit from wills, for instance. Many of my plots, like much of civic Roman Law, derive from family issues. Many of the families I write about go wrong – which, ironically, mirrors the gruesome family of Augustus. You can see his crew in a self-aggrandising procession on the Ara Pacis in Rome; a gathering when the wise probably sent a sick-note.

The paterfamilias

Falco knows Rome is inescapably paternalist. *A man's duty is to honour the gods for his own household.* [TTD] (You're scared of the job, accuses Lenia, as she tries to woo him into acting as priest at her wedding.) Geminus has abandoned the Didii, thus upsetting the social order. Although Falco fulfils his duties, his family fight him off at will. He treats the position drily.

Once, the paterfamilias had the power of life and death; even adult sons had to be given formal 'emancipation' before they could make wills, own property, enter into contracts. The tradition has waned and Falco comments, *Acquiring emancipation from the power of his father is something that only troubles a son who feels bound by his father's power in the first place. In the Didius family this had never applied. Any pleb on the Aventine would probably say the same ...* [PG]

In a divorce, the paterfamilias had legal custody of children he had acknowledged; in practice it looks as if young children were brought up by their mothers.

Marriage

Far too much attention is paid to how aristocratic women were treated as political and financial pawns; this is history as told by men writing for the élite. It affected a very small part of society. Falco knows the system: *Plenty of Roman women of 'good' family are bedded by men they hardly know. Most bear them children, since that is the point. Some are then left to their own devices. Many welcome the freedom. They need not feign deep affection for their husbands; they can avoid the men almost totally. They acquire status without emotional responsibility. So long as acceptable financial arrangements are made, all that is demanded of them is that they refrain from taking lovers. Any rate, they should not flaunt their lovers openly.* [OVTM] What happened in high Roman circles probably had no more contemporary relevance than the cynical hitching of Lady Diana Spencer to the Prince of Wales (complete with an uncle swearing to her virginity – remember that obscenity?). The good part for me is that when a woman's value resides in her dowry, it suggests plots.

Falco and Helena prefer the more idealistic version, as do the equestrians Flavius Hilaris and Aelia Camilla: *The procurator and his lady shared their thoughts as we did. He and I were parties to true Roman marriage: confiding to our serious, sensitive womenfolk things we never even told our masculine friends.* [JM] Even the senator Camillus and Julia Justa have, it emerges, a marriage that is more equable, tolerant and affectionate than Falco first believes; it is, after all, the partnership that produced their three very independent children.

A contract was good practice when the parties brought money to the marriage; this was to say how, and by whom, the money would/could be used during the marriage and what would happen on death or divorce.

Once I discovered it (admittedly, it took a few books), I stuck by the view that marriage was defined as two people volunteering to live together.

Whatever the jokes about keeping wives in ignorance, a Roman expected his domestic partner to bear his children, keep the store-cupboard keys, quarrel with his mother and, if required, to share his confidence. The fact that Brutus failed to share with Porcia what he was planning on the Ides of March, just shows you why Brutus ended up dead mutton at Philippi … [TTD]

Divorce

According to that definition, divorce inescapably occurred when one partner chose to terminate the partnership. For those with contracts and dowries, the party leaving would issue a formal notification, as Helena does to Pertinax.

A special consideration was adultery (with complete horror reserved for adultery by women). *If a man discovers that his wife has committed adultery, he is legally bound to divorce her. Otherwise the husband can be taken to court on a charge of acting as a pimp. Allowing a Roman matron to be dishonoured is something we don't tolerate – if your husband actually catches you in bed with another man, he is entitled to draw a sword and kill you both.* [THF]

Adoption

Adoption for financial and social reasons was common-place. A famous adoptee was the Emperor Augustus, by birth a great-nephew of Julius Caesar, then adopted so that he inherited not only Caesar's money and special status but even a share in his awarded divinity.

Falco explains: *He adopted an heir. Common enough. A presentable young man with no hopes of his own, who was pleased to be welcomed by Marcellus into his noble house, honour his resplendent ancestors, promise to bury him with devoted respect – and in return supervise the substantial Marcellus estates.* [SP]

Falco and Helena will foster and formally adopt Flavia Albia – then eventually another child who is foisted on them in *Nemesis*.

The Concept of Empire

There is a celebrated passage in Virgil's *Aeneid: You, Roman, must remember that you have to guide the nations by your authority, for this is to be your skill, to graft tradition onto peace, to show mercy to the conquered, and to wage war until the haughty are brought low.* Idealistic and slightly patronising to other nations, this shows us what the Romans thought – or claimed – they were about.

Beyond prestige and power, there were practical reasons to expand: to stop other people attacking Italy; to control trade where others held Rome to ransom (the Arabian incense trade; the North African corn supplies; olive oil); to facilitate two-way trade generally; to acquire precious metal mines. The latter was a big reason for invading Britain, though we think the Romans had been misled about what was really available.

Falco knows Virgil: *I was a Roman. As the poet said, my mission was bringing civilised pursuits to the known world. In the face of tenacious opposition, I believed you whacked them, taxed them, absorbed them, patronised them, then proscribed human sacrifice, dressed them in togas and discouraged them from openly insulting Rome. That done, you put in a strong government and left them to get on with it.* [TFL] He also cynically says: *The dear tribes can decide for themselves whether they choose a javelin in the ribs and having their women raped, or cartloads of wine, some nice second-hand diadems, and a delegation of elderly prostitutes from Artemisia setting up shop in the tribal capital.* [BBH] This echoes a famous passage in Tacitus about civilising the British. *Agricola had to deal with people living in isolation and ignorance, and therefore prone to fight; his object was to accustom them to a life of peace and quiet by the provision of amenities … The result was that instead of loathing the Latin language, they became eager to speak it effectively. In the same way, our national dress came into favour and the toga was everywhere to be seen. And so the population was gradually led into the demoralising temptations of arcades, baths, and sumptuous banquets. The unsuspecting Britons spoke of such novelties as 'civilisation', when in fact they were only a feature of their enslavement.*

Tacitus is unexpectedly derogatory; his information must have come direct from his father-in-law, Agricola, who had governed Britain. With such dangerously liberal opinions, Tacitus notoriously put into the mouth of a defeated British tribal leader that scathing indictment of Roman imperialists: *Pillagers of the world, they have exhausted the land by their indiscriminate plunder … They are the only people on earth to whose covetousness both riches and poverty are equally tempting. To robbery, butchery, and rapine they give the lying name of 'government'; they create a desolation and call it peace.*

Falco and Helena are satirical, if not so disparaging: *Helena smiled. 'Here we are – all smart clothes, loud Latin and showing off our love of culture. Perhaps our shy British hosts are smitten with a fear that ghastly politeness will force them to mingle with a bunch of brash Romans … ' We were silent. She was right of course. Snobbery can work two ways.* [BBH] They review their ideas again in *See Delphi and Die* and *Alexandria*.

The Roman Empire endured for half a millennium before the barbarians crashed in. Although the army was the means of seizing and securing a province, the Romans were clearly more practical and, I'm afraid,

Nowhere in the Empire did Romans feel so out of place as in Greece. Imposing democracy on a country that in fact already possessed it raised a few questions. Bludgeoning the originators of the world's great ideas (and blatantly stealing the ideas) did not make us proud. [SDD]

more idealistic than us. Despite Tacitus, they created societies where people wanted to live: with democracy, education and law, with safety from other incursions, with a common currency and language, good transport links for trade, the habit of cleanliness and, in Britain, the blessing of glass windows and central heating. Even if few took the opportunity up, the ambitious could go to Rome and advance socially there.

Triumphs

The ultimate status symbol. A Triumph was a glorious procession to honour a victorious emperor after a major military campaign against enemies of Rome. There were floats, plunder, prisoners and soldiers. As the victor drove in his chariot, dressed as the god, Jupiter, he famously needed a slave to whisper *'Remember, you are mortal.'*

In *The Course of Honour* there is a fulsome description of Claudius' British Triumph; Falco was there, a little tot being sick … He sees much of Vespasian's Triumph for Judaea – even stumbles through the procession. Gallicus' hoped-for Ovation (a minor version for generals) drives the plot of *Saturnalia*. These are grand set-piece occasions – a wondrous gift to a novelist. If one occurred, I eagerly bung it in.

Law and Order

If you're willing to read your way through the records
    of world history
You will have to admit that justice arose from the
    fear of injustice.
HORACE

Roman Law is still studied (I work from a friend's old Roman Law textbook), though what survives is more civil than criminal: wills, heirs and legacies; debt; contract; property and rents; 'agricultural' law – damage by animals; rivers; ownership of fruit. I treat of these with caution because they can be complex and a wrong interpretation could invalidate my plot.

Worrying about crime was a curse of Roman society if you read the poets:

the usual quota
Of theft, embezzlement, fraud, all those criminal
    get-rich-quick schemes,
Glittering fortunes won by dagger or drug box?
JUVENAL

So the authorities tackled it:

Praetorians, Urbans and Vigiles

Rome had a typically stratified response. Let's allow Petronius Longus to spell it out, giving Claudius Laeta a wry, terse lecture:

'*Top of the heap you have the Praetorian Guard; Cohorts One to Nine, commanded by the Praetorian Prefect, barracked at the Praetorian Camp. Duties: one, guarding the Emperor; two, ceremonial swank. They are a hand-picked élite and full of themselves. Next in line and tacked on to them are Cohorts Ten to Twelve, known as the Urbans. Commanded by the Urban Prefect – a senator – who is basically the city manager. Routinely armed with sword and knife. Their unofficial job is* to repress the mob. *Duties officially: to keep the peace, keep their ears open, and keep the Urban Prefect informed of absolutely everything. And at the bottom, doing all the real work, you have the vigiles, commanded by the Prefect of the Vigiles. Seven cohorts, each led by a tribune who is an ex-chief centurion; each with seven centuries who do the foot patrols. Duties: everything those flash bastards at the Praetorian Camp won't lower themselves to touch …* ' [TTD]

The first two appear occasionally and are self-explanatory, but I spend a lot of time on the vigiles, who make a good fit with Falco.

The vigiles

Augustus established the vigiles as a fire brigade. All cooking, lighting and water-heating in Rome was carried out with naked flames. There were rules about leaving fires unattended, but compelling householders to obey rules was hopeless. As the vigiles patrolled the night-time streets looking for fires, they ran into numerous burglars so became the police force too.

The force was paramilitary though neither uniformed nor armed. *The vigiles' life was harsh and dangerous. Most of them had been public slaves. They had signed up because eventually, if they survived, they earned honourable discharge as citizens. The official term was just six years. Soldiers in the legions serve at least twenty. There was a good reason for the short enlistment, and not many vigiles lasted the full term.* [THF] Known as 'espartos' after the mats they used to smother fires, the vigiles were well equipped for fire-fighting with siphon-engines, buckets, ladders, axes and so forth.

They were a scarred-looking crew, though most had affectionate mothers and one or two could even tell you who their fathers were. [SB]

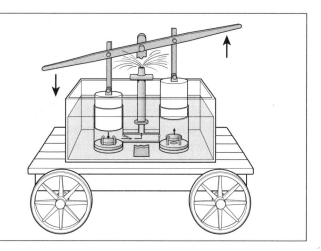

The fire engine was a gigantic tank of water pulled on a wagon. It had two cylinder pistons which were operated by a large rocker arm. As the vigiles worked the arm up and down – something they did with gusto when a crowd was watching – the pistons forced a jet of water up and out through a central nozzle. It had a flexible joint that could be turned through three hundred and sixty degrees. [TFL]

Each cohort patrolled two administrative regions, with a headquarters in one region and an out-station in the other. Some are known to archaeologists, though not Petro's Aventine out-station. A well-preserved *Casa* for the squad guarding the corn supply has survived at Ostia Antica. In these buildings the work might differ, but I imagine the atmosphere much as it is in police stations today – sometimes deserted because everyone is out, sometimes throbbing. In McBain's words: *Telephones rang and typewriters clattered and the place had the air of a thriving, if small, business concern.*

I don't see the vigiles as 'Dad's Army', but they have distinct colour, which I explore. *They cannot parade with their gear highly polished, and insofar as they drill it consists of life-saving tips and equipment practice. They are reluctant to march. A vigiles salute is likely to be derisive. Neat lines don't put out fires. If someone in the crowd had screamed for help, the Fourth would have shown themselves to be good men. But ceremonial was not their strength.* [STH]

Falco readers are expected to give unstinting loyalty to the Fourth Cohort, believing with Petronius that the rest are incompetent, corrupt, or idiots.

The vigiles had investigators called *quaestiones,* which my 'Watch Captain', Petronius Longus, is; I wish now that I had found a more Roman title for him. Petro is often called to murders very early in the morning: *They dump the corpse in the dark, then the dawn patrol discovers it at first light …* [TTD] I have assumed enquiry methods were crude and brutal. *Petronius and Sergius were teasing a statement out of a recalcitrant victim by the subtle technique of bawling fast questions while flicking him insistently with the end of a hard whip … They might close the case in a way that was traditional for the vigiles: find a suspect; say he did it; and if he really wants to get off, let him prove what really happened.* [OB]

I show tension between the vigiles and informers, whom they regard as amateurs. It cuts both ways: *Trust the vigiles; they have to invent a single hypothesis then prove it, whereas informers can cope with several ideas at once …* [THF]

In their work, the vigiles encouraged owners of premises to install fire protection and swooped on clothes thieves at the baths. They assisted aediles in regulating bars and brothels. The 'undesirables' they monitored included secret religions and anything

The two homicide cops looked down at the body on the sidewalk. It was a hot night, and the flies swarmed around the sticky blood on the sidewalk …
MCBAIN

In the detective squadroom of the 87th Precinct, the boys were swapping reminiscences about their patrolman days.

Now you may quarrel with the use of the word 'boys' to describe a group of men who ranged in age from twenty-eight to forty-two, who shaved daily, who went to bed with various and assorted mature and immature women, who swore like pirates, and who dealt with some of the dirtiest humans since Neanderthal ... There, was however, a spirit of boyish innocence in the squadroom in that dreary, rainy March day. It was difficult to believe that these men who stood in a fraternal knot around Andy Parker's desk, grinning, listening in attentiveness, were men who dealt daily with crime and criminals. The squadroom, in effect, could have been a high school locker room.
MCBAIN

If you happen to get arrested, always find out the names of your guards. [VC]

involving magic – not just witches and astrologers, but mathematicians and philosophers. A running joke against Falco is that the secret lists include informers – a forerunner to making private eyes register.

I have made Falco sympathetic to the vigiles' situation: *Sometimes the pressure and danger, and the sheer weight of despair, caused one of them to resign. The others became even more unsettled for a while. But normally they moaned a lot, got paralytic with an amphora, then carried on. Given their lousy pay and harsh conditions, plus the traditional indifference of their superiors, complaint seemed understandable ...* [TTD] Both he and I see them as slightly raffish; of their widows and orphans fund Falco says, *They want the grateful widows to save their thanks for the right people – their late husbands' colleagues. Some are good-looking girls who, being paupers, have to give their thanks in kind, poor dears ...* [AC] I base them on their modern counterparts: the patrol-car occupants Richard and I often saw parked up in a Rome side street while they waited for a call, untidy, with dangling fags, chatting up disreputable-looking women ...

Torture

Torture was a recognised part of the enquiry process, essential in the case of slaves. In *The Accusers,* Second Cohort vigiles accidentally kill a slave they are 'examining'. I bet it happened.

Torture consisted of applying hot flames to the soles of the feet, and using thumbscrews, pincers, and/or whipping. When Amicus is summoned to squeeze information from gangsters and witnesses in *The Jupiter Myth,* he also uses general deprivation (starvation) and psychological pressure (simple terror). Falco and Petronius deploy methods in *Nemesis* that I could only bear to hint at; I felt very squeamish about allowing these much-loved heroes to behave so cruelly but you'll see that the scene has a definite point.

Crime in Rome

Crime, socially and in the streets, is a frequent subject for Roman writers. Some crimes – extortion by a provincial governor, knowingly selling a runaway slave, or wives' adultery – are more their preoccupations than ours. Most is familiar: theft of different kinds, especially aggravated by violence; fencing stolen goods; rustling; embezzlement; forgery; abduction; rape; and of course murder. Anything to do with witchcraft or magic was particularly suspect. Poisoning included abortion. Having someone's horoscope prepared – or simply possessing it – especially that of an emperor, implied that you wished them dead.

Fraud and confidence tricks are regularly mentioned by satirists. Turius in *Ode to a Banker* and Lutea are hustlers: *He would be able to build an extensive career preying on the rich widows of exotic commodity traders … The widows would get plenty out of it. I saw them playing dice with him, their beringed fingers flashing in the light of many lampstands, while they congratulated themselves on their cultured catch. Lutea would leave them flat broke; even so, they would remember him with few hard feelings.* [AC]

In my books, we see both crimes and their effect on people; people who sometimes become clients. Falco pities victims and considers their bereaved associates. Like Petronius, he can be deeply upset: *It had been a terrible day. This was the true face of the Caesars' marble city: not Corinthian acanthus leaves and perfect gilt-lettered inscriptions, but a quiet man killed horrendously in the home and workplace he shared with his brother; a vicious revenge thrust on the one-time slave who had learned a respected profession then repaid his freedom and citizenship with a single act of assistance to the law. Not all the fine civic building programmes in the world would ever displace the raw forces that drive most of humankind. This was the true city: greed, corruption and violence …* [TTD]

Even when less despondent, Falco has strong views on motive, such as: *So often it is the people who have who think they deserve more. Those who lack expect nothing else from life.* [LAP] He is also aware of the domestic source of many murders. *Nemesis* opens with a discussion of this phenomenon. In *Last Act in Palmyra* Falco comments that a killer may be: *someone you eat with; a man somebody probably sleeps with … Someone who has done you kindnesses, made you laugh, sometimes irritated you to Hades for no reason in particular. Someone, in short, just like all the rest in this company.*

Petronius rants at the ambiguity with which society – ours too – views the successful criminal: the 'diamond geezer' syndrome. *A straight villain always respects a straight arrest. He'll shrug and accept that he's caught. But you self-justifying types have to make out that you cannot believe that anyone could so terribly misjudge you. You convince yourselves all that matters in civilised society is for men like you to continue your businesses without interference from officious sods like us. Sods who don't understand. Only I do understand. I understand what you are all too well ...* [TTD]

I am fascinated by street scams, which have a centuries-long history – for instance, the 'craft-rig' used by Gaius and Phlosis at Ostia, and the myriad petty crimes that Falco and Petronius take for granted in city life. Fusculus collects arcane terms – vocabulary invented by me because I cannot use English 'canting' that belongs to a much later period; we don't know the Latin words for criminals like *rat thieves and porch crawlers*.

Legal Procedure

If you did something illegal, your fate depended on what it was and who you were. There was a system analogous to the modern British police caution/ magistrates' court/crown court hierarchy. The vigiles dealt with day-to-day crimes like street theft, burglary, or failure to have statutory fire equipment; they acted either at patrol level or more formally via the Prefect of Vigiles, or they sent repeat offenders and capital cases up a level to the Urban Prefect. Aristocrats could demand to be tried by the Senate, or might even try to wangle a private hearing with the Emperor (*intra cubiculum* – literally in his bedroom). Because a paterfamilias counted as chief magistrate in his own household, even serious matters could be dealt with at home. A domestic tribunal occurs in *Nemesis*, a story about families. Although the accused is not a relative, legal recourse is unavailable and the issue of justice concerns everyone present. (So does the risk, if the proposed action goes wrong.)

Normally, as happens now in many legal systems, a pre-trial hearing before a magistrate determined whether a case went to court. Most important in my

The chief magistrate of Rome may be a blithering incompetent, but when the magistrate makes a pronouncement there is no appeal. [AC]

series is the court where Marponius lurks. *The full title of the murders court is the Tribunal for Poisoners and Assassins. Poisoning is routinely associated with spells, potions and other foul magic. Assassins may be all kinds of murderers, including armed robbers.* [AC] Juries had seventy-five members, free citizens drawn from each of the three ranks; they sat silent and voted in secret, though intriguingly it was possible to know the collective votes of each rank.

It is surprisingly hard to find details of court procedures. In *The Accusers*, I did my best. There is the pre-trial hearing, the award of time for investigation and the right to speak first, the intricate process of selecting the judge: defendants are made up cosmetically to look distressed, an accused nearly fails to appear. We also have a prosecutor (Falco) in danger of a very serious penalty for dropping his case, even though new facts have emerged.

Then as now, a court case involved theatricality, though the Romans were more open about it. *Juries love a man who goes to the trouble of bad acting.* [AC]

Informers and Their Work

Get yourself a proper job and earn some decent cash! [SB]

For the Falco series, I suggest a kind of private eye existed. People called informers certainly did.

Who Were Informers?

'Yours is an unenviable job, Falco.'
'Oh it has its attractions: travel, exercise, meeting new people from all walks of life ... ' [SB]

'The idea is that we obtain facts by our skill and cunning.' I left out theft, bribery and fraud. *'Then in order that we can make a living, other people pay us for those facts.'* [LAP]

He [Anacrites] wore a neutral-coloured tunic with faintly rakish styling, close-fitting boots, and a hard leather belt. Hung on the belt were a small purse, a large note tablet, and a set of nail files to keep him occupied if he ever needed to lean against an Ionic column for hours observing a suspect. Someone must have been giving him lessons. He had the classic informer's look: tough, slightly truculent, perhaps amiable if you got to know him, a curious and faintly unreliable sort of character ... [THF]

INFORMER: *Wings – I need them for my job. I'm a summoner, an informer you know. I work the islands.*
PEISTHETAERUS: *A noble profession. I congratulate you.*
INFORMER: *Rigging up prosecutions and so on ...*
PEISTHETAERUS: *And is this how you earn your living? A young man like you, with nothing better to do than go round laying information against foreigners?*
INFORMER: *What else can I do?*
PEISTHETAERUS: *There are lots of respectable jobs a man like you could do. You could earn an honest living instead of hanging around the lawcourts all the time.*
ARISTOPHANES

So what was an informer, a *delator?* Their pedigree goes back at least to the Greeks; Aristophanes' comedy *The Birds*, source of 'Cloud-cuckoo-land', has an informer, who flies about the Greek islands handing out subpoenas.

An excellent book by Steven H. Rutledge discusses the First Century informer: *He is one who is a fierce opportunist, a ruthless careerist who will climb to the top and create peril for all who cross his path, who disregards danger to himself, who gains access to the princeps' ear. He is lowborn, advances from poverty to wealth, and is a threat to those of high rank. In short,* delatores *constitute a negative social category, often based on the social and political prejudices, as well as the status-conscious nature of Roman society; it was a way Romans communicated with one another concerning perceived abuses of the legal system and of political privilege as well.* Falco is acutely aware of informers' behaviour under Nero and of why, therefore, the public despise them: *Those vermin skulking behind temple pillars to overhear unguarded comments from the pious, or even using private conversations at dinner parties to betray their last night's hosts. The political parasites who, before Vespasian purged public life, had put fear into the whole Senate. The slugs who had empowered bad emperors' favourites, and oiled the jealousies of worse emperors' mothers and wives ...* [PG] Late in my series, at the start of *The Accusers,* Falco says: *I had been an informer for over a decade when I finally learned what the job entailed ...* Then we see the traditional version.

But initially, instead of making him a full-time prosecutor, I devised Falco from scratch rather differently. *Shedding a putrid body from the Censor's list of citizens was up to standard for my work. It was unhygienic, irreligious, and put me off my food ... In my time I had operated for perjurers, petty bankrupts and frauds. I swore court affidavits to denounce high-born senators for debauchery so gross that even under Nero it could not be covered up. I found missing children for rich parents who would better abandon them and pleaded lost causes for widows with legacies who married their spineless lovers the very next week — just when I had got them some money of their own. Most of the men tried to dodge off without paying, while most of the women wanted to pay me in kind. You can guess which kind; never a sweet capon or a fine fish.* [SB]. We know Falco has experience of tracing lost children; however, his response to Albia's plea to find her family is glum: *It was always the most painful question an informer could be asked. Either you cannot trace the missing ones, and you never stood a chance of doing so, or you do find them and it all goes badly wrong. I had never known a good outcome. I refused to handle such requests from clients any more.* [JM]

It was important to establish Falco as a recognisable fiction genre type. Raymond Chandler discussed this, seeing him as: *a lonely man, a poor man, a dangerous man, and yet a sympathetic man ... I think he will always be awakened at some inconvenient hour by some inconvenient person to do some inconvenient job. It seems to me that is his destiny,*

Who's next? An informer.
He turned in his noble patron,
And soon he'll have gnawed
   away that favourite bone of
   his,
The aristocracy. Lesser
   informers dread him, grease
His palm with ample bribes,
   while the wives of trembling
   actors
Grease him the other way.
JUVENAL

possibly not the best destiny in the world, but it belongs to him. This is certainly true of Falco's life on the Aventine when we first meet him. It fits comfortably with the Roman Stoic's attitude: *Such is more or less the way of the wise man: he retires to his inner self, is his own company. So long in fact as he remains in a position to order his affairs according to his own judgement, he remains self-content even when he marries, even when he brings up his children.* Falco says, half joking, *We informers are tough men. Our work is grim. When not treading a solitary path we like to be surrounded by other grim, tough men who feel that life is filthy but that they have mastered it.* [STH]

In modern detective writing the 'gritty' protagonist is frequently a depressed alcoholic chain-smoker, with a failed marriage and disastrous parental relationships, at odds with the boss and unable to handle subordinates. I could not have spent twenty years with that; Falco scoffs: *I had met informers who implied that to succeed they needed not just sore feet, a hangover, a sorry love life and some progressive disease, but a dour, depressing outlook too. I disagree. The work provides enough misery. Being happy gives a boost that can help solve cases. Confidence counts.* [LAP] However, he never forgets the downside: *Bratta showed his teeth. They were a sorry set. Too much bad food munched at cheap food stalls while he was watching people and places. The usual. He was one of us all right.* [AC]

As time went by I gained enough confidence to make fun of the genre. There are occasions, usually when Falco addresses us directly, when he and I mock traditional crime novel clichés. *I had made him drunk. Now I had to sober him up again. That's because the theory is wrong. When you bring a witness to the point of passing out, he does not know he is supposed to tell you all before he quits – he just goes ahead and drifts into oblivion …* [JM] Eventually we reach the double-take, where our hero, loosely undercover as a playwright, acts in a play as himself: *My role was tiresome. I played the informer. In this otherwise witty satire, my character creeps in after the ghastly poet, the twisting fortune-teller, the rebellious youth and the cranky philosopher,* grumbles Falco (incidentally listing the kind of cast I am prone to using). *Once they have come to Cloud-cuckoo-land and all been seen off by the Athenians, an informer tries his luck. Like mine, his luck is in short supply, to the delight of the audience.* [LAP]

The Workload

Many of the murders and frauds Falco has to investigate are unusual, as is common in mystery novels. Regarding murders, he is always conscious that most unnatural deaths occur for trivial reasons amongst close acquaintances. In *Nemesis,* where he will be thinking about families and crime, he asks very early in the book: *Why are more kitchen cleavers not sunk between the fat shoulders of appalling uncles who get the slaves pregnant? Or that sneaky sister who shamelessly grabs the most desirable bedroom, with its glimpse of a corner of the Temple of Divine Claudius and almost no cracks in the walls? Or the crude son who farts uncontrollably, however many times he is told …* It's not the first time he has mused gloomily like this: *Cronies fall out. They sit in a tavern having a drink, then they quarrel about money, or women, or political philosophy, or simply about whether their boat home leaves on Tuesday or Thursday. Then it's natural that somebody gets stabbed and his pal legs it …* [PG]

For other kinds of crime, especially deception by confidence tricksters, I am heavily influenced by what Latin authors say. Clearly Rome was full of chancers. According to Horace, wills were eyed up jealously:

> *You must fish cunningly around*
> *For old men's wills. If one or two are clever enough*
>   *to nibble*
> *The bait off the hook and escape your clutches, don't*
>   *give up hope …*

Juvenal adds other disreputable types:

> *Don't you just want to cram whole notebooks with*
>   *scribbled invective*
> *When you stand at a corner and see some forger*
>   *carried past*
> *On the necks of six porters, lounging back like*
>   *Maecenas*
> *In his open litter? A counterfeit seal, a will, a mere*
>   *scrap*
> *Of paper – these were enough to convert him to*
>   *wealth and honour.*
> *Do you see that distinguished lady? She has the*
>   *perfect dose*

For a thirsty husband – old wine with a dash of
toad's blood.

Since official forces of law and order exist, Falco inevitably gets cases where the crime has been cunningly disguised, the victim has no one to speak for them, or the mystery is so old nobody else thinks it can be solved.

Clients

They come pleading with you to save their skins,
then when you've given up weeks of hard effort for
some pitiful reward, you take them the answer and
they stare at you as if you are mad to bother them
with these puny facts ... [PG]

While they are working as partners, Petronius Longus devises an advertisement (which disgusts Falco) where he claims they offer *a select service for discerning clients,* making *specialist enquiries,* and offering *no charge for preliminary consultation.* As Falco fears, they are inundated with unsuitable customers and he has to admit, *I hate barristers, but their work might make the difference between survival and going under.* [THF] We see him taking legal casework at the beginning of *The Accusers.*

Falco does constant routine work that he never bothers to tell us about. He has been hired by all sorts, from the Emperor, through the vigiles when they are short-handed, down to freedmen; a six-year-old girl tries to hire him in *One Virgin Too Many* but he puts her off. He will investigate corruption or serial killings for the state, but the ultimate Falco client tends to be an oddball who comes uninvited, with a case that sounds ghastly (yet is compelling), where the fee is uncertain, the encounters annoying and dangerous, the outcome most likely disappointing.

They saw us as devious political sneaks; we knew they were incompetent thugs. They could put out fires. We possessed more sophisticated expertise. [OB]

Skills

In writing about an ancient period, there are benefits; you don't need knowledge of modern ballistics or forensic science. Falco has to 'keep 'em peeled': eyes, ears, nose (my smells!). That, plus understanding human nature, will see him through. He says pragmatically: *Investigating consists mainly of failure. You need thick boots and a strong heart, plus an infinite capacity for staying awake while parked in a draughty pergola, hoping that that strange scuttling sound is only a rat, not a man with a knife, though all the time you know that even if the person you are watching for ever does turn up, they will be a dead loss* ... [PG]

I have tried to deduce actions an informer could take: checking public records, looking up geographical information at a public library, looking for a missing person at the Aesculapius hospital on Tiber Island or seeing if they have been arrested by the vigiles. Falco knows useful people personally – or he knows Rome enough to winkle out those who hold information.

He likes to give us professional insights, for instance when discussing the rather strait-laced Marius Optatus: *Some people are eager to gossip, but a few unusual souls do find discussing their neighbours distasteful. These are the ones who are best value to an informer. They are offended by offers of payment, and better still they tell the truth.* [DLC] Or, *Many a craftsman's lock-up is overrun by children; people dislike being interviewed about their life-or-death problems while an energetic baby hurls porridge at their knees.* [OVTM] And: *I was hoping that the witness would cave in out of sheer anxiety. In life, they never do.* [BBH] Or: *She spoke like a woman who was being quite honest. Women who are lying always know just how to do that.* Above all, Falco's take on the job is humane:

> 'When I look at a corpse I remember "he must have parents somewhere; he may have had a wife." If I can, I find them. I tell them what happened. I try to be quick; most people want time to react alone. But some of them come back to me afterwards and ask for details all over again. That's bad enough.'
>
> 'What's worse?'
>
> 'Thinking about the ones who want to ask but never come.' [SB]

In the Appendix, I have reproduced a recent archaeological find, tentatively translated as *The Forum Informer's Handbook,* though it may be spurious.

Some Other Aspects of Roman Life

I can't produce a Roman encyclopaedia, but these are subjects people regularly ask about:

The Roman Home (and Its Frequent Refurbishment!)

The Roman domus turned a blind, unbroken wall on the street and all its doors and windows opened on its interior courts. The insula, on the other hand, opened always to the outside and when it formed a quadrilateral around a central courtyard, its doors, windows, and staircases opened both to the outside and to the inside. The domus was composed of halls whose proportions were calculated once for all and dictated by custom in advance. These halls opened off each other in an invariable order: fauces, atrium, alae, triclinium, tablinium (doorway, hall, colonnades, dining room, and terrace) and peristyle. The insula combined a number of cenacula, that is to say, distinct and separate dwellings like our 'flats' or 'apartments', consisting of rooms not assigned in advance to any particular function. The plan of each storey was apt to be identical to that above and below, the rooms being superimposed from top to bottom of the building.

This was my template from the outset, from Carcopino's *Daily Life in Ancient Rome*. It gave me both tenements and grand houses. My task was to show that most people lived in tenements, so grand houses would be, for a man like Falco, a matter of wonder, envy and distrust. I found it easy to impose squalor on the tenements; I trowel on dirt, pongs, crawlies, noise, fear. Andrew Wallace-Hadrill's work on the houses of Pompeii and Herculaneum helped firm up my vision of wealthier spreads with their frescos and gasp-inducing sightlines; For example, *A public figure went home not so much to shield himself from the public gaze as to present himself to it in the best light.*

We know from premises where builders were at work when Vesuvius erupted that places were frequently rearranged, refurbished and rebuilt for new uses. Jobbing craftsmen with various levels of competence must have swarmed everywhere, exploiting general fashions or owners' personal taste. This proved topical to write about in the age of the TV makeover (how Roman designers would have swooned over *feng shui* and that darling, the 'colour accent cushion'). It also fits my own life as a home-owner, with its glorious highlights of Fruiting Bodies, putting up an Anaglypta frieze, and those energy-sapping encounters with swine who inspired Gloccus and Cotta. For legal reasons I cannot reveal from whom I recovered the price of a defunct central heating boiler using the Small Claims Court; threatening to name the maker at all my public events and saying I would have better service from a Roman hypocaust did work. This was a highly satisfactory by-product of writing the Falco series.

To illustrate Roman curse tablets, try this:
I curse Peter and Kevin and Roy and Young Roy and their life and mind and memory and liver and lungs mixed up together, and their words, thoughts and memory ... May he who cheated me over the gravity-feed hot water tank become as liquid as water!
DAVIS

Food and Drink

> *First there comes the complex science of flavours*
>   *which has to be mastered.*
> *And it isn't enough to sweep fish off an expensive*
>   *slab*
> *Without knowing which are better with sauce and*
>   *which should be grilled*
> HORACE

It's vital to remember that Roman food included nothing from the New World. No tomatoes, pasta, potatoes, aubergines, peppers, sunflower seeds, and certainly no cocoa, chocolate or real ice cream – ruling out the main ingredients of modern Italian cuisine. There was no sugar, but people used a great deal of honey.

Think Roman, think Apicius. Think several of them, though the original lived early in the First Century; Falco can go to dinner parties and eat such lush cuisine – Roast Kid stuffed with Ginger Sausage, Peas Vitellian, Sea Urchins in Wine Sauce. I've had fun implying that a Chicken Vardanus or Chicken Frontinian might be spoken of like Chicken Biryani or Chicken Tikka ...

Most people ate more simply, as Falco does normally. Cooking at home for many was frying in a skillet or boiling in a saucepan; grilling was feasible on a kind of indoor barbecue but Falco has to build his own. It was healthy food, using fresh ingredients from markets; there was meat if you could afford it, fish and shellfish, dry-cured meats and sausages, vegetables and fruit, salads and herbs; not much dairy, though various cheeses. Needing an oven meant taking your food to a baker at the end of the day, just as it did throughout more modern history for the urban poor.

Otherwise, people ate at the many 'fast food' outlets we see in archaeological remains, or bought snacks from pedlars' trays of pies and sausages. Not good for cholesterol – though frescos don't show many as obese. They probably worked too hard.

Caupona, *popina* or *thermopolium*? – well, what's the difference between a café, a trattoria and a hosteria? I tend to use 'caupona', a shop, inn or tavern, consistently

Typical caupona counter pots

for streetside snack or wine bars, to avoid confusion. Strictly speaking, a *thermopolium* served hot drinks and a *popina* was an eating house. Most would have offered sexual services upstairs because the definition of a waitress had the same connotations as 'masseur' nowadays.

A Lucanian Sausage was clearly a loukaniko. When I say 'rissole' I mean something equivalent to a doner kebab. When I say 'big rissole' I mean either a bumper kebab or a master criminal.

For Roman writers, shorthand for luxury was a turbot. Yes, I cooked one; it was delicious. Caraway sauce may be an acquired taste.

Americans get confused by 'corn' – which amazes us in Europe with our much older languages and wider world view …

Garum/liquamen

A perennial curiosity! Sally Grainger needs almost fifteen pages to untangle Roman fish sauces, so I am at the edge of my précis skills here.

Evidence from Pompeii attests the wide use of *garum* and *liquamen* which may, or may not, be the same thing. There were different versions, perhaps many. My mum, without question, would have boiled up her own in a saucepan at home (especially when she was book-keeping for a stall at the fish market!).

The finest was a gourmet's condiment, but humble houses and foodshops used fish sauce. It could be made from whole small fish (dissolved), from entrails and/or blood or chopped parts (fermented in the sun); it probably had extremely fresh ingredients, so because of the fast-acting salt was less smelly than we think. Mackerel was a preferred base. It could be made in barrels or amphorae, with the fish layered with salt and herbs, or on an industrial scale in tanks. The fermentation time could be thirty days or three months. When the liquid sauce cleared, a thick paste, called *allec*, formed at the bottom of the container; this was a real fermented 'pickle' and had different uses.

Spain was a centre for fish sauce production. In *A Dying Light in Corduba*, Falco mentions that the best came from Cadiz; there was a version considered inferior, called Muria (tuna based).

If you are recreating Roman food, either anchovy essence or the Far Eastern *nam pla* or *nuoc mam* are reckoned acceptable substitutes. I imagine boys slathered it on as heavily as modern teenagers do ketchup.

Silphium

The so-called silphium was disgusting. Still, nobody eats raw garlic, and I myself had a high disdain for truffles. Owning a world monopoly was the aim. Luxuries only have to be scarce, not nice. Participants' enjoyment is in thinking they have something other people can't acquire or afford. [TFL]

Silphium, a large plant, was so highly prized that the city of Cyrene, which controlled the trade, had its emblem on coins. Its uses were many. It became extinct either through over-cropping or because the local tribes wanted the land; Nero was supposed to have eaten the last shoot. An inferior alternative is said to be asafoetida.

When Helen and I were in Libya, we heard rumours that silphium was growing again, around Tobruk, on land which has lain undisturbed because it is heavily infested with landmines. We met the proverbial man who knew a man who had seen it ... we never saw it ourselves.

Drinks

What did people drink when they had no tea, coffee or soft drinks, when less milk is drunk around the warm Mediterranean than in Northern Europe, and when water was unpurified? It's a problem for historical novelists. I think people must have drunk the water regardless of flies, sewage and dead sheep. *Mulsum* (wine mixed with honey, sometimes diluted like cordial) may have been fairly common and was a staple for soldiers. I have Falco and Helena frequently imbibe herbal tisanes, but clearly they are cranks.

Of course there was wine. Respectable people diluted it, though Falco has a fad of taking his water in a separate beaker. Wine could be sweetened with honey or flavoured with herbs. I use authentic varieties:

Falernian, Setinum, Caecubian, rotgut ... Because vine-
yards across Europe were devastated by the phylloxera
epidemic in the late Nineteenth Century (the bugs
were introduced from America where vines were resist-
ant), it is almost impossible to drink the same wine as
the Romans, though it seems to me that grapes grown
on the same soil and in the same sun may produce a
vintage in the same spirit.

Fine wines were kept to a great age, for example
twenty years. I assume people also drank much younger
wines, particularly in a domestic setting where they
may have produced their own or had it sent to town by
country relatives. There is a strong Mediterranean tradition that everyone, including children, drinks well-
watered local wine with meals. People everywhere
liked the stuff; it was traded over long distances.

The *Daily Gazette*, or *Acta Diurna*

No middle-ranker passes on without an
announcement in the Daily Gazette *to warn the*
gods in Hades that the shade of an eminent person is
expecting the best seat in Charon's ferryboat ... [SB]

See under 'Novels', *Scandal Takes a Holiday.*

Games

The Romans had several board games, of which the
best known are *latrunculi*, or Soldiers, and *duodecim
scripta*, or Twelve Lines; the former was probably like
chess or draughts and the latter akin to backgammon.
Numerous sets of counters in two colours have been
found at archaeological sites, with occasional evidence
of playing boards; examples are scratched by the Basilica
Julia in Rome. While despondent and wounded in *The
Silver Pigs*, Falco has to fill in time playing draughts and
says he hates board games, especially when playing
against an Egyptian physician who always wins.

When I mention *latrunculi*, there is an extra reference to 'Stuff that for a game of soldiers' (where 'stuff',

though onomatopoeic, is not my actual word), modern slang for, 'I won't do that because it sounds unpleasant and likely to go wrong'. I might use this, for example, while thinking, 'shall I meticulously distinguish between *latrunculi* and *duodecim scripta?* – oh, ★★★★★★ that for a game of soldiers!'

Although public gambling was illegal, there was much dicing, as seen in a very famous wall painting of two men quarrelling at an inn. I'd like Falco to use dicing argot, but we know very little. He must confine his metaphors to weighted dice – of which surprising numbers are known to archaeologists.

Kottabos

Falco gives a world-weary description when faced by young men engaged in this messy Greek party game: *kottabos was invented by a group of uproarious drunks. You have a tall stand with a large bronze disc suspended horizontally halfway up. A small metal target is balanced on the top of the stand. The players drink their wine then flick their cups to expel the dregs. They aim to make the flying lees hit the target so it falls off and hits the lower disc with a noise like a bell. All the wine they flick splatters the room and themselves.* [DLC]

There are other references to the pastime which, according to our jaded hero, explains why the Greeks no longer rule the world. He is in Athens when he says that; the boy knows no fear.

Roman Names: the *Trianomina*

> *I refrained from saying that only select members of my family were permitted to use my personal name …* [PG]

This subject really worries some readers.

A certain Ján Ludwig Hoch renamed himself Ian Robert Maxwell, then used the *second* of his forenames because he believed that was what British aristocrats did … In Rome, the complexities may have been as subtle. Rules existed, so textbook writers regurgitate them, apparently believing the Romans were a law-abiding people.

Ideally, a free man had three names: *praenomen, nomen, cognomen;* a woman had two. A man was officially described according to the *lex Julia municipalis;* so in documents or inscriptions our hero is:

Marcus Didius, son of Marcus, of the Falerina voting tribe, Falco

You didn't know his voting tribe? No, I just chose it. Aren't you glad you bought this book?

(1) The *praenomen* is the 'personal' name, though clearly not used like 'Darren', since every male in a family could have the same one. Vespasian, his father and grandfather, his brother, his two sons and his nephews were *all* called Titus. A nightmare at the breakfast table, this would be unbearable in a novel.

There were only twelve common *praenomina*: Aulus (abbreviated to A); Appius (Ap); Gaius (C); Gnaeus (Cn); Decimus (D); Lucius (L); Marcus (M); Publius (P); Quintus (Q); Servius (Ser); Titus (T); and Tiberius (Ti). I chose Marcus specifically because it is modern English too.

(2) The *nomen,* a family name. I chose Didius because my dictionary said it was plebeian. A later emperor had it, but that's coincidence.

(3) The *cognomen*. Textbook writers call this a nickname, like 'Baldy'. Really? How many of us, when naming a baby, can guess its character or appearance? Incidentally, Brutus, 'the noblest Roman of them all', was in strict translation 'Heavy' – Marcus Junius *Fatso?* – or even 'Stupid'. *Et tu, Dumbo!* gives an intriguing gloss, infrequently noted by scholars. Mark Antony never had a *cognomen;* who can blame him?

A *cognomen* was often geographical: Vespasian's brother Sabinus ('the Sabine'); Rutilius Gallicus who came from near Gaul; Silius Italicus. Or there were family reasons. Vespasian was named after his mother, Vespasia Polla; he named his second son Domitianus, after his wife, Flavia Domitilla.

Why Falco? I wanted a Latin word for a tool, as in Sam Spade or Mike Hammer. So, I lay in bed for several nights diligently reading the entire *Smith's Smaller Latin Dictionary*. Most promising was falx, a sickle. It failed to roll off the page, but turned into Falco – which could allude to *The Maltese Falcon*. It was important that my three chosen names, Marcus Didius Falco, went together well when spoken aloud (a lesson to all parents). I only learned later that Flaco is a natural typing mistake.

Women had no *praenomen*. We can only speculate on why they needed no 'intimate' name. Textbook dogmatists insist women were always named after their fathers. Oh but look, trusting textbook writers! Vespasian's daughter was called Flavia Domitilla after Mum, and his grand-daughter likewise.

Helena should perhaps be Camilla. Camilla is just *so* English toff!

Some experts maintain women took their husbands' names in the genitive case. I have seen this only occasionally. On tombstone after tombstone, women have their own names – even when a widower is paying for the inscription.

Perhaps she really is; perhaps this is why Marcus can never find her birth certificate at the Atrium of Liberty. Perhaps as a child she decided she didn't like her name and decreed her relations must call her something else!

Other naming points

We know one affectionate diminutive: Cicero sometimes called his daughter Tullia, Tulliola. So watch out for Juliola, Favoniola, Albiola (they sound like cooking oils, full of saturated fats …)

Slaves conventionally had a Greek name: Caenis, Narcissus. On manumission, they adopted their patron's first name: Antonia Caenis, Tiberius Claudius Anacrites. In the provinces, those granted citizenship took the Emperor's name: Flavia Albia.

Adoptees would add a set of names to gratify their new relatives, as in Quintus Julius Cordinus Gaius Rutilius Gallicus.

For great deeds, an *agnomen* might be earned: Scipio was called Africanus for defeating the Carthaginians. C. Julius Caesar Octavianus (NB: he had first been adopted by Julius Caesar), on becoming emperor allowed himself to be called Augustus; subsequent emperors were all Imperator Caesar Augustus.

Emperors' official titles show how flexible the system was: Augustus used his flashy *agnomen*. Vespasian used his *cognomen,* but Titus always distinguished himself from Dad by using the 'intimate' *praenomen*. Gaius had set this precedent – though Gaius is better known to us as 'Caligula', a nickname he acquired as a child ('Little Boots').

I don't believe we know how the Romans talked to each other. They were a volatile Mediterranean people; did they jab a finger to get noticed? Snatch at someone's tunic sleeve? Grip a wrist? Gesture rarely shows up in literary sources.

Degrees of formality were important though: *Towards Helvidius Crispus who was the only man to greet him by the private name of 'Vespasian', he showed no anger until he felt himself virtually reduced to the ranks by Priscus' insufferable rudeness. Thereupon Vespasian banished him and presently gave orders for his execution.* [SUETONIUS]

I decide by 'feel'. Russia gives some clues. On a TV programme about the man we called 'President Yeltsin', I noticed that journalists and fellow politicians referred to him as 'Boris Nikolayevich'. (That included the rival politician, subsequently removed from office, who was calling him an inept drunk …)

My Roman system works like this: a man's full three names or a woman's two are most formal. Marcus Didius Falco would be on a writ; he is Marcus Didius when his family mention him to others, Marcus when they are badgering him directly; polite outsiders say Didius Falco. Falco is for strangers, enemies or when he is in trouble with his wife.

I don't think he knows about 'Mickey Spartacus'.

Religion

Religion was a very visible aspect of Roman life, with temples to gods of all types dominating Rome. Festivals, mainly religious, filled the calendar; they involved street processions and, like Bank Holidays now, they affected civic life. There could be ten named festivals a month, some celebrations taking place over several days or as long as a fortnight. Many went back to the mists of time and it is no longer certain exactly what deity or concept was being commemorated. Falco comments on festivals with resignation; in a plot they are a useful way to give a scene focus or just to cause him hassle.

There were numerous permitted religions. The Olympian pantheon was 'official', with the Roman versions of the old Greek gods and goddesses: first, Jupiter 'Best and Greatest', with Juno and Minerva; then Venus, Mars, Neptune, Vulcan, Ceres, Mercury, Apollo, Diana and Vesta. There are also: Fortune; the implacable Fates who spin man's thread of life; the Three Graces; the nine inspiring Muses; and of course Nemesis, the even-handed goddess who cancels out undeserved good fortune. The demigod Hercules was very popular. The Bona Dea had secret rites attended by matrons (e.g. Julia Justa). Quirinus was the deified Romulus. Other cults were tolerated in Rome, chiefly the Eastern Cybele and Egyptian Isis. Mithras, the soldiers' god, was perhaps not widely popular at this period; archaeologists have found fabulous mithraea (e.g. London and Ostia), but of later date. However, Falco thinks that Festus experimented.

Deified emperors gained cults, even Vespasian, who had mocked the idea. Gaius Baebius yearns to be an affiliate. To deny the Emperor's divinity was blasphemy, as the early Christians found. However, they were not thrown to the lions under the Flavians and the contemporary attitude is shown by a famous instruction from Trajan to Pliny: *These people must not be hunted out; if they are brought before you and the charge against them is proved, they must be punished, but in the case of anyone who denies that he is a Christian, and makes it clear that he is not by offering prayers to our gods, he is to be pardoned as a result of his repentance however suspect his past conduct may be.*

The old Roman state religion involved priestly 'colleges', such as the Arval Brethren; although membership might boost an aristocrat's career, Falco says: *The fanciful rites of the ancient cults, where only the favoured may communicate with the gods, are about power in the state.* [OVTM] The most important priest, the Flamen Dialis, was present at state occasions; you can pick him out in

Festus had tried the whole Mithraic ritual of lying in a trench in the dark and having the blood of a sacrificial bull rain down on him. I doubt if he ever progressed beyond the first level … [STH]

procession on the Ara Pacis, thanks to his strange pointed hat. Peculiarly Roman were the Vestal Virgins, who tended the fire that must never go out on the sacred hearth which represented the life, welfare and unity of the state. Their role as guardians of wills, mainly for the aristocracy, comes up several times.

Falco is a man with a conscience though he despises superstition. He does not pray; in a typical crisis he doesn't have time. He rules his own life but does not interfere in other people's beliefs.

> *'Do you believe in the gods?'*
> *'Enough to have cursed them many times …*
> *I believe in human endeavour. I believe that most*
> *mysteries have a logical explanation; all you have to*
> *do is find it.'* [SDD]

At a black moment in *Nemesis*, he merely says, *I don't annoy the gods; I don't encourage them either.*

He wore a shaggy double-sided cloak and on his head a birchwood prong set in a wisp of wool; this contraption was held on by a round hat with ear-flaps, tied under his chin with two strings, rather like an item my baby daughter used to pull off and throw on the floor. [OVTM]

Medicine, Dentistry, Contraception

> *I was unwell. You hurried round, surrounded*
> *By ninety students, Doctor. Ninety chill,*
> *North-wind-chapped hands then pawed and probed*
> *   and pounded.*
> *I was unwell; now I'm extremely ill.*
> MARTIAL

Falco has a similar brush with a doctor and his students, when he nearly suffers a leg amputation in an army hospital in *The Silver Pigs*.

The best doctoring was given to gladiators (the expensive, trained kind); Galen worked with them. Ancient medicine traditionally derived from the teachings of Aesculapius and of Hippocrates, whose compassionate oath doctors still swear. Both Falco's parents have operations we know existed in Roman times (for cataracts and piles), Veleda wants trepanation and Scaeva has his tonsils removed – with the risk of haemorrhage that still applies today. Consultancy was profitable in ancient Rome; in *Saturnalia* I have fun discussing rival disciplines and techniques. There are fads among the

There are doctors who would agree anything. Plenty of dead patients could testify to that. [TFL]

rich. Women who have difficulty conceiving attend a specialist clinic ... It all sounds familiar.

> *Insomnia causes more deaths among Roman invalids*
> *Than any other factor (the most common complaints,*
>   *of course,*
> *Are heartburn and ulcers, brought on by over-eating).*
> JUVENAL

As a crime-writer I have learned a fair bit about botanical poisons; hellebore, hemlock, corn cockle – don't try these at home. For *Alexandria* I described an autopsy, though it would be illegal in Roman society.

Dentistry

Dentistry was surprisingly sophisticated. The Etruscans made successful bridgework (for the rich, as the wires were gold) and long before titanium, a man in Gaul survived having an iron post fixed into his jaw. Great-Uncle Scaro's home-made false teeth have a basis in archaeology (bone, dogs' teeth or metal were used) – though Scaro's choking to death on the fourth prototype is my invention.

Unfortunately I have lost the newspaper article that inspired the fake dentist in *A Body in the Bath House*; it was about two men in a North African country who were arrested after carrying on an unauthorised dental practice, where they used such tools as tyre irons ...

Contraception

Contraception was legal, though abortion was not (it deprived the father of his rights). We know of spermicides and other contraceptive methods, though evidence of use is hard to obtain. Falco gives Larius a lesson: *There are ways to avoid it: holding back manfully in moments of passion, or eating garlic to put the women off. Some people swear by a sponge soaked in vinegar. Festus told me once, if you know where to go and are prepared to afford it, you can buy scabbards sewn from fine calfskin to guard delicate parts of your anatomy from disease; he swore he had one though he never showed me. According to him, it helped prevent the arrival of curly-haired little accidents.* [SB]

On that hot August night in Palmyra when Julia Junilla is conceived, I wanted to show that the main reason contraception fails is that people omit to use it.

The Armed Forces

The army

In Falco's time there was a professional standing army of more than twenty legions, with the highest concentration in the most restless frontier provinces. Briefly, each legion had between five and six thousand men, in six cohorts, each divided into ten centuries (confusingly, only about eighty men). The training was superb, as was equipment and nourishment, though there must have been high degrees of boredom except on campaigns.

The army provided opportunity for the poor, citizenship for foreigners, and career postings for the aristocracy. My knowledge of how armies work is drawn from what I heard in my childhood after the Second World War and my work in the civil service. Falco encounters a rather high proportion of dodgy military characters but this is to suit plots.

It goes without saying the legions were a fine fighting force, but their role in peacetime was significant, as Falco muses in *Alexandria: Who really ran Egypt for Rome were the centurions. Men who acquired geographical knowledge, legal and administrative skills, then used them. They would resolve disputes and root out corruption in the nomes, where appointed locals supervised local government and taxation, but Rome was in overall charge* ... Based on archaeological evidence, Falco lists the kind of situation a centurion might tackle: *Embezzled land, sheep stealing, house burglary or threats against a local tax gatherer (especially if the taxman's ass was stolen or he himself had gone missing.* [AL]

Ballista, or military crossbow

The navy

The Romans were not a seafaring nation, unlike the Greeks. Naval protection was essential, however. Italy itself, being a difficult long narrow shape, had two fleets, one at Ravenna, for which Falco's Uncle Fulvius has worked in some murky capacity, the other at Misenum. Pliny the Elder was in charge of the Misenum fleet when Vesuvius blew its top. We glimpse that fleet, behaving ashore as navies 'showing the flag' tend to do. *Their capacity was enormous and their expertise at steering a course home afterwards while singing jolly songs in fabulously obscene versions made sober men blench.* [SB] Things haven't improved much when a hard-drinking officer called Canidius features in *Scandal Takes a Holiday.*

Headquarters staff were out-stationed in Rome: the Misenum Fleet's in the Praetorian Camp and the Ravenna Fleet's in the Transtiberina.

The air force

No, Falco really is *not* Biggles.

Music

When levered off its carriage, the water organ stood over twelve feet high. The upper portion looked like a gigantic set of syrinx pipes, made partly of bronze, partly of reed. The lower part was formed from an ornamental chest to which bellows were attached. One of Thalia's men was pouring water carefully into a chamber. Another was attaching a footboard, a huge lever, and a keyboard. [LAP]

Falco seems ambivalent about music, especially if it has 'ethnic' overtones. Scenes, such as Oplontis on Silvana's birthday, with slightly worn country dancers, evolve directly from occasions I have attended during coach tours or on holiday in Croatia with my family; Max and I had one of those unplayable flutes ... Folk dancers trying to earn a crust from tourists just seem good value as satire. If you are a folk dancer, I apologise (everyone else knows what I mean). Another lot do their stuff at Anacrites' dinner party in *Nemesis;* I'm afraid in that book there is also a singer who moans the Roman equivalent of *lieder* or *The Dream of Gerontius* or what they play on Radio 3 in mid-afternoon when you are stuck in bed with flu ...

Falco either can or can't play the cithara well enough to teach it. Decide for yourselves.

A special feature of the Roman world was the water organ, or *hydraulus,* which so fascinated Nero. It appears in art and on coins, generally played by a smart young lady, which may have been its appeal. A water organ springs the plot of *Last Act in Palmyra.* My friend Rosalie's uncle, Dr Laurence Picken, a Cambridge musicologist, suggested gently that a water organ might not have been quite so loud as I described.

The Baths

The strenuous types are doing their exercises, swinging weight-laden hands about … some ball player comes along and starts shouting out the score … someone starting up a brawl, and someone else caught thieving … the man who likes the sound of his voice in the bath … people who leap into the pool with a tremendous splash … the hair remover making his client yell for him … the man selling drinks, and one selling sausages, and the other selling pastries …
SENECA

The baths were central to Roman life, an institution that probably came from the East. Supplied by the aqueducts, ornamented with statues and mosaics, they were heated by hypocausts and wall flues. Turkish baths or old-fashioned European spas give the idea. The public baths offered all kinds of social intercourse, though I suspect many people tried to keep to themselves. The classic client trick was to try to meet someone who would invite you to dinner.

You paid your *quadrans,* stripped and left your clothes on hooks or shelves in the *apodyterium* (hoping they would not be stolen). Sandals were useful on the hot floors. You could exercise first, then move through a series of rooms; how many depended on the size and luxury of the baths. The basic three were the *tepidarium* (warm), *caldarium* (hot), and *frigidarium* (cold); many baths also had a plunge pool or swimming pool.

Cleanliness was achieved through scented oils, scraped off with a strigil, either managing yourself, or having a slave (yours, or hired) do it. Professional masseurs were available. So were poems and pies, manicurists and barbers. Painful kinds of depilation were practised – though not by Falco. In *Nemesis* a vain man with louche tastes avails himself of the ancient version of 'back, sac and crack', as attested by Persius:

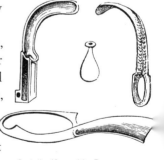

Strigils (found in Roman baths)

On your jaws you keep a length of rug which you comb and perfume;
So why is your crotch plucked smooth around your dangling worm?

Though half a dozen masseurs in the gym uproot
    this plantation,
Assailing your flabby buttocks with hot pitch and the
    claws
Of tweezers, no plough ever made will tame that
    bracken.

It can only end in tears.

Money and Measurement

Do you not realise what money is for, what
    enjoyment it gives?
You can buy bread and vegetables, half a litre of
    wine,
And the other things which human life can't do
    without.
Or maybe you prefer to lie awake half dead with
    fright, to spend
Your days and nights in dread of a gang of burglars
    or fire
Or your own slaves, who may fleece you and
    disappear?
HORACE

These were the coin denominations in Falco's day:

Aureus	= 25 denarii (gold)
Denarius	= 4 sestertii (silver)
Sestertius	= 4 asses (brass)
Dupondius	= 2 as (brass)
As	= 2 semises (copper)
Semis	= 2 quadrantes (brass)
Quadrans (copper)	

Basic pay annually for a legionary was 225 denarii, and they were well paid (though subject to deductions for uniform, burial club, etc.). An aureus would have been a rare sight; the unit of account was the sestertius, but even those would chink infrequently in most purses. Coins in daily use on the streets would be 'coppers'. A famous price list from Pompeii offers wine for an *as*, best wine for two or Falernian for four (though it might be fake). A loaf would be a dupondius, a tunic fifteen sestertii (Falco probably owns too many tunics, incidentally; perhaps he claims them as expenses, under 'disguise').

Measurement

Weights and measures tables are easy to find. I'll just mention that the Roman foot and therefore the Roman inch, or in Falco phraseology, digit, were slightly shorter than ours, as was the Roman mile; when Falco mentions miles, I try to work out *Roman* miles but it is rough and ready.

All decent markets had sets of standard weights and measures. Most sellers probably cheated strangers, though not old ladies unless the sellers were extremely stupid.

Clothes and Accessories

Clothes were woven on looms, so the tunic was the basic garment: a rectangle, long for women, short for men, very short for male re-enactors who want to show off their legs. The neck-hole was a weak point, prone to tears and ladders. Shaping is difficult on a loom, hence togas, with their curved edges, were a sign of the élite. Sewing flat braid on to a curve is a nightmare too. And togas took an enormous amount of cloth. Look elsewhere for diagrams of how to don a toga; you dropped one end down your front, wrapped the other end behind your back, then down under your arm and across your front, then slung it back over your left shoulder; this left your right hand free to hold a scroll or make dramatic gestures. Togas were heavy and men made a fuss, longing to leave them off (they could in the country).

Most clothes were made of wool, so were hot, hard to wash, and prickly to sensitive skins. On the other hand, southern people wore more than North Europeans would, just as Mediterranean men nowadays wear summer vests. Augustus, a sickly chappie, wore several layers of tunic.

Neither aniline dyes nor dry cleaning had been invented, with the results you would expect. Colours were natural, but tended to leak in the wash, getting paler each time. Body odour is earthy in a world without antiperspirants.

There were all kinds of cloaks, hats and shoes. Women, and some men, loved jewellery; cheap stuff was basic (stones on a string) while the best had astonishing craftsmanship, filigree gold, pearls and precious stones – though facet-cutting was difficult so coloured gemstones predominate over diamonds. Wigs were worn by both sexes (human hair, often imported, like extensions today). Everyone knew blondes had more fun.

Make-up existed, with a tendency to be composed of wine-lees and dung, or wicked substances like antimony and lead. There are books on Roman fashion; or just look at frescos and tombstones. Personally, I am no fan of the brief vogue for the Flavian ladies' curly court hairstyle.

In my period good Romans were clean-shaven. *No honest Roman wears a beard. Access to good razors is what singles us out from the barbarians.* [AL]

A court beauty having a bad hair day

Falco mentions all this because style helps him evaluate witnesses' and suspects' status and character. Hats and boots have been clues. Hats and cloaks have been disguises. A painted face always provides a chance to purse disapproving lips, while – in Falco's case – probably smacking them.

Latin Words and Pronouncation

I was asked to discuss Latin words. I don't know why, because I use very few. I write to be accessible to people who know neither Roman history nor Latin. I like to use the original names for places and people, because that adds period flavour; I get twitchy over my Spanish and Italian translations, where national convention is rigidly followed instead, so Falco is 'Marco Didio'.

Otherwise, I loathe books where show-off authors repeatedly use foreign phrases, so I shun that. Everything has to be understandable in context. (First, I have to understand it myself!)

I did intend to include a pronunciation guide, honest. There are various types of oral Latin: classical, church, singers' Latin which differs according to period … You can find instructions in books and on websites. You can play with it for hours.

The problem is not just that we don't know for certain how classical Latin was pronounced. We can make deductions from inscriptions and the rhythms of poetry, though this may only give the sound of the educated classes. Think how pronunciation has changed just from early films to now. Throughout the Empire there would be wide variations; even in Rome, the man in the street might be unintelligible to a senator – and vice versa. Vespasian, who was born not so very far from Rome, was mocked for pronouncing the word for 'wagons' as 'plostra' rather than 'plaustra'.

Trying to be 'correct', you fall at almost the second consonant: 'c' should be hard. Julius Caesar should be pronounced like Kaiser Bill. It gets worse: 'i' should be 'y' and certain syllables are long – so Helena's nice brother mutates into Yusteenus. Yuk. When I was at school, a new system had been introduced which included saying 'v' as 'w'. This would make my emperor 'Wespasian'. Even if true, I refuse to do it. I have always in mind the consoling history of Sellar and Yeatman: *Julius Caesar … set the memorable Latin sentence 'Veni, Vidi, Vici', which the Romans, who were all very well educated, construed correctly. The Britons, however, who of course still used the old pronunciation, understanding him to have called them 'Weeny, Weedy and Weaky', lost heart and gave up the struggle, thinking that he had already divided them All into Three Parts.*

Ginny sent me her teaching-guide, but not all of it fitted what I learned, which is, mostly, how I still speak. When I tried her rules, redolent with long 'a's where I think they are short, I was soon pronouncing Latin with a Texan accent.

A novel should tell a story, smoothly and naturally, so the sense takes precedence and you are not held up by oddities. Even though I hear the words as I write, I am listening to their rhythm as it imparts ideas and jokes; I'm not being picky about vowels. Half my vowels are Brummie anyway if I get excited. People who ask for guides don't want the Corieltauvi dialect.

So my advice is, don't worry. Never put the stress on the last syllable. Roll your 'r's if you can. Then say what seems natural and just pretend you live in a barbarian province where the elocution teachers haven't yet been sent out from Rome.

Frequently Asked Questions

HIC…

·HAEC HOC··

Peter Godfrey

These are perennials from my postbag.

Would you write a prequel (about Falco and Petro in the army in Britain)?
No. Two reasons: I would not want to write a book that could not include Helena. And I myself don't want to address whether Falco and Petronius were as laddish as they both make out. Some things are better left open. Other authors write books about a couple of blokes who are best pals, bonding and fighting. It is not my style. Falco and Petronius are the kind of men real women like: grown-ups.

Is Festus really dead?
Yes.

Might he not be secretly in hiding somewhere?
No.

But he's one of life's survivors; wouldn't it be fun if …
Nope. I couldn't stand the bloke for five minutes. I don't have to do this!

What will happen when Vesuvius erupts?
I am loath to write about the eruption. Pliny described it so well (his classic and very famous description is still used by vulcanologists); there is nothing left for a descriptive novelist to say. And this was a real tragedy. The Boxing Day tsunami sealed my view that such an event is unsuitable for light, entertaining novels.

How will Falco survive under Domitian?
Stoically.

Will you ever kill off Falco?
No. Nor Helena.

What is fish-pickle? What is silphium?
See the section on Roman food and drink.

Ashes were already falling, hotter and thicker as the ships drew near, followed by bits of pumice and blackened stones, charred and cracked by the flames …
Meanwhile on Mount Vesuvius broad sheets of fire and leaping flames blazed at several points, their bright glare emphasised by the darkness of night.
PLINY THE YOUNGER

How do Roman names work?
See Some Other Aspects of Roman Life.

Is Falco telling the story from some future time/writing his memoirs?
I suppose Falco is writing his memoirs but I'm not sure why some readers get so intrigued by this. First-person narratives are just a convention in some novels. I don't think about it.

An extended joke is that Falco is bound by rules of confidentiality to 'protect his sources'. As the project manager of Fishbourne, he is silenced by the Roman equivalent of the Official Secrets Act: *A problem arises when working for clients who demand confidentiality clauses: the investigator is required to keep silent forever about his cases. Many a private informer could write titillating memoirs, full of slime and scandal, were this not the case. Many an imperial agent could produce a riveting autobiography, in which celebrated names would juggle in shocking juxtaposition with those of vicious mobsters and persons with filthy morals of both sexes … Want to hear about the Vestal, the hermaphrodite and the Superintendent of Riverbanks? You won't get a sniff of it from me.* [BBH]

If this were other than irony, we would have no Falco novels.

I do always remind people that the books are fiction – but fiction written by a fairly laid-back, and perhaps mischievous author (well, two of them: him and me both). I reserve the right to bury Falco in Vesuvius ash and say the books are really written by Helena afterwards. Or indeed (and how tempting this is!) that they are scrawled by Anacrites in some psychologically weird wish to emulate. However, to become Falco's Boswell requires Anacrites to survive whatever adventures await *him* …

When will Falco and Helena get married?
I think they are married. So do they, which is what matters.

From the moment Helena turns up with her luggage in *Venus in Copper* they are married in the strict sense. If the situation seems unclear after that, it reflects both the state of the author's research and their mutual insecurity. The definitive scene occurs at the end of *Poseidon's Gold*.

Subsequently Falco gives extra explanation to soothe the perturbed: *We were both free to marry and if we both chose to live together that was all the law required. We had considered denying it. In that case our children would take their mother's social rank, although any advantage was theoretical. As long as their father lacked honorific titles they would be stuck in the mud like me ... So when we came home from Spain* [i.e. after the birth of Julia] *we had decided to acknowledge our position publicly. Helena had stepped down to my level. She knew what she was doing; she had seen my style of life, and faced up to the consequences. Our daughters were debarred from good marriages. Our sons stood no chance of holding public office, no matter how much their noble grandfather the senator would like to see them stand for election. The upper class would close against them, while the lower ranks would probably despise them as outsiders too.* [THF]

Falco refers to his wife in *The Silver Pigs*. Does anybody really want to imagine this is not Helena?

Will you do the Christians?
I affirm not.

I doggedly stand by my tenet that those of my characters who would have been pagans stay that way. I want to correct all those earlier, Christian, novelists who implied that every First Century Roman was bursting for conversion.

While writing *Last Act in Palmyra* at a furious pace, Jehovah's Witnesses interrupted. I particularly resent being evangelised in my home. *As soon as they smiled and said how pleasant it was to meet us, we knew they were bastards ... So, When the fanatical sales-talk moved to offering us a guarantee of eternal life, we beat the Christians up soundly and left them whimpering.*

Emboldened by Christians sneakily liking that scene, I did have Falco refuse to buy a Christian slave. *'They drink their god's blood while they maunder about love, don't they?' My late brother Festus encountered these crazy men in Judaea and sent home some lurid stories. 'I'm looking for a children's nurse. I can't have perverts.'*

'No, no, I believe they drink wine ... These Christians just pray a lot, or try to convert the master or the mistress of the house to their beliefs.'

'You want to get me arrested because some arrogant slave says everyone should deny the sanctity of the Emperor?' [BBH]

'There, there, Cornelius, don't cry; they wouldn't have hurt you. They just like to smile and tell you they have found the answer.'
'The answer to what?'
'To the question.' [SDD]

Now at rock bottom, the slave master can only offer a Briton instead …

Why are you so rude about Britain?

Because the Romans were.

Americans, with their dangerous ideal of 'My country, right or wrong', find it hard to grasp that Britons love most what they disparage most. I illustrate the Roman view of the impossibly remote place they invaded. Take it from Tacitus: *The climate is wretched, with its frequent rains and mists, but there is no extreme cold. Their day is longer than in our part of the world. The nights are light, and in the extreme north so short that evening and morning twilight are scarcely distinguishable … The soil will produce good crops, except olives, vines, and other plants which usually grow in warmed lands. They are slow to ripen, they shoot up quickly – both facts due to the same cause, the extreme moistness of the soil and atmosphere.*

We liked Britain more than Marcus Didius admits. I think if ever informers are barred from Rome we might even retire there; Marcus dreams of a quiet farm in a fertile river valley … [THF]

We know from the Vindolanda Tablets that Britain was a hard posting whence officers desperately begged for more beer for the lads, while the lads themselves requested underpants. So Falco sees Britain according to the stereotype, a stereotype he has experienced: *The fine mist that tangles sticky as fishglue in your hair; the cold that leaps straight into your shoulders and knees; the sea fogs and hill blizzards; the dreadful dark months when dawn and evening seem hardly separate … [SP]*

Lucius shows his bottom (and grows up to hate family sculptures)

I spent long childhood holidays camping on Holy Island, off Anglesey. When it comes to weather I know what I'm talking about.

Did the Romans wear underpants?

The fastidious, no doubt.

As with '*What does the Scotsman wear under his kilt?*', who will be brave enough to lift the tunic and look?

The Vindolanda soldiers wanted *subligaculi*. Which proves pants existed.

On the lesser-known side of the Ara Pacis in Rome, I found 'thought-to-be-Lucius Caesar', a toddler in the procession of Augustus' family. He was hard to photograph, but this indicates his choice on pants.

Where Next for Falco?

*'Maybe we should emigrate to some far province away
from everyone.'*
    'You belong in the city, Marcus.'
    *'Perhaps. Or perhaps one day I'll set up home with
you in some villa in a river valley – choose your spot.'*
    *'Britain!' she quipped wickedly. I returned to my
original dream of a town house above the Tiber, with a
garden on a terrace with a view across Rome ...* [DLC]

Of course people want to know.

I have always been fairly relaxed about this. I have
generally never planned more than a book ahead. I
don't worry about where Falco and Helena are heading. Their significantly changed situation in *Nemesis*
came as a surprise to me, settled only when I wrote a
synopsis for that book.

I always said I would never kill Falco off – why
would I need to? I once thought if I finally did him in,
that might deter those unspeakable, unoriginal, money-
grubbing writers who carry on another author's creation. I curse anyone who ever thinks of doing that to
me (see my curse laid on plumbers in the section on
Roman homes). So long as I can totter into a courtroom to bend the feeble plagiarism laws, or am at least
alive to shake an angry fist, it should be possible to keep
those ghouls at bay. When I'm dead you – my readers –
must do it for me. Once I choose to stop writing, I will.
Conan Doyle fostered the ridiculous notion that pressure from the public could *force* a novelist to continue
with a popular hero. Nonsense; Doyle wanted the
money, the fame, the security that writing Holmes provided. Nobody can compel a strong-willed woman to
write against her will.

I keep all options open. But in 2009 I turned sixty;
becoming a pensioner, by golly, makes you think! The
fear of losing your grip, losing the hunger, losing your
judgement is monstrous for anyone whose work
depends on their energy and brainpower. The hope of
staying sharp is encouraged, however, by all those

intrepid English women writers, many of whom do their best work in their eighties. I could have another twenty books to go ... Since the publication of *Rebels and Traitors*, it is pretty certain that I will want to write on different subjects. I used to say I expected to continue to write Falco novels in between.

But the passage of time brings changes a writer may neither anticipate nor welcome. In the autumn of 2008, after thirty-two years, I lost Richard. I have said he wasn't Falco – but he *was* an intricate part of the series, because he encouraged me, travelled with me, read and scoffed at my drafts; besides, there is hardly an exchange between Falco and Helena that does not owe something to our crazy, sparky, loving conversations. When Richard died, I was contracted for *Nemesis* and due to start writing more or less immediately. Completing it without him was extremely hard.

Then, before I finished, my editor, Oliver, resigned from Random House. Readers would normally neither know nor care about this, but we were a particular author/editor team and after more than twenty books together, it matters. I could work with another editor, but do I want to do so on Falco? So, unexpected decisions will have to be made. By the time you are reading this, the way forward may be obvious. As I write it, I don't know what I shall do. I never expected this to be how the *Companion* would end, but I am going to be honest.

Don't be downhearted. *Wait and see!* is one of the most exciting answers an author can give.

Appendix:
Fragments from the *Casa della Spia Principale*, Rome

During stabilisation work to the lower Palatine Hill, remains came to light of a Roman house dating from the Republican era. Archaeologists made tentative links to a Tiberius Claudius Anacrites (previously unknown), possibly a mid-First Century imperial freedman granted grace-and-favour occupation of the building in return for unspecified services.

Fragments of documents were recovered, which it was hoped would be as important as scrolls from the Villa of the Papyri *at Herculaneum, currently being studied with ambitious new techniques. Results so far on the Rome fragments, however, are disappointing. It would appear the occupant was a man of no great culture; his library contained only disparate documents with no literary merit. Several show an unhealthy interest in the murky world of informing.*

CSP.1 Appears to be a speech, or draft of one, by the noted orator Paccius Africanus, accusing a low-born informer of calumny. It is not known whether this seriously revisionist speech was ever delivered.

CSP.2 Some kind of handbook for *delatores*. The writer had written it on the back of an old recipe.

CSP.3 Reverse of the above. The recipe.

CSP.4 Mutilated fragments of a play, tentatively identified as *The Spook Who Spoke*, author unknown, text otherwise lost.

CSP. I: Speech of Paccius Africanus

Let me turn to the character of Marcus Didius Falco, distasteful though this must be. Consider what type of man he is. What is known of his history? No distinguished ancestors adorn his pedigree. We shall search in vain for consuls, senators or generals. He was born, in extreme poverty, in one of the anonymous buildings close to the Temple of Ceres, an infamous haunt of outsiders and the lower class of plebeian. His education was meagre and he grew up fatherless.

As a young recruit he was sent to the province of Britain. It was the time of the Boudiccan Rebellion. Of the four legions then in Britain, some were subsequently honoured for their bravery and the glory of their victory over the rebels. Was Falco among their number? No. The men in his legion disgraced themselves by not responding to the call from their colleagues for help. They stayed in camp. They did not fight. Others were left to achieve honour while the Second Augusta, including Didius Falco, abandoned them, earning only disgrace. It is true that Falco was obeying orders; others were culpable – but remember, as a servant of the Senate and People, that was his heritage.

He claims he was then a scout. I can find no record of this. He left the army. Had he served his time? Was he wounded out? Was he sent home with an honourable diploma? No. He wheedled himself an exit, under terms that are shrouded in secrecy.

We next hear of this man, operating as the lowest type of informer from a dingy base on the Aventine. He spied on bridegrooms, destroying their hopes of marriage with slanders [*text lost*] He preyed on widows in their time of bereavement [*text lost*]

Didius Falco did seedy work, often for unpleasant people. Some time around then he had a stroke of enormous luck for a man of his class. The daughter of a senator fell in love with him. It was a tragedy for her family, but for Falco it proved a passport to respectability. Ignoring the pleas of her parents, the headstrong young woman ran off with her hero. Her noble father's fortunes declined sharply from that moment. Her brothers were soon inveigled into Falco's web, subject to his incorrigible influence. Now, instead of the promising careers that once lay ahead, they are facing ruin with him … [*manuscript corrupt*]

By means I dread to guess, Didius Falco managed to ingratiate himself with those in the highest positions. Pitying, perhaps, the plight of his once-noble wife, the Emperor allowed him to conduct work of a sensitive nature, which might otherwise be entrusted to worthier men. Before her death, Caenis considered him for honours, but quickly saw through him. Acting with a partner whose sinister identity to this day remains hidden, Falco was permitted to work on the Census. His efforts brought ruination to many who had previously flourished, businessmen whose industry had benefited our city, men who had won everyone's admiration for their talent and self-sacrifice. It made no difference: Didius Falco laid them low, ruthlessly profiting from their fall. He had been poor. After plundering with impunity, he was suddenly a man of substance.

Whenever things grew too hot for him in Rome, he disappeared from the city to hideaways abroad. He even travelled outside the Empire, shamelessly venturing among barbarians who shun Rome and even those who have openly waged war upon us. Veleda, our most implacable enemy, played host to him before she was brought to justice.

Putting on a habitual show of ambition for his children's sake, it was inevitable that Falco would seek honours. To everyone's amazement, he was made Procurator of the Sacred Geese of Juno and the Augurs' Chickens. What more respected position could there be, connected with the safety of Rome and one of our oldest festivals? But it ended badly. Before [*text lost*] years expired, Falco was summoned before the Praetor on the most terrible charge: impiety. His accuser, plainly a man of great rectitude, was reluctantly compelled to accuse Falco of irreverence to the gods and dereliction of his temple duties. Though the evidence was clear, the case was dismissed, one more example of him avoiding accountability.

[*Manuscript ends*]

CSP.2: *The Forum Informer's Handbook*

Eat before surveillance. Be meticulous about *what* you eat. Diarrhoea on watch is disastrous.

Always know where to find a public latrine.

Identify the nearest vigiles station-house.

Carrying a weapon in Rome is illegal. Don't let that stop you.

Clothes: dress to meld in. Have some professional pride though: be stylish.

Your belt is an ornament, a sign of taste and character. Choose one that won't break while being used as a whip or garrotte. If things get really bad, you can hang yourself with it.

Your boots should be sturdy and comfortable. It is polite to clean off the mule-dung when visiting decent houses.

Denied access in the morning? Try again in the afternoon; you may get a different door-porter. Same one? Try a bigger bribe. Don't thump him. He may let out the watchdog. Never thump a dog. You don't want a bad name.

Don't encumber yourself with shopping, however brilliant the bargain.

Never sleep with clients, suspects, slaves or unattractive barmaids.

Always know this week's festivals and entertainments. *You* may hate the Games and the theatre, but one day you may need to concoct an alibi. Or to check the fake alibis of suspects and witnesses.

Have money on you. Hide it.

Don't hide it so well you can't get at it when you need to pay a bribe or buy a rissole.

Learn Greek. It makes you seem like a clerk, but saves paying an interpreter.

Don't drink and delve.

CSP.3: Recipe

Ingredients: Turbot. Sauce

Method: First find your fish kettle.
Poach turbot gently in oil, wine vinegar, water, bay leaves, pepper, to taste.

Sauce: Combine pepper, lovage, caraway seed, celery seed, finely chopped onion (go easy), wine, wine vinegar, fish stock and olive oil. Boil. Simmer. Thicken with flour.

CSP.4: *The Spook Who Spoke*

[*margin corrupt*]

CHARACTER: What, has this thing appeared again tonight?

GHOST: That bastard's done me in; hire an informer …

MOSCHION: The question is … [*text missing*]

CLOWN: I say, I say. A customer returns to the slave market. That slave you sold me died last night! Slave-owner replies, That's funny, he was perfectly all right when I had him!

[*margin corrupt*]

? FEMALE CHARACTER: I'm worried about Moschion.

? OTHER FEMALE CHARACTER: He's just a lad. They all get like that – hate their parents, can't find a girlfriend, give up their studies after your husband has spent all that money – it's just his age … [*text missing*]

… MOSCHION: In the most noble city of Rome, a little before the mighty Julius fell, the graves stood empty and the dead all squeaked and gibbered in the Roman streets …

CLOWN: I say, I say, a stranger is passing the funeral of a woman. Who is resting in peace here? Her husband answers, Me, now I've got rid of her! …

… MOSCHION: Oh mother! [*end of scroll*]

Acknowledgements

Note: Serious efforts have been made to contact copyright owners. Where this has been impossible, the author and publisher are willing to acknowledge any rightful copyright owner on substantive proof of ownership and would be grateful for any information as to their identity.

Creating a heroine from advice for entrants in the CWA Debut Dagger competition, edited by Liz Evans
The Course of Honour from an Afterword for St Martin's Press (not used) and Marco Tropea
Website from an article by Ginny Lindzey for a Random House Newsletter

Quotations

All quotations from *The Course of Honour* and the Falco novels are © Lindsey Davis, reproduced by permission of the Random House Group Ltd

Aristophanes, *The Birds,* translated by David Barrett, (Penguin Classics, 1978) © David Barrett and Alan H Sommerstein/ reproduced by permission of Penguin Books Ltd

Jérôme Carcopino, *Daily Life in Ancient Rome,* Translated E. O. Lorimer, 1941 © reproduced by permission of Taylor & Francis/ Yale University Press

Raymond Chandler, *The Simple Art of Murder,* (1934) © Raymond Chandler/reproduced by permission of Ed Victor Ltd
Selected Letters of Raymond Chandler, ed Frank MacShane, (1981) © Raymond Chandler/reproduced by permission of Ed Victor Ltd
Raymond Chandler, *The High Window,* (1942) © Raymond Chandler/reproduced by permission of Ed Victor Ltd
Raymond Chandler, *The Big Sleep,* (1939) © Raymond Chandler/reproduced by permission of Ed Victor Ltd

Stella Gibbons, *Cold Comfort Farm,* (1932) © Stella Gibbons/ reproduced by permission of Curtis Brown Ltd

John Henderson, *A Roman Life: Rutilius Gallicus on paper and in Stone,* (University of Exeter Press, 1998) © John Henderson/ reproduced by permission of University of Exeter Press

Horace's *Satires,* translated by Niall Rudd, (Penguin Classics, 1973) © Niall Rudd/reproduced by permission of Penguin Books Ltd

Horace, *Odes,* translated by James Michie, (Penguin Classics, 1964) © James Michie/reproduced by permission of the Estate of James Michie/David Higham Associates Ltd

Juvenal, *The Sixteen Satires,* translated and introduced by Peter Green, (Penguin Classics, 1967) © Peter Green/reproduced by permission of Penguin Books Ltd

Livy, *The Early History of Rome,* translated by Aubrey de Sélincourt, (Penguin Classics, 1960) © Estate of Aubrey de Selincourt/ reproduced by permission of Penguin Books Ltd

Martial, *The Epigrams,* translated by James Michie, (Penguin Classics, 1978) © James Michie/reproduced by permission of the Estate of James Michie

Ed McBain, *Cop Hater,* (Permabooks, 1956) © Ed McBain/ reproduced by permission of Curtis Brown Group Ltd
Ed McBain, *Give the Boys a Great Big Hand,* (Simon & Schuster Inc, 1960) © Ed McBain/reproduced by permission of Curtis Brown Group Ltd
Ed McBain, *The Heckler,* (Simon & Schuster Inc, 1960) © Ed McBain/reproduced by permission of Curtis Brown Group Ltd

Persius, *Satires,* translated by Naill Rudd, (Penguin Classics, 1973) © Niall Rudd/reproduced by permission of Penguin Books Ltd/ David Higham Associates Ltd

Petronius, *The Satyricon,* translated by J P Sullivan, (Penguin Classics, 1965) © J P Sullivan/reproduced by permission of Penguin Books Ltd/David Higham Associates Ltd

Letters of Pliny the Younger, translated by Betty Radice, (Penguin Classics, 1963) © Betty Radice/reproduced by permission of Penguin Books Ltd

Steven H Rutledge, *Imperial Inquisitions,* (Routledge, 2001) © Steven H Rutledge, reproduced by permission of Taylor and Francis Books Ltd

Walter Carruthers Sellar and Robert Julian Yeatman, *1066 And All That,* (Penguin Books, 1930) © Walter Carruthers Sellar and Robert Julian Yeatman/reproduced by permission of Penguin Books Ltd

Seneca, *Letters from a Stoic,* translated Robin Campbell, (Penguin Classics, 1969) © Robin Alexander Campbell/reproduced by permission of Penguin Books Ltd

Suetonius, *The Twelve Caesars,* translated by Robert Graves, (Penguin Classics, 1957), revised by Michael Grant, 1979: © Robert Graves/ reproduced by permission of Carcanet Press Ltd/A P Watt Ltd on behalf of the Robert Graves Copyright Trust

Rosemary Sutcliffe, *The Eagle of the Ninth,* (1954/OUP, 2004) © Anthony Lawton 1954, reprinted by permission of Oxford University Press

Tacitus, *Histories,* translated by Kenneth Wellesley, (Penguin Classics, 1964) © Kenneth Wellesley/reproduced by permission of Penguin Books Ltd

Tacitus, *Agricola* and *Germania,* translated by H Mattingley, (Penguin Classics, 1948) © Estate of H Mattingley/reproduced by permission of Penguin Books Ltd

Virgil, *The Aeneid,* translated by W P Jackson Knight, (Penguin Classics, 1956) © W P Jackson Knight/reproduced by permission of Penguin Books Ltd

Andrew Wallace-Hadrill, (Princeton University Press, 1994) ©Andrew Wallace-Hadrill/reproduced by permission of Princeton University Press

Emails and letters from readers © Iola Robertson, Vanessa Terry, Dave Lee Tripp, Barbara Young
Emails about 'the Camel Joke' © Dave Morris and Oliver Johnson

Feature from *Metro, 'And finally…'* © Associated Newspapers Ltd

Picture Acknowledgements

Index

See also Key to Abbreviations (book titles) vi and Gazetteer of place names pp. 186–92. *m* refers to marginal matter.